THE

CHARITY

OF THE

PRIMITIVE CHURCHES.

HISTORICAL STUDIES UPON THE INFLUENCE OF CHRISTIAN CHARITY DURING THE FIRST CENTURIES OF OUR ERA, WITH SOME CONSIDERATIONS TOUCHING ITS BEARINGS UPON MODERN SOCIETY.

BY

REV. STEPHEN CHASTEL,

OF GENEVA (SWITZERLAND).

TRANSLATED BY

G. A. MATILE

PHILADELPHIA:

J. B. LIPPINCOTT & CO.

1857.

TRANSLATOR'S PREFACE.

EACH of the four Academies which compose the Institute of France, holds a meeting every year to decide upon the merits of works submitted in competition for prizes offered for the best essays upon questions proposed one or more years previously. One of them, moved, no doubt, by the disturbed state of society in 1852, proposed an extraordinary meeting on the subject of Charity in the early ages of Christianity, a subject so perfidiously perplexed and envenomed by the heroes of 1848.

"The Academy had reason to congratulate itself on having pointed out this subject and proposed this work. Excellent essays on history and moral jurisprudence have resulted from it. The monuments of early Christianity, pagan legislation, philosophy, religious eloquence, carefully compared, have offered, in answer to anarchical paradoxes, a precious tradition of incontestable facts, just and true ideas, virtuous and powerful sentiments."

It is thus that Villemain, permanent Secretary of the French Academy, expresses himself on the result of the meeting. He adds:

"This subject, worthy of our times, has attracted serious minds. Twelve manuscript treatises have long occupied the judges. Two works, especially, have gained their approval by a profound knowledge of the subject; a judicious and firm method; a tendency towards the true and the useful, inseparable here as everywhere; and finally, by a disgust towards those falsifications of the past, which would bend it to the service of existing paradoxes, and, among other impostures, assimilate things which have the least possible resemblance, namely, the severe self-renunciation and pure spirituality of Gospel morality, with the intense egotism and materialism of Thomas Paine and others."

"Of the two works considered the best, one bears for its epigraph this beautiful sentiment of St. Augustine: "Where charity is not, justice cannot be."

" Ubi caritas non est, non potest esse justitia."

"It is worthy of such a device. It is a learned work, written with the feelings of a good man. The highly interesting texts of profane and Christian literature, of the Roman jurisconsults, and of the Fathers of the Greek and Roman Churches, of emperors and sophists, are there skilfully employed and everywhere referred to or transcribed. We may find there the full testimony of antiquity on a grave question arranged with the accuracy of a critic; and sometimes the views of a thinker, in whom science sharpens reflection, and who, under forms somewhat unusual, brings to his work studious scrutiny and unflagging interest, with occasional displays of eloquence both in feeling and language.

"The other work on Charity bears for its epigraph: "To God, in the poor."

" Deo in pauperibus."

"If it is less enriched by quotation from ancient authorities, and proceeds by less complete deductions, it is written after no less profound and protracted study of the early periods of Christianity."

"This appears even in the easier style of the author. What he says, suggests a knowledge of that which he omits. Familiarized by previous labors, which have been crowned by the Academy of Inscriptions, with the history of the fall of Paganism, and, consequently, with the establishment of Christianity and its immediate and progressive benefits, he finds his way with ease through this immense question of Charity; he knows it, he develops it like a judicious antiquary, like a historian who knows its scope, and like a friend of humanity, who is a friend of Christ; he approaches it with the full power of earnest, sacred eloquence; and he opposes it to our modern speculations and experiences, with a skill and science analogous to that of his learned competitor, and in a form and by a process, different, but not inferior."

"These two works appear to us to sustain and complete each other, and to offer a most instructive, moral solution of the problem proposed. The decision of the Academy, which divides the prize between them, will appear, we think, to every attentive reader but a just tribute to the rare merit of two, between whom even esteem forbids a preference."

The Academy, consequently, awarded two equal prizes to the two learned authors, Charles Schmidt, Professor of Theology in Strasburg, and Stephen Chastel, Professor at Geneva. The adjudication of these prizes to two Protestant theologians made a sensation in the Catholic world.

From men so eminent as those who were arbiters

in this case, such impartiality was to be expected, even if the names of the two authors had been known to them before the solemn opening of the sealed letters, bearing the corresponding epigraph on the outside and the author's name on the inside.

"We cannot positively decide," says the editor of the *Revue Britannique*, "whether the author before us is Catholic or Protestant. Is not this in itself a eulogy? For it is truly to be deplored that so many books on this Charity, which should unite us all, should also be works of controversy. In the work of Chastel we may love each other instead of supporting a thesis. The citations from the Fathers of the Church are addressed to all religions and all sects. The author uses these citations with perfect fairness in reference to modern economists. It is this erudition which has charmed us in a work which will have also its practical utility; it may and should be consulted by governments as well as by charitable societies."

This is the work of which I now offer a translation to the public, with the approbation of the author, with whom I have the pleasure to be personally acquainted and on the most friendly terms. At the same time, it is my earnest wish that, for the sake of the great subject of Charity, the work of Schmidt may soon be translated. These two works, which complete each other and have received the same honors, ought not to be separated in their career. I would have myself undertaken that translation had not other urgent business prevented me from doing so. How gladly would I give Mr. Schmidt this mark of my affection! The hours I should spend with his book in my hands would afford me pleasure like that recently enjoyed in his society. I should be very happy to bring into direct communication with Mr. Schmidt the person who would undertake the translation of his work.

That I might not fall too far below the difficult task of a translator, especially when it concerns a work written with the truth, ardor, and eloquence which are to be found in the original, I have procured fortunately the friendly and able assistance of W. F. Roe, a member of the bar at Elmira.

While occupied in this work, I learned that my author had just been translated into German by a man whom all Germany reveres, Dr. Wichern, of Horn, near Hamburg, whose name is well known among us.

The idea of this translation was suggested to me by one to whom I am bound by ties of gratitude and affection, Stephen Colwell, in whose ample library I met, for the first time, with the works of Chastel. No one has studied more faithfully than he this great question of Christian Charity, especially considered in its relations with political economy, and no one could judge better of the utility of the publication of Chastel's work in America.

In some respects, this work is European: in so far as it treats of the social state of the Old World, it seeks to apply a remedy to its evils and to prevent the return of grave crises. But what serious lessons may not we of the United States draw from its teachings! Doubtless we are—thanks to Divine Providence—far from the social state of Europe, and have no cause for present anxiety. But, is there nothing to fear for the future? If I have not erred in the conclusions drawn from thirty years' historical studies, there are grounds of apprehension. It is true that some of this gloom may come from the social state of Europe, and especially of Switzerland, my native and formerly happy country left by me on account of the political disorders of 1848. But in this young and vigorous country, history has still continued to occupy my leisure, and, trusting to its light, I cannot conceal from myself that the horizon is not as clear as it appears to many others. Though they have entered more recently the lists open to all nations, the United States of North America are hastening no less rapidly toward the end common to all; in many respects they have distanced their competitors, and often run with more ardor than prudence. Ah! could they only remain temperate and not become intoxicated by success! Could they profit by the career of other nations, without boasting of advantages which they possess over others, and glorify, not themselves, but Him to whom they owe all. Let them reflect upon what they would be with a population as numerous in proportion to their territory as that of the States of Europe!

It appears to me that the Fathers of America, if they could return to us, could not observe, without some uneasiness, certain tendencies, certain habits which are developing every day, and which may become more and more dangerous in the course of time, if not more strongly counterbalanced by the true spirit of Christian institutions.

This work is addressed to governments as well as to individuals, for Chastel is not only a scholar and an erudite theologian, but a man profoundly versed in Social Economy; his work is full of realities. He reconciles perfectly, with the Gospel in his hand, the rights of the rich with their obligations, and the rights of masters with those of slaves; the reader will learn from these pages that it is only by Christianizing master and slave, by teaching each his duties, that the position of both can be ameliorated and a way prepared for the final suppression of Slavery much more certainly and promptly than could be done by employing violent means, which neither religion nor sound policy justifies. He points out the grand social duties of the Christian in relation to the charity to be exercised towards his fellows; how this charity is to be exercised in order to bring forth the most fruit; and, while always admitting that collective benevolence neither should nor can be dispensed with, dwells particularly on private charity, the action of the individual; in a word, the duties which devolve upon Christians to prevent misery. All these doctrines, systematically arranged and supported by historical facts, testify to great erudition and sound criticism on the part of the author.

The reader will be convinced of the immense utility of studying, for the interest of Christianity itself, the annals of the primitive churches; of turning his attention more than heretofore to ancient Christian literature; he will find in Chastel an interpreter worthy of the purest Christians of that period, and in his work a noble monument to their honor.

The volume of Chastel is, besides, an edifying work, impregnated with the true spirit of the Gospel. The heart warms as we proceed; our souls are purified and elevated; we are filled with regret that we are not better, and with a desire to become so. Herein lies the success of Chastel's work, rather than in the honors with which he has been loaded by one of the greatest scientific bodies in the world, or in the translation of his work into two languages. It is in the name of God that he speaks to his readers; it is God whom he exhibits to them in the poor, as is expressed in the motto of his book, "*Deo in pauperibus*," and in the exhortation of the last page, which contains the substance of the whole:

"To the work then! The times urge, not because of the dangers which misery could beget; if our sole aim were to conjure them, perhaps already it would be too late; the times urge, because our brothers suffer, and it will never be too soon to relieve them. Were the shocks which still threaten social order to reach us to-morrow, to-day even, it is necessary to labor for the good of the disinherited classes: we must do for them, and for God in them, what it would be no longer time to do for ourselves."

We heartily concur in the last thought expressed by Dr. Wichern in the preface to his translation of our common original:

"May the advantage which we enjoy in viewing the monuments of the Christian charity of former ages recall to us our destiny as Christians, and make it still dearer to us; may it be given us to see, beyond the brilliant light of history, whose veil we raise, the features of Him who presents to us the image of His Heavenly church; and may we behold it reflected in that in the midst of which we have still to live out our appointed time in this lower world!"

G. A. M.

PREFACE.

THE power of charity has seldom been questioned before our days. Most men revered in it a celestial virtue, as efficient as admirable in its spontaneity, and which, wherever practiced with zeal and discernment, contributed powerfully to the relief of misery. Some even feared that it might go too far in this respect. Pre-occupied with certain absolute maxims of the political economy of the English school, they charged beneficence, by blunting the salutary spur of want, with a tendency to relax the efforts of the poor, to destroy in them the disposition of prudence, to increase population beyond the means of subsistence, and, thus, to extend the scourge by a too great ardor for its relief. Any alms, any charitable institution appeared dangerous to them in this respect; at most they spared some establishments, indispensable for curing evils which it is impossible to foresee; and they would willingly have reduced charity to the opening of gratuitous schools for the poor, where the principles of Malthus were to be taught to them.[1]

At the present day those fears seem to have been calmed, and charity is subjected to a very different reproach. It is no longer charged with imprudence and indiscretion, but with impotence; it is no more accused of doing too much, but of not doing enough; it is pretended that, in its most ingenious, its most heroic devotion, it can do absolutely nothing to lessen misery. "To meet," they say, "such pressing and multiplied wants, to fill such a gulf, what are a few crumbs from the table of the rich? What are a few drops of water to calm a consuming thirst? As long as the relief of the poor is made to depend upon the caprice of the opulent, nothing will have been done for the well-being of the most numerous class. Recourse must be taken to a more efficient and less precarious remedy. There is no grant of a favor to be made here, but there is a right to be recognised. Every human being that is born has the right to live; society owes him either work if he has none, or a subsistence if he cannot obtain it by his labor. The State must secure to him the one or the other; or, better still, it is necessary that all the resources of

[1] To be just, let us acknowledge that these ideas are less those of Malthus himself, than of his most exclusive disciples. See chiefly, *Westminster Review*, 1824, on *Charitable Institutions.—Extracts of Reports on Poor-Laws*, London, 1837, pp. 180, 283, &c.

society, put in common and concentrated in its hands, should be distributed to each one according to his needs. Then no one will suffer. The riches of the few will no longer be seen insulting the misery of the many; no one will have a superfluity, but all will have what is necessary; the unfortunate will no longer be reduced to wait till a look of disdainful compassion falls upon him, till a humiliating and meagre alms is tossed to him by some one of the happy of this world."[1]

To appreciate the justice of this new reproach against charity, and the value of the remedy pretended as a substitute for it, excellent reasons have been and can be given. But, if it is true, as we think it to be, that in the moral, as well as in the physical sciences, the method of observation is at the same time the shortest and the surest,[2] if experience is the true touchstone of all social systems, nothing better can be done to judge the assertion in question than to submit it to this test. You accuse voluntary charity of impotence: well, without throwing ourselves into abstract

---

[1] "Charity," says de Melun, "has not only been depreciated, it has been calumniated. Its works have been mistrusted, and its sacrifices suspected. The motive which incites the strong to succour the weak, has been rejected as a humiliation and a shame." (*Annales de la Charité*, March, 1851, p. 137.)

[2] Thiers, *De la Propriété*, Liv. I. c. 2.—"It is especially in the study of the past," says De Gérando, "that we have sought rules for the future." (*Bienfaisance publique, Intro.*, p. 79.)

discussions, wherein we always run the risk of only seeing one side of the question at once; without engaging in divinations regarding the future, let us question the past; let us examine what charity has produced, wherever it has been unconstrained, and moved solely by religious persuasion; then, as is always necessary in like cases, allowing for the diversity of times and of circumstances,[1] let us judge from the effects which it has produced, of those which it can still produce under the same impulse.

These useful and conclusive researches in the past, are what the French Academy aimed to provoke, in its programme for 1849; and it was to render them more conclusive still, that it directed them specially upon the first centuries of our era. Christian charity, then in all its fervour, displayed itself in an empire of a civilization which has more analogy with ours than that of any other of the ancient States. What influence did it exert on that empire? What institutions did it found there? With what new spirit did it penetrate it? What relief, what remedies did it bring to its evils? Such is the question, wholly scientific in appearance, but indeed full of reality, proposed by the Academy. It has wished to call forth, for the instruction of the present generation, the too much for-

[1] "Societies progress and transform themselves," says Passy, "and the past does not always contain the true measure of the possibilities of the future." (*Journal des Economistes*, Vol. XII. p. 53.)

gotten recollections of the charity of early times; and that, while recalling the essential characteristics which then distinguished this virtue, the principle from which it came, and the spirit which animated it, its effects on Roman society should also be related.

We believe that we have not passed the limits fixed by this programme, in extending our researches a little beyond the fall of the Western Empire. Besides that the Empire of Byzantium, in the age of Justinian, offers to us, in regard to the influence of charity, more than one memorable and instructive example; besides that the conquests of this prince brought back, for a short time, under the Roman government, many provinces of the west, already conquered by the barbarians; it is known that, even under the domination of the latter, the civil and ecclesiastical institutions of the Roman world had still a certain duration; that the Goths, the Burgundians, and even the Vandals and the Franks made it a point of honor to maintain, for the most part, the *régime* of the civilized people they had conquered, and that it was hardly before the beginning of the VII. century that civil and religious society in the west took a decidedly barbarian stamp.

Our investigation, to be complete, ought then to embrace the first six centuries of the Christian era. Thus it will comprehend two periods of equal extent, but perfectly distinct, and separated from each other by the conversion of Constantine.

Not only the decline of the empire, and consequently the multiplication of the evils to be remedied by charity, date from the predecessor of this prince, but it is from Constantine that, Christianity being adopted and sustained by the State, the principles of charity began to penetrate Roman legislation more directly; so that the epoch when this virtue became the most necessary, was also the one in which it acquired, at least by legal means, the most influence.

After having related the efforts and the action of charity, in each of these two periods, we will doubtless be indulged in drawing some general inductions therefrom, relative to the part which it is called upon to fill in modern times. It would be impossible for us, we confess, to remain silent on such a subject. But the lively and powerful interest which it offers to us, will not cause us to lose one instant from view that of historic truth. We know that if the past throws light upon the present, it is only on condition of being studied with impartiality, and freedom from the trammels of system. The Academy demanded an historical work, and it is such, above all, that we have had the design to present to it. To collect, in the original monuments of the first centuries, all the facts of any importance connected with the influence of charity—to raise ourselves to the general spirit which sways them, thus to render an exact account of the effects of this virtue in the Roman world—such is the real object which we have proposed to ourselves in this work. Those of greater skill will doubtless find lessons there which have escaped us, and will derive consequences therefrom which we may not have perceived. The principal merit to which we aspire is to collect from this period, with somewhat of abundance, and, above all, with entire fidelity, the historical materials necessary for the solution of one of the greatest problems of our times, the remedies for want.

CONTENTS.

RECAPITULATION AND CONCLUSION.

PAST AND FUTURE OF CHARITY.

HISTORICAL STUDIES

ON

THE INFLUENCE OF CHARITY.

INTRODUCTION.

SURVEY OF THE TIMES BEFORE CHRISTIANITY.

In forming the heart of man, God has implanted in him, besides the instinct which makes him look to his preservation and well-being, an instinct of sympathy, which gives him an interest, also, in the happiness of his fellows. Whilst the former would engage him to live exclusively within himself, and to take himself for the only object of his affections, the latter draws him out of himself and forces him to live, to feel, and to suffer, to a certain degree, in others. There is, between these two instincts, the same relation that exists between the two forces, the concurrence of which keeps up the harmony of the universe; on their precise equilibrium depends the welfare of society and the harmony of the moral world. Who has not heard, in the depths of his heart, the often importunate voice of pity? Who has not yielded to it, sometimes, even at the expense of his own interest? The most selfish, themselves, are saddened by the sight of suffering; the most cruel have involuntary flashes of sensibility and compassion.

Thus we learn, without surprise and without incredulity, the humane deeds which history relates to us of the ancients. When it speaks to us of the generous zeal with which hospitality was practised among them, when it shows us, in the Island of Crete, at Athens, at Argos, at Corinth, public halls destined to receive travellers,[1] when it extols the liberality of a Cimon and of a Pelopidas, when it shows us the Romans, themselves, so inferior to the Greeks in this respect,[2] receiving in their own houses and waiting on the soldiers of Fabius,[3] and the wounded of Fidenæ,[4] we do not rack our minds to invent interested motives for these generous deeds; we do not treat them all as *bright and shining sins*, and, if we refer the glory of it all to God, who spoke in the hearts of these heathens, we are pleased with them for having obeyed His voice, even without knowing it.[5]

But with them it was with these humane sentiments, as with so many other natural and exalted instincts, which their religion, far from strengthening, tended rather to suppress, and to destroy.[6] Without speaking of those barbarian forms of worship, even in our

---

[1] Barthélemy, *Voyage en Grèce*, c. 34; de Gérando, *de la Bienfaisance publique*, Vol. IV. p. 274, &c.

[2] De Gérando, *ubi supra*, Vol. IV. p. 468.

[3] Livy, *Decad.*, I. b. 2, c. 47.

[4] Tacit., *Annal.* IV. 63.

[5] Augustine himself acknowledges among the heathen the influence of those natural feelings of benevolence. Ep. CLV. *ad Maced.* c. 14.

[6] Meiners, *Gesch. der Relig.*, Vol. I. p. 77.

days, which command the forgetfulness of the most legitimate affections, compel the mother herself to kill her child or to give it up to the most horrible sacrifices, deify cruelty, and even consecrate cannibalism, every form of polytheism, even among the most civilized people, was little favorable to the development of the sentiments of fraternity. To what love, to what reciprocal services could men believe themselves bound, who did not adore the same God, who did not recognise the same Ruler in Heaven? While there were, for each of the fractions of the human race, different protectors, different gods, what religious bond could exist between them, or rather what free career was there not open to national egotism? The laws of justice were hardly recognised between people and people; how could those of charity have been? Each nation believed itself permitted to seek its interest at the expense of that of the others: the right of the strongest was the common law. Had a people enriched itself by its labor, its neighbors, like greedy hornets, hastened to dispute with it its prize. Wars, colored with the most honorable pretexts, generally had no other motive than pillage. No equity for the weak, no pity for the vanquished. When the conqueror, moved to compassion, might have wished to spare, religion was opposed to it. "What hast thou in common with this people? Its laws, its gods are not thine. It has succumbed; let it die or let it serve thee!" And the captive, treated as without country, without a god, excluded from the temples, festivals, and sacrifices,[1] was, with his posterity, given up to the

[1] Vico, *Philosophy*, &c.. IV. 4, p. 312.

contempt and barbarity of his masters. How many citizens were there at Rome and at Sparta, who seemed to suspect that the slave was a man as they were.[1] The slave, according to the classification of Varro, was an agricultural instrument, which differed from cattle only by speech. He was a vile being, protected by no law, bought and sold according to need or caprice, which the owner destined, according to aptitude, to trades, arts, agriculture, beggary, or prostitution; that was enchained at night in the *ergastulum*, like an ox in his stall; cared for only according to the measure of service that might be derived from him; that was marked, whipped, put upon the cross for the least offence; that, when dead, was thrown into a den, to the animals; but which, when old, it was deemed preferable, generally, to sell, as Cato advised, "with old cattle and iron," or to be sent to the island of Esculapius, to finish as he could.[2]

Had they much more regard for strangers, whom, truly, they suffered among them, to profit by their riches or their industry, but whom they turned off with contempt to servile functions, and loaded down with exorbitant taxes,[3] and then, at the least fear of famine, at the least symptom of troubles, drove out by thousands.[4] In general, in the ancient republics, man

---

[1] Juvenal., Sat. VI., "O demens! Ita servus homo est!"

[2] Wallon, *Histoire de l'Ésclavage*, Vol. I. & II.; Dezobry, *Rome sous Auguste*, Lett. X. XXVI., Vol. I. p. 100, 271 &c. Dureau de la Malle, *Economie politique des Romains*, Vol. I. p. 410, &c.

[3] Blanqui, *Hist. de l'Econ. pol.*, Vol. I. p. 25; Boeckh. *Polit. Econ. of the Ath.*, translated into French, Vol. I. p. 74, 237.

[4] Sueton., *in Aug.*, c. 42; Dio Cass., IV. 26; Dureau de la Malle, *ubi supra*, Vol. II. p. 246.

was nothing as man; he had importance only as citizen.[1] Religion, born with the State, united to its constitution, fitted to its interests and its wants, limited itself in inculcating the love of country, obedience to law, bravery in battle, and respect for civil obligations.[2] It was not religion that pacified nations, that united tribes, it was rather the approximation of nations and of tribes that determined different forms of worship. It was not she that softened manners, it was the manners that, in becoming refined, compelled religion to grow more mild. Jupiter was not originally, either *hospitable* or *protector of suppliants*;[3] these were attributes which he owed to the new-born civilization of the Greeks much more than to the virtues which he inculcated to them.[4]

Even between citizens, whom the sentiment of their common nationality should have closely united together, religion still raised strange barriers. Each class, each family, each *gens* had, in remembrance of its distinct origin, its gods, and its domestic genii, its particular rites,[5] which it transmitted within itself from generation to generation, and which separated it from all the others.[6] The Roman patricians, for example,

---

[1] Blanqui, *Hist. de l'Econ. pol.*, Vol. VI. p. 48, 49; De Champagny, *les Césars*, Vol. IV. p. 264, &c.

[2] Briegleb. *Comment. de moment. moralibus rel. Gr. et Rom.*, *Goetting*, 1799, p. 17; De Rhoer. *Dissert. de effect. rel. Chr. in Jurisp. Rom.*, Groning, 1776, p. 5—7, 104.

[3] Πρόξενος, ἱκετήσιος.

[4] Therefore Rome had a temple in honor of *Jupiter Depredator.*

[5] *Sacra Gentilia.*

[6] Lebas, *Hist. Rom.*, Vol. I. p. 123; Moreau Christophe, *Du problême de la misère*, Vol. I. p. 12, &c.

had mysterious ceremonies in which the people could not take part; and when it was agitated to form alliances between them and the plebeians, they pleaded against it these ancient ceremonies which they were not permitted to profane. Thus, what a profound separation and what a perpetual conflict of interests between these two classes! What desperate efforts to wrest from each other rights, riches, and dignities! What incessant struggles between inhuman creditors who speculated on the misery of their debtors, and unjust debtors who formed coalitions to frustrate their creditors;[1] between the rich, fraudulently appropriating to themselves the property of the State, and the poor, ever ready forcibly to invade the rights of private property! While a few patricians kept up the immense estates which they had usurped, thousands of families, ruined by war or by usury, dragged from province to province a wretchedness no one thought of relieving. The complaints of suffering were neglected, the cry of revolt alone came from time to time to make itself heard. Then some concessions were hastily made, they abolished debts, they sent off colonies of proletarians,[2] they divided conquered lands, they distributed food to the poor citizens, and they even went so far as to proclaim the Agrarian law. But, the danger passed, all the concessions were withdrawn; the old egotism, the old barbarity regained the ascendant.[3]

---

[1] Naudet, *Du Prêt à intérêt chez les Romains*, (Acad. des Inscr., séance annuelle de 1849, p. 75, &c.

[2] Dureau de la Malle, *ubi supr.*, Vol. I. p. 234.

[3] Naudet, *Des secours publics chez les Romains*, (Acad. des Inscr., Vol. XIII., nouvelle série, p. 88.

"Homo homini ignoto lupus est."

These words of a character of Plautus paint better than was ever done, perhaps, the relations of men to each other in the ancient Roman society.

Doubtless, as common interests brought different classes together—as commerce, migrations, and conquests mingled populations—some prepossessions were dissipated, some prejudices effaced; men, brought into contact by more frequent relations, began to regard each other with not so fierce an eye. Some, even, over the barriers erected by customs, forms, and institutions, began to see, to suspect, at least, the existence of the primitive ties of relationship which united them; and philosophy, the depository of these new things, the organ of these new dispositions, attempted to give credit to more humane maxims. Socrates, who was so great a philosopher only because, better than all others, he knew how to listen to Nature, and to read what she had engraved on his heart, compared men to the members of a body, which, far from injuring each other, are made to lend to each other a mutual support.[1] Plato, in his book of Laws, rejected this maxim of the Lacedemonians, that each State, being naturally the enemy of its neighbors, all its institutions ought to be calculated in view of war.[2] Cicero, speaking of the distinctive attributes of Divinity, exclaimed, "What better, what more excellent, than goodness and beneficence? Is it not a grave error to qualify as weaknesses such

[1] Xenoph., *Memor. Socrat.*, B. II. 3, 18.

[2] Plato, *De Legibus* B. I., transl. of Cousin, Vol. VII. p. 5, 13.

noble virtues? Is there not, among the good, a kind of natural charity? The name even of love, whence that of friendship comes,[1] indicates a disinterested affection; for to love others for one's self, as we love the meadows, the fields, the flocks, from which we derive profit, is traffic, and not love. The characteristic of charity, as well as of friendship, is to be gratuitous."[2] Further, who does not know these beautiful words of the same philosopher: "Among human virtues nothing is more beautiful than union among men, than this association, this rendering their interests common, this love of the human race,[3] which, commencing with the family, progressively extends itself abroad to parents, relatives, friends, neighbors, fellow-citizens, allies, and finally to the whole of mankind."[4]

But all schools of philosophy did not profess such noble maxims. Lactantius reproaches them, in general, with having overlooked the principles of sociability innate in the human heart, in attributing the foundation of human societies to a simple and cold calculation of utility.[5] It is known that the Stoics erected insensibility and the Epicureans egotism into a system, and the former branded pity as a feebleness unworthy a sage; and the latter, as an affection of the soul injurious to its repose. Aristotle himself has not, in this respect, elevated the sentiments of the Greeks very high; in his view, anger and vengeance were legiti-

---

[1] The French has the words *amour, amitié.*

[2] Cicero, *De natura deor.*, I. 44.

[3] Caritas generis humani.

[4] Cicero, *De finib. bonor et malor.*, V. 23.

[5] Lactant., *Inst. div.* VI., 10, p. 532, &c.

mate passions, without which the human heart would lack one of its most powerful energies.[1] As to benevolence, he saw in it hardly anything more than a means of popularity for those who practised it, and for the State a pledge of tranquillity, a means of preventing seditions and troubles.[2] To him, as to the most of the ancients, the citizen was more than the man; the interest of the State prevailed over that of humanity. "One is confounded," says M. Cousin,[3] "on seeing the imperturbable coolness with which Aristotle analyses the nature of this special property, called a slave, as he would any object of natural history, without any scruple of humanity troubling for a moment his sad analysis, and staying his pitiless deductions. The slave is, in some sort, an animated property, he partakes of reason only to the degree necessary to modify his sensibility, but not enough to permit one to say that he possesses reason. Thus, according to him, nature makes men free and slaves, as she makes animals and men, souls and bodies."

Even the most spiritual philosophers, those whose admirable maxims we have just cited, did not always know how to free themselves entirely from the ideas and the genius of their age. Plato, who recognised human dignity even in a slave, and who would have others treat him with still more justice than they would their equals, does not, however, dissemble that, if he advises to do so, it is, above all, for the interest of the

---

[1] Seneca, *De irâ*, III. 3.
[2] Aristot., *Ethic.*, IV. 2.
[3] Cousin, *Œuvres de Platon*, Vol. VII.; pref., p. 83, &c.

master himself, and he accuses of imprudence rather than of harshness those who conduct their slaves by the lash.[1] If, to avoid the reproach of a want of sociability, he consents to admit strangers into the *State*, whom he excluded from his *Republic*,[2] he forbids under any consideration, that they should be naturalized, and would have every beggar, even of free condition, driven from its territory.[3] Cicero, forgetting his own principles regarding the disinterestedness which ought to guide charity, insists upon the civil advantages of this virtue much more than on its intrinsic excellence. Hence, he prefers the redemption of prisoners, or the relief of poor citizens, to expenditures for public games.[4] If, in imitation of Theophrastus, he praises hospitality, it is because nothing is more honorable, according to him, than to see the house of a citizen open to illustrious guests, the renown of his wealth and liberality spread afar among other nations, and his own fellow countrymen united to him in bonds of gratitude.[5] Besides, for this very reason, he advises every one to choose well the objects of his gifts, and in general to use much prudence and discretion in pecuniary largesses; "for, he adds, the inconvenience attached to such favors is that they dry up the sources of benevolence itself, so that the more prodigal one is in them, the more he is deprived of the means of

---

[1] Plato, *De leg.*, B. VI.; transl. by Cousin, Vol. VII., p. 361, &c.
[2] Ibid., B. XII., Vol. VIII., p. 356.
[3] Ibid., B. XI., Vol. VIII., p. 331.
[4] Cicero, *De offic.*, II. 15.
[5] Ibid., II., 15, 18.

giving them for the future."[1] This is much foresight for a virtue, which, above all, calls for unreserved impulse.

Had the philosophers used less reserve in the advocacy of benevolence, had they better recognised the bonds of mutual devotedness which ought to unite men together, they would not in this, any more than in many other matters, have succeeded in conquering the egotism and in destroying the prejudices of their contemporaries. Devoted, as has been said,[2] too exclusively to speculation, they knew little of the art of popularising their maxims; scarcely even did they feel the need of it; they had not that ardor which makes one wish, at any price, to spread around him the truth which he possesses; the temperate glow of their generous affections hardly warmed their most assiduous disciples who were near them, and they could not teach others to give themselves up when they knew so little how to do it themselves.[3]

Philosophy, then, among the ancients, had but a feeble influence in ameliorating the social relations. It doubtless enlarged the sentiments, it increased the affections of some men, it inspired, perhaps, Terence and Virgil with those beautiful verses, in which vibrates the pure accent of humanity;[4] but its action was little felt by most men. The lot of the slaves, so unhappy in the last days of the Roman Republic, grew

---

[1] Cicero, *De offic.*, c. 15.

[2] Troplong, *Influence du Christianisme sur le droit Romain*, p. 56, 57.

[3] Lactant., *Inst. div.*, II. 3, p. 126, &c.

[4] "Homo sum: humani nil a me alienum puto,
Sunt lacrymæ rerum, et mentem mortalia tangunt."

worse and worse down to the end of the first century. The crowd was as much captivated as ever with the cruel sports of the amphitheatre; human life was not more respected; the great majority continued to be the victim and the sport of the few.[1] The people of Rome, it is true, received its regular distributions of provisions, the *sportula* was delivered each day at the doors of the rich, the sacred repasts of the *epulones*, the profusions of the generals and consuls spread from time to time joy and intoxication among the lowest orders of the people; but benevolence had little share in these gifts; they were rather sacrifices wrested from vanity, ambition, politics, or fear,[2] tributes paid by the rich to the poor that they might not be disquieted by them.

In all antiquity, we know only one people whose civil and religious institutions really were marked with the spirit of fraternity: the people whose only God was Jehovah. He, the Protector of Juda, was also the Protector of Ephraim and Manasseh; each member of each tribe found in Him not only a firm guardian of his rights, but also a faithful supporter of his interests, a friendly intercessor with his brethren. In the land of Canaan, all the Hebrews were to have an equal lot. Every fifty years each family was to re-enter into possession of the domains, of which it had been stripped by whatever events.[3] Every seven years

---

[1] "Paucis nascitur genus humanum," said Cæsar.

[2] Naudet, *Des secours publics*, pp. 36, 37, 38. The same happened with public distributions to the people of Athens—Boeck. *Economie politique des Athéniens*, transl. Vol. I., p. 351, &c., 359.

[3] Leviticus, xxv. 10, 23, 24.

the land was to remain without culture, and the spontaneous growth of this year was common to all.[1] Each seventh day all labor was to cease, that the slave, the workman, and even the domestic animal might repose.[2] Each Jew, when he cut his harvest, or gathered the grapes of his vineyard, was to leave the sheaf for the gleaner, and the bunch for the indigent.[3] They were to recruit their slaves only among strange nations,[4] and if any Jew was forced, by want, to engage himself to service, he was not subjected to the same treatment as other slaves; he became of right, free, at the seventh year, unless he preferred to continue to serve.[5] As a member of the family, he was admitted to celebrate the passover with them. The stranger even, who, because of uncircumcision, was excluded from this right, was recommended warmly to the humanity of his hosts. "Thou shalt neither vex a stranger, nor oppress him, for ye were strangers in the land of Egypt."[6] Loans on interest might be made with a stranger, but not with a Jew;[7] a pledge delivered by the latter had to be restored to him before sun-set. Every debt was extinguished on the Sabbatical year, and yet every one ought to be at all times disposed to lend to the poor.[8] These precepts, and some others like them, which may be criticised as matters of political economy, and which, in our days, would gravely

[1] Levit. xxv. 6, 12.
[2] Exod. xx. 8–10.
[3] Deut. xxiv. 19–21.
[4] Levit. xxv. 44–46.
[5] Levit. xxv. 39, Exod. xxi. 2, 5, 6.
[6] Exod. xxii. 21; xxiii., 9.
[7] Exod. xxii. 25; Levit. xxv., 36; Deut. xxiii., 19, 20.
[8] Levit. xxv. 36, 37.

injure credit,[1] were less objectionable among an isolated people, exclusively devoted to agriculture; and, taking the legislator's point of view, we cannot but admire the humane spirit with which they are marked. What solemnity in these recommendations in favor of the widow and the orphan! What penetrating accent in these words: "If thy brother be waxen poor and fallen in decay with thee, then thou shalt relieve him. If there be among you a poor man of thy brethren, within any of thy gates in thy land which the Lord thy God giveth thee, thou shalt not harden thy heart, nor shut thy hand from thy poor brother. For the poor shall never cease out of the land. Thou shalt open thine hand wide unto thy brother, to thy poor, and to thy needy, in thy land!"[2] Giving of alms was like a sacrifice of thanksgivings offered to God for His goodness.[3] It was one of the works of expiation for which remission of sins was promised. "Break off thy sins by righteousness," says Daniel, "and thine iniquities by showing mercy to the poor." "By mercy and truth," said Solomon, "iniquity is

---

[1] Moreau—Christophe supposes that such was indeed the intention of the Hebrew legislator, and that, the loan being always a source of misery, Moses wished to prevent it by discouraging the loan (*Du problème de la misère*, Vol. II., p. 39–40.) This hypothesis seems to us more ingenious than solid. It is contradicted by the passages which the author quotes in the same place. Moses had a very simple way of preventing loans, by prohibiting them, whilst he recommended it formally. Deut. xv. 9; xxiii. 20; Levit. xxv.; 36–37.

[2] Levit. xxv. 35; Deut. xv. 4, 7, 11.

[3] "O Lord, said David, my goodness extendeth not to thee, but to the saints that are in the earth." Ps. xvi., 21.

purged."[1] These exhortations had penetrated profoundly into the spirit of the Jewish people. Old Tobit, on his death bed, repeated them to his son.[2] The son of Sirach taught them to the Jews of the dispersion. Job, in his misfortunes, bore witness to himself that he had always been a father to the poor, and that he had nourished the orphan.[4] The Emperor Julian remarked that in his times, there was not to be seen a beggar among the Jews: and to-day the Israelite has always an offering ready for his indigent brothers, and the mutual support which the members of this nation render to one another, has almost constantly preserved it, till now, from the touch of poverty.

Let us remark, however, that the charity of the Hebrew people was far from being entirely free and voluntary. Besides the alms which a Jew was exhorted to bestow voluntarily, there was a triennial tithe, raised on the property of each family, for the benefit of strangers, of widows, and of orphans, and this tithe was obligatory. It was the same with the first fruits of the crop,[5] and, as has been seen, the same, too, with the precepts relative to the Sabbatical year, to the year of jubilee, and the gratuitous loans; this was a consequence of the theocratic character of the Jewish constitution. Jehovah, the Chief and Legislator of the nations, declared himself also to be the sole owner of its property,[6] which He gave, in lease, to the Israel-

[1] Dan. iv. 27; Prov. xvi. 6. [2] Tob iv. 7–11, 18; xiv. 11, 12.

[3] Eccl. iv. 1–9 &c. [4] Job xxix. 13–17.

[5] Deut. xiv. 28, 29; xxvi. 2, 12; Levit. xix. 9, 10.

[6] Levit. xxv. 23. "The land shall not be sold for ever; for the land is mine; for ye *are* strangers and sojourners with me."

ites, only on certain obligations, certain rents, fixed and guarantied by the law. Even after the Jews had passed under foreign domination, benevolence as well as piety preserved among them, more or less, this compulsatory character. Ecclesiastical law, in the absence of civil law, exacted the offering, determined its quota, made of it a ceremonial prescription from which the Jew, except by abjuring, could not escape. He therefore observed the literal precept, rather, without the spirit of it; his charity proceeded often from the hand rather than from the heart, and Jesus could reproach the Pharisees, that while they paid so exactly the tithe of the smallest herbs, their hearts were void of all sentiment of justice and charity.[1]

It was not liberty, spontaneity alone, that was wanting to Jewish charity: above all it was breadth, extent; it did not reach beyond the chosen people. To have a right to it, it was necessary to belong one's self to the posterity of Abraham, or be admitted to reside upon his inheritance. The Eternal, although Creator of the Universe, and King of all nations, only protected the one with which he had contracted solemnly a covenant. "Thou shalt love thy neighbor, and hate thine enemy,[2] thou shalt aid those of thy nation, thou shalt bow the others under thy yoke:" such was the ultimate expression of the Jewish law. David, in this respect, was scarcely more advanced than Moses; the prophets hardly more advanced than David;[3] and, later, if the dispersion modified the

[1] Matth. xxiii. 23.

[2] Levit. xix. 18; Deut. vii. 1–24; xxiii. 6; Matth. v., 43.

[3] The beautiful precept of Solomon, which deserved to be repro-

national prejudices a little, if the intercourse of the Jewish with the Greek mind, at Alexandria, inspired Philo with maxims more liberal to strangers,[1] if, from time to time, this author recognised the primitive equality of men among themselves, and their relationship by nature, their common mother,[2] he nevertheless exalts to excess the prerogatives of his own nation, and, besides, is not exempt from all passion of vengeance.[3] And so the son of Sirach, who with touching precepts of charity towards the Jews, manifests a profound hatred against the Gentiles.[4]

And yet, the dogma, from which was to proceed the largest, the most disinterested charity, the dogma of the divine unity, was proclaimed in Israel. The God of the Universe could not eternally restrain his solicitude to one people alone; a time was coming when he would teach his worshippers to love, in Him, all His children. Moses had laid down the principle: Jesus was to derive the consequence from it, and thus to give the signal of the greatest, of the most beneficent of revolutions.

---

duced by Paul: "If thine enemy be hungry, give him bread to eat; and if he be thirsty, give him water to drink," (Prov. xxv., 21), applied itself to personal enemies rather than to those of the nation.

[1] De Wette, *Christliche Sittenlehre,* Vol. II., part I., p. 90, 100, &c.

[2] Philo, *De Decalogo,* p. 749, &c., ed. Hœschel, fol.

[3] Id., De execr., p. 937, &c.

[4] Eccles. xxxiii. 9, 10; L. 25, 26; De Wette, *ubi sup.*

FIRST BOOK.

THE INFLUENCE OF CHARITY ON THE THREE FIRST CENTURIES OF THE CHRISTIAN ERA.

CHAPTER FIRST.

THE FIRST PREACHING OF CHARITY BY JESUS CHRIST.

It is impossible to comprehend well the precepts of Jesus, relative to charity, if, before all things, we do not take into consideration the end for which he preached.

This end, according to some authors, was exclusively temporal and worldly. Jesus was a social reformer, who had taken upon himself the mission of elevating the suffering classes and of removing here below the scourge of poverty. Some have even attributed to him, in this regard, socialist views. The levelling of conditions, a community or equal partition of property, the abolition of all distinction of rank and fortune, such, according to them, is the kingdom of God that Jesus came to establish upon earth.

If such is, in effect, the end which Jesus proposed to himself, we must acknowledge that he proceeded in a strange and inconsistent way to attain it.

Having come, as they say, to change the social organization of the present world, yet he himself declares that his kingdom is not of this world. He affects to call it the "Kingdom of Heaven." He affirms that he does not wish to touch the established order of things. "Render unto Cæsar the things which are Cæsar's."[1] Having come to do away with the misery of destitution and slavery, to call men to a state of universal well-being, instead of making them desire that well-being, instead of expatiating on the evils of poverty, he commences by proclaiming blessed are the poor, blessed are those who suffer, blessed are those that hunger, blessed the poor Lazarus who lies covered with sores at the rich man's gate.[2] Happy! and why? Because they shall be indemnified, sated here on earth, because the spoils of the rich will fall to them? No; but because Lazarus, after his death, "will be carried to Abraham's bosom," and because "great is their reward *in heaven.*" He promises them that they shall be indemnified in heaven; it is there that he invites them to lay up for themselves, treasures, "where neither moth nor rust doth corrupt, and where thieves do not break through nor steal." And that they should "take no thought, saying, what shall we eat? or, what shall we drink? or, wherewithal shall we be clothed? (for after all these things do the Gentiles seek:) but seek ye first the kingdom of God and His righteousness."[3]

Finally, this Jesus came as they say to make a more just distribution of worldly goods, to re-establish the primitive and natural equality, to have restored to the

[1] Matth. iv. 17; v. 6; John xviii. 36; Matth. xxii. 21.

[2] Matth. v., 3, &c.; Luke, vi. 20, &c.

[3] Matth. and Luke, ib.; Luke xvi. 22; Matth. vi. 19, 25, &c., 33.

poor that which belonged to them, yet he preached charity instead of preaching justice; he solicits that which he ought to exact, he asks as a favor that which he ought to claim as a debt, and, generous to excess, he promises to recompense the restitution of usurped wealth. Far more; the first time that he is required to make a division of an inheritance, he declines, and, instead of the arbitration expected from him, he gives a lesson of contentment of mind, and shows himself against the love of riches.[1]

But what fundamentally destroys the opinion which we are examining, is the declaration of Jesus concerning the imminent ruin which awaited His nation.[2] What! Jesus is persuaded that Jerusalem is about to perish, that the generation he addresses will see this great catastrophe, and it is this moment that he chooses to change its social order! Strange revolutionist, who takes pains to reform that which is about to be destroyed, and dies in order to redress abuses which an inevitable overthrow was about to do justice to!

No! Jesus was not this social reformer, in whom many a humanitarian of our day complacently admires, and pretends to recognise himself.[3] He has thought

[1] Luke xii. 13, 15. [2] Matth. xxiv.

[3] Ought we take for serious the admiration of which writers of that party show, in our times, for Christianity, or are the quotations which they borrow from it, under their pen, but arguments *ad hominem?* They disclose too well on this point, their thoughts. They look as if they said to their contemporaries: "As for us, we have known, long since, what to think of those obsolete traditions; but as for you, who still believe in them, you, for whom the gospel is still a law and Jesus Christ a God, listen to their evidence in behalf of our doctrines." Now, I doubt, if by speaking thus, any one ever was persuaded.

so little of changing the established order here below, of founding a new temporal kingdom, that it is precisely for having refused that, that he was abandoned and sacrificed by his nation. Had he proclaimed himself king, a worldly liberator, all the people would have been at his feet. But his aim was higher. It was a spiritual welfare that he brought to the world. He came to preach conversion to men, which would lead them to the celestial kingdom. He came to show them life eternal, and the way they should follow, and the conditions they should fulfil in order to enter upon it.[1]

What are these conditions? The first is piety. To live with God in heaven man must have lived with Him on earth. He must love him, Him, the Perfect, with all his heart, with all his soul, with all his mind. But how love God without seeking to imitate him, and, if God is Love, how not imitate him in his love and goodness for his creatures? How love the Father and not love the children? There is then a second commandment like unto the first, a second condition inseparable from the first: "Thou shalt love thy neighbor as thyself. This is the law and the prophets. Do that, and thou shalt live."[2]

Such is the spirit in which Jesus preaches charity,

---

[1] Matth. iv. 17; Mark i. 14, 38; Luke i. 76—79; x. 25.

[2] Luke x. 25, 28; Mark xii. 33; Matth. xxii. 37—38. These precepts were literally inscribed in the ancient law; but Jesus, by borrowing them from it, gives them a higher meaning. Piety is not only the regularity of offerings and sacrifices, it is the full gift of the heart to God. Charity is not only the strictness and abundance of alms; it is the sincere and cordial affection for our neighbor. Matt. xxiii. 4, 23.

such is the part He assigns to it. It is not a political virtue that he comes to establish among men; it is a religious sentiment that he desires to teach them, and this much less for the present happiness of those who will be the objects of it, than for the eternal felicity of those who are called upon to exercise it. It is piety, the first fruit of this new birth, which alone can render them worthy of the celestial kingdom, it is the robe with which they must adorn themselves to be admitted to the "marriage supper of the Lamb." How pure and perfect, then, it should be! In image of God's charity, which embraces in an equal love all his intelligent creatures and makes his "sun to shine upon the just and upon the unjust," the Christian's charity ought to elevate him above all difference of origin or condition, above all egotism and all scheming, above all conflict of passions and of interests. "Who is my neighbor?" asks Jesus of a doctor of the law. "This Samaritan, whom the traditions of thy people teach thee to curse, as well as this Jew, whom thy law commands thee to love.[1] But when thou makest a feast, call the poor, the maimed, the lame, the blind; and thou shalt be blessed, for they cannot recompense thee."[2] "How often," asks St. Peter, "shall I pardon my brother? seven times?" "I say not unto you seven times, but seventy times seven. You have heard that it hath been said, Thou shalt love thy neighbor and hate thine enemy. But I say unto you, love your enemies, bless them that curse you, do good to them that hate you, and pray for them which despitefully use you

[1] Luke x. 29–37.

[2] Luke xiv. 13, 14.

and persecute you. For if you love them which love you what reward have ye? do not even the publicans the same? And if ye salute your brethren only, what do ye more than others? do not even the publicans so? But love ye your enemies, and do good, and lend, hoping for nothing again; and your reward shall be great, and ye shall be the children of the Highest; for he is kind unto the unthankful and to the evil. Be ye therefore merciful as your Father also is merciful."[1] What a pure and sublime ideal! Who else had the right to speak thus to men but Him who gave himself to them without reserve, and who went on Calvary to offer himself up for the salvation of all?

But if the horizon of charity, such as Jesus has traced it, is infinitely more extended than that of beneficence, wherever charity is, there is beneficence. Every true sentiment expresses itself in acts. How sincerely love our brothers as ourselves and not do for them whether for the body or the soul all the good in our power?[2] The love of one's neighbor once in the heart, beneficence flows naturally from it, as a stream from its source. It is because Jesus loved, that while announcing the gospel of the kingdom of heaven, He healed "all manner of sickness and all manner of disease among the people."[3] This same compassion, which seized him at the sight of the multitudes that fainted and were scattered abroad,[4] moved him also for other sufferings; he went from place to place doing good and leaving everywhere some testimony of his

---

[1] Matth. v., 43-48; Luke vi. 27, &c.

[2] Matth. vii. 12. [3] Matth. iv. 23, 24. [4] Ib. ix. 36.

inexhaustible sympathy.[1] Among his disciples the same sentiment ought to inspire the same deeds. Hence the recompenses which he promises to almsgiving; not, doubtless, to that which announces itself with the sound of the trumpet and seeks only the regards of men, not to those pompous tithes on which the Pharisees counted to whiten their sins and to excuse themselves from compassion, not to interested favors, which call for other favors in turn, but to modest alms, given for the eye of God alone, and proceeding from a heart full of love. "Go and do likewise," Jesus said, when relating the story of the good Samaritan. "Give, and it shall be given unto you; good measure, pressed down and shaken together and running over, shall men give into your bosom." "Make to yourselves friends of the mammon of unrighteousness; that, when ye fail, they may receive you into everlasting habitations." But wo to the egotist "that layeth up treasure for himself and is not rich toward God!" Wo to the evil rich man who has no compassion for the indigent![2]

Beneficence prescribed by Jesus as a pledge, as a natural fruit of charity, was so, still, for another reason. Cruel treatment awaited the disciples of the Saviour; the persecutions which assailed him, were soon to assail them also. Sent into the world like sheep in the midst of wolves, they were to be seized, delivered up to the synagogues, and into prisons, being brought before kings and rulers, hated, accursed of all for his name's sake, delivered up even by their rela-

[1] Acts x. 38; Matth. ix. 35; Mark i. 39, &c.

[2] Matth. vi. 1–4; xxv. 23; Luke vi. 38; xii. 21; xvi. 9.

tives and their friends.[1] What trials for their faith! How could it resist, if they could not count at least upon the support of their brothers? Jesus never ceases to solicit this support for them. In this point of view, beneficence, a duty towards all men, became an obligation still more strict between the disciples. To aid, to succor, to defend them, to do good, to any one of those who believed in Him, was to co-operate in the work of his salvation. "He that receiveth you, receiveth me," said he. "And he that receiveth a righteous man in the name of a righteous man shall receive a righteous man's reward. And whosoever shall give to drink unto one of these little ones, a cup of cold water only, in the name of a disciple, verily I say unto you he shall in no wise lose his reward."[2] "Then shall the King say unto them on his right hand, Come, ye blessed of my Father, inherit the kingdom prepared for you from the foundation of the world. For I was an hungered and ye gave me meat: I was thirsty and ye gave me drink: I was a stranger and ye took me in—sick and ye visited me: in prison and ye came unto me. Be not astonished—inasmuch as ye have done it unto one of the least of these my brethren, ye have done it unto me."[3] In the same thought, at the moment of quitting them, he returns with so much urgency to the new commandment, that they should love one another. This mutual love which should make them to be recognised by all as his disciples, which was to mark them in the eyes of the

[1] John, xvii. 14; Luke xxi. 12, &c.
[2] Matth. x. 40–42.
[3] Matth. xxv. 34, &c.

world with a distinctive and inimitable seal, was also to be their firmest support against persecutions. The world hates you "because you are not of the world. Love one another as I have loved you. Greater love hath no man than this, that a man lay down his life for his friends. Ye are my friends if ye do whatsoever I command you."[1]

But in these critical circumstances, benevolence was not useful only to those whom it sustained; it was useful, also, to those who imposed upon themselves this sacrifice. Wealth has its dangers as adversity has. Those thousand bonds wherewith it attaches us to the world — those factitious wants with which it enthralls us — those fantastical desires with which it fills the soul — that ease in which it lulls it — that vain fascination wherewith it dazzles it — that need of enjoyment which increases with the facility of satisfying it — that thirst of gain — that fear of loss, which increases with possession — were so many obstacles which closed against Jesus the hearts of those even who were the best disposed. How many of the rich who, after having put their hand to the plough, looked behind them! How many, possessed of this idolatry, wandered from the faith! How many, in whom the good seed was choked by the cares of this world, by the disquietude of avarice, by the attractions and the seductions of pleasure! How hard is it for them that trust in riches to enter into the kingdom of God![2] To fol-

[1] John xv. 12–19.

[2] Luke viii. 14; ix. 62; 1 Tim. vi. 10; Mark iv. 18, 19; Luke xviii. 24.

low a poor, wandering, despised, and persecuted Master, who had not where to lay his head, and for whom the cross was to be the bed of death — to follow this Master through opprobrium — to devote one's self, under his guidance, to the most painful of apostleships! Even as it was necessary in advance to have taken up this cross, to be ready to abandon father, mother, wife, children, and even one's own life, for a still stronger reason was it necessary to renounce one's goods, if they were obstacles in the way of salvation — to sell all, if it were necessary, to obtain the pearl of great price.[1] And what better use could be made of these goods, in renouncing them, than to employ them in freeing other souls from absorbing cares, from the temptations of want? This is what Jesus advised the rich young man: "If thou wilt be perfect, go and sell that thou hast, and give to the poor, and thou shalt have treasure in Heaven; and come and follow me."[2] Here, evidently, Jesus had in view much less the relief of the poor than the salvation of the rich; benevolence was here, to his eyes, an auxiliary to renunciation. So that he did not always demand the same sacrifice. When Zaccheus stood before Jesus, saying, "Behold, the half of my goods I give to the poor; and if I have taken anything from any man, I restore him fourfold," Jesus appeared satisfied:[3] he saw the publican cured of his avarice, and, even by that, salvation entered his house.[4] But the rich young man, still a

[1] Luke xiv. 26; Matth. xix. 12. [2] Matth. xix. 21.

[3] Luke xix. 1–10.

[4] It is the matter of a judicious observation of Clement of Alexandria. *Quis Div. Salv.*, c. xiii. (opp. fol. Oxon., 1715, p. 942.

slave to his wealth, could only find by its total abandonment the courage to follow Jesus. Hence the advice Jesus gives to him;[1] and, in the same spirit, addressing his apostles, he said to them,[2] "As for you who have forsaken all and have followed me, ye shall sit upon twelve thrones, judging the twelve tribes of Israel. And every one that hath forsaken houses, or brethren, or sisters, or father, or mother, or wife, or children, or *lands*, for my *name's sake*, shall receive a hundred fold, and shall inherit everlasting life." It is not the gift even that he promises to recompense; it is the devotedness, the fidelity in following him.

This is what Augustine hath very well explained in his sermon upon the contempt of the world: "'I have given to the poor,' thou sayest to me, 'what more have I to do?' Give thyself, to make the measure full. Thou hast not yet obeyed the Master, who says to thee, 'Sell thy goods; after that come and follow me.' 'Follow where?' thou wilt say. Everywhere; where he will conduct thee; through torments, outrages, and opprobrium."[3] So thought Paulinus, when, after having sold all his

---

[1] Hence, too, these declarations: "Wo unto you that are rich! for ye have received your consolation. Wo unto you that are full! for ye shall hunger," etc. Luke vi. 24, etc.

[2] Matth. xix. 28, 29; Luke xviii. 28–30.

[3] Augustin's Serm., 345, *De contempt. mund.*, c. vi., opp. 8vo., V. 21, p. 269. See, too, Ep. 157, c. xxv., V. xl., p. 264. Jesus says not, "If thou wilt enter into the life, sell thy riches;" but simply, "Observe the commandments." It is in order to have him perfect, that he tells him to sell his riches and to follow him; thus showing that it would be of no use for him to sell his property if he should not follow him.

goods and those of his wife, opened his granaries to the poor and discharged his debtors, he said to those who felicitated him upon having attained the height of Christian perfection: "Alas! I am only at the beginning. Like the wrestler, I have stripped myself for the fight, but it remains for me to fight and to conquer. I have left that which would have hindered me from following my Master, now I must follow him even unto death. I have renounced my goods, but it remains for me to conquer my passions and purify my heart.[1]"

Upon the whole, it is difficult to find even one declaration of Jesus where benevolence is presented as having for its principal end the amelioration of the temporal fortune of man. When he praises and prescribes this virtue, it is now as a pledge of the sentiments of fraternal charity, whereon he makes salvation to depend; now as the bond of the community of the faithful, the stay of each one of them against recantation and apostasy; and now, finally, as a means of aiding the rich in the way of renunciation. But in proposing this purely spiritual end, Jesus was to attain so much the more surely the temporal end which is attributed to him, and, by a contrast paradoxical in appearance, but which it will be easy for us to explain hereafter, the worldly good of individuals and of nations, that good which those who make it the sole object of their seeking pursue vainly, was to come out abundantly from a teaching which had for its first and principal object the regeneration and salvation of souls.

[1] Paulin., Ep. 24, ad Sever, c. 7, vit. Paulin., p. 17; Ed. Murat., 1736, fol.

CHAPTER II.

CHARITY IN APOSTOLIC DAYS.

THE disciples of Jesus showed themselves, after him, worthy heralds of his charity. Soon it is no more at Jerusalem alone that they preach it. Dispersed by persecution in the different cities of Palestine, conducted afterwards by their zeal into the most distant countries — into Syria, Phœnicia, Asia Minor, Greece, Italy — everywhere, where they carried the message of Christ, they published at the same time his law of love. Each apostle, each evangelist, in establishing new churches, essays to stamp upon them this divine mark. Each, in accents peculiar to himself, re-echoes in his preaching and his epistles the new commandment which Jesus left as a farewell.

In writing to the faithful who were dispersed in Asia Minor, St. Peter recommends to them to "love one another with a pure heart fervently;" to "be all of one mind, having compassion one of another, love as brethren, be pitiful, be courteous. And above all things, have charity among yourselves; for charity shall cover the multitude of sins. Use hospitality one to another, without grudging. As every man hath received the gift, even so minister the same one to another, as good stewards of the manifold grace of God."[1]

---

[1] 1 Peter i. 22; iii. 8, etc.; iv. 8–10, etc.

St. James calls charity the *royal law.* "Pure religion and undefiled before God and the Father is this," he writes to the faithful of the twelve scattered tribes, "to visit the fatherless and widows in their affliction." He reproves those who were content with having faith and had not works, and who said to their brothers and sisters in need, "Go in peace," without giving them those things of which they had need. He fears, above all, to see pagan selfishness stealing over Christian communities; he thunders in prophetic style against the rich, who, forgetful of the poor, only thought that they might sate themselves as on a day of sacrifice. "Go to, now, ye rich men, weep and howl. Your riches are corrupted, your garments are moth-eaten, your gold and silver is cankered; and the rust of them shall be a witness against you, and shall eat your flesh as it were fire."[1]

St. John, more pacific, limits himself to a repetition of the order which he received from the mouth of Jesus, and which, according to tradition,[2] he did not cease to the last to have upon his lips: "He that sayeth he is in the light and hateth his brother, is in darkness even until now. He that loveth his brother abideth in the light, and there is none occasion of stumbling in him. But he that hateth his brother is in darkness; for how could he love God whom he does not see, he that hates his brother whom he sees, and who, possessing the goods of this world and seeing his brother in want, closes his compassion upon him?

---

[1] James i. 27; ii. 8, etc.; v. 1, etc.

[2] Hieronym, Comment. in Gal., c. 6, opp. fol. Ed. Ben., V. iv., part 1, p. 314.

If we love God and believe in Christ, we ought to love one another; we ought to be ready to give our life for our brothers, as Christ has given his life for us."[1]

But it is in the mouth and under the pen of St. Paul that the preaching of charity acquires all its fullness and all its force. This great apostle, who, without having known Jesus, had so well penetrated the depths of his thoughts, insisted upon this duty as no other apostle had done before, and as no one after him had done. Since he had devoted himself, soul and body, to him whom he had at first persecuted, since he had made the entire sacrifice of himself to the cause of Christ, he knew no more reserve, and, if I may so say, observed no measure in the accomplishment of any duty; he raised himself without effort to the most sublime precepts of Christian morality, and with gigantic step attained its most difficult summits. There are men to be seen who by the vivacity of their imagination, strongly conceive and eloquently preach virtues which they are incapable of clothing themselves with; there are others, who, by favor of a happy instinct, practise virtue better than they teach it. With St. Paul the power of the idea responds to the energy of the sentiment. As gold in a furnace purifies and refines itself and throws out a dazzling light, so with this apostle, from the ardor of the sentiment springs the vigor of the conception and the plenitude of the thought. What elevation, what newness of views, when, in the midst of a society divided by a thousand

[1] 1 John ii. 9; iii. 10, etc.; 16 etc. 23; iv. 7, etc.; 16, 20; 2 John 5.

distinctions of rank, condition, and nationalities, he shows all these distinctions to be effaced, and as if dissipated, before God, who, after having created all men in nature, has created them all anew in grace, and has wished to make of the church one body whose head is Christ, and whose bond is charity.[1] With what superiority he defines this virtue, recalls its principles, retraces the characters of it, presses the motives for it, and derives its applications!

Like his master, he makes it, above all, a sentiment, whose seat is in the heart, and of which no external work could take the place. "Though I bestow all my goods to feed the poor, and though I give my body to be burned, and have not charity, it profiteth me nothing." There is no charity without the love of God.[2] A sincere faith, a pure heart, a good conscience, these are the roots from which it comes. As to its characteristics, "charity suffereth long, and is kind; charity envieth not; charity vaunteth not itself, is not puffed up, does not behave itself unseemly, seeketh not her own, is not easily provoked, thinketh no evil, rejoiceth not in iniquity but rejoiceth in the truth; beareth all things, believeth all things, hopeth all things, endureth all things, charity never faileth."[3] As its most deadly poison is pride, its most indispensable support is humility. It is in the sentiment of

---

[1] Col. iii. 11–15; 1 Cor. xii. 12, &c.

[2] It was with a view to unite more intimately these two feelings, in order that the love for our neighbor may be tempered by the love of God, that Paul ceases not exhorting Christians to pray the one for the other. 1 Tim. ii. 1, 8.

[3] 1 Cor. xiii. 3–7.

his feebleness and imperfections that the Christian finds the force to conquer resentment and hatred. As much as his heavenly Father has pardoned him, as much of celestial clemency as each day he stands in need of, so much he ought himself to pardon and endure from his brethren, that mercy may be his in turn. In imitation of Christ, who annihilated himself in taking the form of a servant, he ought to be always ready to regard others as above himself, and to subordinate himself to them, in the fear of God. Then he looks "not only on his own things, but also on the things of others." [1]

After having thus described charity, and the sentiments from which it proceeds, with what philosophy and what eloquence St. Paul shows his appreciation of it! "Though I speak with the tongues of men and of angels, and have not charity, I am become as sounding brass or a tinkling cymbal. And though I have the gift of prophecy, and understand all mysteries and all knowledge; and though I have all faith, so that I could remove mountains, and have not charity, I am nothing." [2] Thus, he places it above all the gifts which then conferred the most authority in the church. Charity adds infinitely to the price of all these gifts, making them serve for the common good of the faithful, and to the glory of God, rather than to the particular honor of him who possesses them. It is equally superior to them by its duration. All the others must have an end; the gift of tongues must cease; faith itself and hope will pass, since they will

[1] Col. iii. 11; Phil. ii. 3–7.

[2] 1 Cor. xiii. 1–2.

be changed into sight; charity alone will abide, and, fortified by the eternal contemplation of Him who is love, far from passing away or from being transformed, it will take new life.[1]

From these general views upon charity, Paul, descending to practical applications, presses by turns the numerous duties which it embraces, the maintenance of peace, union, mutual support, compassion for the feeble, kindness to inferiors, humanity to slaves, reciprocal services between equals, hospitality, the giving of alms; finally, benevolence under all its forms.[2] It is the livery which the saints and elect of God are to put on, here on earth. It is the least equivocal proof of the sincerity of their love. It is a sacred debt to Jesus, who, being rich, made himself poor for them.[3] Should they be withheld by the love of perishable goods? Could they fear, from sharing with their neighbor, that they would come to need? How would they not rather repose their confidence in Him who has said, "I will never leave thee nor forsake thee." "They must enrich themselves with good works." Through the hands of the selfish, riches pass and flow away like water; given to the poor, they form a treasure, safely invested, the benefit of which is eternal life, a sowing whose harvest shall be gathered in heaven. Sure as they are, concludes Paul, to reap the fruit of their good works in due season, let them do good unto all men, especially unto them who

---

[1] 1 Cor. xiii. 8, 13.

[2] Rom. xii. 10–13; xv. 5; Gal. vi. 9–10; Col. i. 10; iii. 12, 13; Eph. iv. 28, 31, 32; Heb. xiii. 1–3, 16; Philem., 16.

[3] Eph. v. 2; 2 Cor. viii. 8–9; Heb. xiii. 16.

are of the household of faith. Then unfurling with enthusiasm the standard of his Master, and raising in the midst of them the cross, on which he expired: "Walk in love," he exclaims, "as Christ has loved us and hath given himself for us." [1]

In these lively and fervent exhortations of the apostles, does there ever mingle, as in the ancient law, the appearance of a constraint, the shadow of an obligatory precept? No; the new law, in enforcing, with the old, the sovereign rights of God, to whom all the earth belongs,[2] ever wishes to act only by persuasion. "I speak not by *commandment*, and herein I give my *advice:* for this is expedient for you, who have begun before not only to do but also to be forward a year ago. Now therefore perform the doing of it; that as there was a readiness to will so there may be a performance also out of *that which ye have.* For if there be first a willing mind, it is accepted according to that a man hath, and not according to that he hath not. Every man according as he purposeth in his heart, so let him give; not grudgingly, or of necessity: for God loveth a cheerful giver." And to Philemon, "Wherefore though I might be much bold in Christ to *enjoin* thee that which is convenient, yet for love's sake I rather *beseech* thee. I would have retained Onesimus with me, but without thy mind would I do nothing; that thy benefit should not be as it were of necessity, but *willingly*." [3]

Thus the apostles preached. They left each one

[1] 1 Tim. vi. 17–19; Heb. xiii. 5; Gal. vi. 9–10; 1 Thess. iii. 12; Eph. v. 2.

[2] 1 Cor. x. 26.

[3] 2 Cor. viii. 8–12; ix. 7; Philemon, 8, 9, 13, 14.

free as to the measure of his gifts, and as to the gifts themselves. They did not order; they advised, exhorted, supplicated; and this preaching of persuasion, advice, especially of example, was understood by the Christians of every nation to whom they addressed themselves. They extolled the favors of a Caius, a Philemon, a Stephanas, an Epaphroditus, an Onesiphorus, and of many others.[1] They relate how, at Joppa, when St. Peter ascended into the chamber of Dorcas, the widows, weeping, showed to him the coats and garments which they had made for the poor;[2] how Mary at Rome, Phœbe, a deaconess, at Cenchreæ, had assisted St. Paul and with him several brethren; and how Aquila and Priscilla had exposed their own lives for him.[3] It was not individual charity alone which showed itself thus ingenious and devoted. All the churches founded by the apostles constituted themselves, from the beginning, into veritable benevolent associations, and the most of them were admirable in the exercise of this virtue.[4]

Let us judge of this by the portrait which St. Luke traces for us of the Church of Jerusalem. "All that believed were together, and had all things common; and sold their possessions and goods,[5] and distributed them to all as every man had need." And elsewhere, "and the multitude of them that believed were of one

---

[1] 3 John, 6; Philem. 5; 1 Cor. xvi. 17; Philip. ii. 25, 30; 2 Tim. i. 16. [2] Acts ix. 39. [3] Rom. xvi. 1–4.

[4] See the praises given by the apostles to the churches of Corinth, Philippi, Thyatira, &c., Rom. xv. 26; Philip. iv. 10–18; Rev. ii. 19; Heb. vi. 10–11.

[5] Κτήματα καὶ ὑπάρξεις

heart, and of one soul; neither said any of them that aught of the things which he possessed were his own; but they had all things common.[1] Neither was there any among them that lacked; for as many as were possessors of lands or houses sold them and brought the prices of the things that were sold, and laid them down at the apostles' feet, and distribution was made unto every man according as he had need."[2]

These words, taken literally, have made many believe that the Church of Jerusalem formed, at its origin, a community like that of the Essenians or of the Therapeutics, in which all individual property was abolished, and, into which, according to Josephus and Philo, no one was admitted if he did not, on entering, give all his goods to the association and put into the common fund the daily product of his labor.[3]

But the continuation of the recital of St. Luke shows formally that this supposition is false.

In effect, when Ananias and Saphira pretended that they laid down, at the apostles' feet, the whole price of their possession which they had sold, of which they really brought only a part, St. Peter did not reproach them with having broken the rules of the community; so far from it that he declares that whiles it remained it was *their own*, and after it was sold it was *in their power;* he reproached them only with their lie and

---

[1] Ἦν αὐτοῖς ἅπαντα κοινά.

[2] Acts ii. 44–45; iv. 32–34, 35.

[3] Joseph. *De bell. jud.*, II. 8; *Ant. jud.*, XVIII. 1 (Opp. Oxon., 1720); Euseb., *Præpar. evang.*, VIII. 11–12 (Par. 1728); *Hist. eccles.*, II. 16.

their hypocrisy.[1] The Church of Jerusalem was not, then, constituted into a strict community; it had not substituted property in common for private property; each one, on entering it, was free to keep what belonged to him. We have even reason to believe that many took this liberty; for if, among the seven or eight thousand persons who already composed the Church of Jerusalem, *all* those who possessed property had sold it, would the sacred author have taken the pains to cite one sole example, in the midst of so many? much more, would he have chosen for that example a Levite, who, being called to him at the altar in this quality even, could, without grave prejudice to his interests, sell land, which he had in the Isle of Cyprus?[2] We see, besides, in the 12th chapter of Acts, that Mary possessed a house, in full property, at Jerusalem.[3] It may be observed still, that, on the supposition of an absolute community of goods, the complaints of the hellenised Jews about the inequality of the daily distributions would not have concerned their widows alone, but their entire families, and that St. James would not have reproached the Church of Jerusalem with despising or neglecting the poor.[4] As for these words, "all was in common among them," it has long since been shown that, in a crowd of authors, whether sacred or profane, there are analogous expressions, which can only be understood in the sense of a moral or figurative community. Such, among others,

---

[1] Acts v. 4, 9. See on this matter the observation of Jerom. Epist. ad Hed. 6, opp. Ed. Ben., V. IV. part 1, p. 171.

[2] Acts iv. 36. [3] Acts xii. 12. [4] Acts vi. 1; James ii.

is this maxim of Socrates: "Among friends all is common;"[1] a maxim repeated, in nearly the same terms, by Aristotle, who energetically rejected, as all know, the community of goods advocated by Pythagoras and Plato.[2] In the same sense the words of St. Luke are understood by the best commentators.[3] They only see a figurative expression of that spirit of union, that perfect fraternity which prevailed among the Christians of Jerusalem, and which made each one of them, in place of enjoying his property as a personal and exclusive advantage, to be always ready to share it with his brethren, and even to sell it, if necessary, for the good of the poor. The expectation of the great events which the Christians then considered as near at hand, made this sacrifice more easy to them. Persuaded that not only Jerusalem but the whole world was about to perish, and that Jesus was about to come to judge mankind, they thought only of securing for themselves, by a liberal distribution of their goods, the recompenses which he had appointed for his disciples.[4]

Besides, even the authors who admit a real community of goods among the first Christians, acknowledge that it soon ceased, and that no other trace of it

---

[1] Mosheim. *De verâ nat. commun. bon. in eccl. hieros* (Dissert. ad hist. eccl. pertin., ‡ V. II. p. 22, &c.)

[2] Πάντα τὰ τῶν φίλων κοινά. [3] Aristot., Polit., II. 2.

[4] Mosheim (ubi supra, p. 43–51) shows that Luke's words have commenced being otherwise interpreted but from the fourth century, when the propagators of monastic life, to bring into honor that mode of living, pretended to have found this type among the first Christians.

[5] Pætz, Comment. de vi rel. chr. per 3, pr. sæcula, Gottingen, 1799, 4to. p. 27, 28. Stickel and Bogenhard, *De moral. prim. chr. conditione.* Neust. 1826, p. 76, not., 136.

was left but the repasts in common[1] of which Luke makes mention, and the origin of which we will proceed to recall.

It was a custom among the Jews, on their festival days, sometimes even on their ordinary Sabbath days, to invite to their family repasts ten or twenty of their relatives, neighbors, or friends. Towards the end of the repast, there was served a bread prepared more carefully than usual. The head of the family distributed pieces of it to each of the guests; then, touching a cup of wine to his lips, he passed it around, pronouncing words of edification and of thanksgiving.[2] Jesus, on the eve of his death, with unwonted solemnity celebrating a repast of this kind, wished that thereafter his disciples should celebrate it constantly in memory of him. In effect, they did so, from their first meeting at Jerusalem, and every time they assembled for worship.[3] For then it was a commemoration of the death and last farewell of their Master; but it was also an emblem of their sentiments of mutual fraternity, and a means of providing

---

[1] The assertion of Chrysostom is very express on this point. "When Paul," says he, "addressed the Corinthians with those words of blame (1 Cor. xi.), the primitive community had already decayed, but there were still some traces of it. As rich and poor began to be among them, they did not bring all their goods together (τὰ μὲν ἑαυτῶν οὐ κατετίθεντο πάντα εἰς μέσον), but they prepared, on certain fixed days, common repasts, to which the rich invited the poor; then this very custom degenerated." (Chrys. hom. 27, in 1 Cor., c. i., Opp., Vol. X. p. 240, Ed. Ben.)

[2] Moerlin, *De orig. agap.* (Volbeding *Thesaur. comm.*, Vol. II. p. 184.

[3] "Breaking bread from house to house, and eating their meat with gladness and singleness of heart." Acts ii. 46.

for the subsistence of their poor. From this comes the name of *agapæ*, by which these repasts were soon designated. Whilst in Lacedemonia, according to Aristotle,[1] the poorest citizens, unable to pay their monthly portion, were on that account excluded from the common repasts, in the Christian agapæ the poor were entertained at the expense of the rich; almoners attended at the tables and distributed what was left, either to the poor guests themselves, or to those whose age or infirmities had kept them from the repast.[2] The importance of these distributions may be judged of from the complaints which the Hellenized Jews made when they believed that their widows "were neglected in the daily ministrations;" complaints which gave occasion to the election of seven new almoners, under the name of *deacons*.[3]

From the church of Jerusalem, the institution of the agapæ easily passed into the other churches. If it recalled the family repasts of use among the Jews, it also recalled the repast of the tribe of the ancient Greeks.[4] So that it was admitted by the converted Greeks and Jews with equal readiness, but everywhere it had the same destination. Saint

---

[1] Aristot., *de Rep.* II., 7, 4. In Athens, however, if we believe the Scholiast of Aristophanes, there was always at the sacrifices of Hecate a distribution of bread and other provisions to the poor by the sacrificers.

[2] Bœhmer, *De coitionib. Christ. ad capiend. cibum* (in dissert. juris eccles. Lips., 1711, p. 237). Drescher, *De agap. vett. Christ.*, Giessen, 1824, p. 6, 8, 10–12, 25.

[3] Acts vi. 1–6.

[4] Φρατρία, φυλετικά. Moerlin. De orig. agap. (ub. sup., Vol. II. Part I., p. 185, etc.)

Chrysostom refers to this charitable end the origin of the agapæ, or love-feasts. "The faithful," he says, "after the holy teachings, the prayers, and the partaking of the sacred mysteries, did not separate immediately; but the richest and they who were most at their ease had provisions brought from their homes, and invited the poor to a repast prepared in the place of the assembly itself. This common repast, and the holiness of the place where it was celebrated, drew closer together their mutual union, and from it resulted for all a great joy and an advantage not less great; the poor were relieved, and the rich, objects of the gratitude of those whom they nourished, and of the favor of God for whom they did it, returned to their homes charged with an abundant measure of blessings."[1]

The first epistle of St. Paul to the Corinthians informs us, it is true, that abuses contrary to the spirit of those meetings began to creep into them. In imitation of what passed in certain repasts of the Greeks,[2] where each one consumed alone the meats he had brought, the rich at whose expense the agapæ were given did not always await those of their brethren who were retained rather late by their work; they hastened to take their repasts by themselves; the poor, on arriving, did not always find wherewith to satisfy their hunger, and the disciples of Christ were no longer there to break bread in his name.[3] Yet it is probable that this abuse, and those to which Peter

[1] Chrys., Hom. in 1 Cor., xi. [2] Συμπόσια φιλικά.

[3] 1 Cor., xi., 20–22, 33, 34; Schlegel, *De agap. ætat. apost.* (Volbeding, l., c., p. 170.)

and Jude allude in their epistles,[1] were but rare exceptions, which did not hinder this institution from bearing good fruit during the first three centuries.

That of deacons, to which it had primitively given occasion, took further extension and stability. Doubtless, the charity of Jesus Christ was to be manifest in all his ministers; and St. Paul wishes the bishop to be "a lover of hospitality," and "a lover of good men."[2] But it was the deacons who, in each church, were specially charged with the cares of benevolence; and the same apostle shows the importance which he attaches to the deaconship by the urgency with which he traces its duties.[3]

In conformity to the exigencies of oriental manners, and in order to avoid all that could occasion evil suspicions to the deacons, very soon were attached deaconesses, who were charged with the same cares to the poor and sick women which the deacons offered to the other sex.[4]

Among the indigent whom the church cared for, the most worthy of compassion, without doubt, were those whom death had deprived of their natural pro-

---

1 2 Peter ii. 13; Jude 12.

2 Tit. i. 8.

3 Rom. xii. 7–8; 1 Tim. iii. 8–13.

4 Rom. xvi. i. Neander's *Hist. de l'Egl. apost.*, French transl., v. I., p. 128. Lucke, *Comment. de eccles. apost.*, p. 100. The deaconesses were more or less confounded at that time with the assisted widows (χῆραι) and with the πρεσβύτερας, of whom Paul often speaks; 1 Tim. v., 2, 3, etc.; Tit. ii. 3. It is likely, in the churches composed of heathens converted, that the office of deaconess was first instituted. The Jewish almoners had to the women of their nation a freer access than Grecian habits allowed. (Augusti, Lehrbuch der Christlichen Archæologie, Vol. I. p. 251.)

tectors; and it was they whom the apostles, in imitation of the old law, recommended most warmly to Christian charity. Every widow over sixty years of age, and who did not find sufficient resources in her own family, was, according to the order of St. Paul, inscribed upon the book of the poor who were assisted by each church,[1] a list in which were also inscribed the orphans, the destitute old men, the infirm, and those who could not subsist on the product of their labor.

Already the bonds of charity began to unite together churches most distant from each other.

In the forty-fourth year of our Lord, when that famine raged in Palestine of which so many persons perished,[2] the Christians of Antioch made an abundant collection in favor of those of Judea, which they sent by Paul and Barnabas.[3] They were not alone, indeed, in giving this example; Helena, a proselyte of the Jews, and Queen of Adiabene, in Syria, sent at the same time, to those of her religion, wheat from Alexandria, and figs from Cyprus, and caused these provisions to be distributed to the poor in Jerusalem.[4] But Jewish benevolence wearied before the Christians' did. About fifteen years after, when a new famine afflicted Judea, St. Paul, who was then founding the churches in Asia Minor, in Macedonia, and in Greece, resolved to try the charity of the new followers of the faith, and to turn it to the profit of the cause which he preached. If his plan succeeded, not only the

---

[1] Acts vi. 1; 1 Tim. v. 1–9.
[2] Sueton. *Claud.*, c. 28.
[3] Acts xi. 27, 30.
[4] Joseph. Antiq. Jud. xx. 2.

Christians of Jerusalem would be delivered from a cruel trial, but also, succored by converted heathens, they would be reconciled to that principle of the vocation of the Gentiles, which, till then, had remained a mystery and almost a scandal. By the generous sympathy of which they would themselves see the object, they would recognise among their new brethren the fruits of a living faith, worthy of salvation.[1] Paul commences, then. He solicits the Christians of Galatia, of Macedonia, of Achaia, to give a share of their temporal goods to those from whom they had received spiritual advantages of a much greater price; to assist them this time in their famine, that they might afterwards be assisted in turn, so that there should be some equality.[2] St. Paul knows all that can be done by an accumulation of small offerings; he knows that a sacrifice, which, demanded all at once, would appear costly, even to the rich, but if made successively, and in an imperceptible manner, is easy to those in moderate circumstances. He invites the faithful, then, not to await his coming, or that of his delegates, in order to collect their alms, but that each one should put aside, on Sunday, the fruit of his saving, and each week to increase this little treasure, till the moment was come to deliver it.[3]

Finally, in order to leave them entire liberty, and, at the same time, to put his ministry beyond all suspicion, he invites them to name of themselves the per-

[1] Gal. ii. 10; 2 Cor. ix. 12–14. [2] Rom. xv. 26; 2 Cor. viii.
[3] 1 Cor. xvi. 1–2.

son who would carry their alms to Jerusalem.[1] Thus all that could make their liberality active and profitable, all that could gain their confidence, he exerts on this occasion, and gives an example of zeal and prudence, which the apostles of charity cannot too closely imitate at all times.

The success much surpassed his expectations. He gives this testimony to the faithful of Macedonia, that notwithstanding their great trials, they had given of good heart, according to their ability, and even beyond, and had appeared rich by their generosity. He gives the same evidence in favor of the faithful of Achaia and of Galatia, and the praises, which he gives to all, do not admit a doubt that his end was fully attained.[2]

Who would not admire these first prodigies of Christian charity, which, notwithstanding the distance of the places and the difficulties of the route, already averted the most frightful of scourges. During one of the three famines which had desolated Rome under Augustus, that prince, seeing provisions in his capital for only three days, had resolved to poison himself rather than to fall a victim of the anger of the people.[3] Later, under Tiberius, the delay of the fleet which brought the grain from Alexandria, had almost occasioned a sedition. From the height of his rock, at Caprea, the tyrant watched with anxiety the arrival of the convoy, on which depended his life or his crown.[4] Claudius had just escaped a still graver danger; in

---

[1] 1 Cor. xvi. 3–4. [2] 2 Cor. viii. 1–5; ix. 2; Rom. xv. 26.

[3] Dezobry, *Rome sous Auguste*, Vol. III., p. 93.

[4] Dureau de la Malle, *Econ. pol. des Romains*, Vol. II., p. 248.

short, in the most prosperous times, even, the fortune of the large cities was ever, says Tacitus, at the mercy of the winds and the waves.[1] Charity already possessed more certain resources. To nourish a famished population, it depended neither on the seasons nor on the crops; its granaries, its treasures, were everywhere, wherever Christians were found; a prayer, a word, addressed in the name of Jesus, brought abundance to the scene of distress.

But it was little, even in the interest of the poor, to cause the rich to fulfil the duty of benevolence, if the sentiment of his own obligations were not awakened in the poor also.

A disposition of inertness, which a deplorable prejudice kept up among so many of the pagan nations, by other causes had been also introduced among the Christians. The expectation of the speedy return of Jesus on earth kept up, among many of them, an agitation of mind but little favorable to regular and peaceful labor. Constantly believing that they saw the end of time, that they heard the sound of the last trumpet, and only inquiring after the signs that were to announce that great day, they abandoned their ordinary occupations, superfluous, they thought, for those who, from one moment to another, might be called before their Redeemer; their days were passed in inaction, sometimes in culpable idleness, and, when their resources were exhausted, they counted upon the charity of their brethren. "For we hear," St. Paul writes to the Christians of Thessalonica, "that there are some which walk among you disorderly, working not at all, but

[1] Tacit., *Annal.*, III., 54.

are busy bodies."[1] Thus, whatever may be done, an error the most innocent in appearance may have disastrous consequences. This belief that the end of the world was near at hand, which, among some, tended to detach them from it, if it multiplied the alms of the rich, increased the number of the poor; if it filled the treasury of the church, emptied it still more promptly, and, little by little, charity would have been weary of having to nourish so many pious sluggards. This is what St. Paul studied to prevent. While calming the too ardent expectations of the faithful,[2] he reminds them of that strict obligation to labor perseveringly, which he had not ceased to preach to them, both by his word and by his example. "Neither did we eat any man's bread for nought; but wrought with labor and travail night and day, that we might not be chargeable to any of you. Not because we have not power, but to make ourselves an ensample unto you to follow us. For when we were with you, this we commanded you, that if any would not work, neither should he eat."[3] He exhorts them then to work peaceably, not only that they might have wherewith to live upon, but above all from a sense of duty, "for the sake of their Lord Jesus Christ," in consideration of their dignity as Christians, to the end that they might have need of no one; finally from charity for their brethren, in order that they might have something to give.[4] He goes still farther. He wishes to have cut off from the communion of the church all

[1] 2 Thess. ii. 1–2; iii. 11.
[2] 2 Thess. ii. 1–3. [3] Ibid. iii. 8–10; Conf., Act., xx. 34–35.
[4] 2 Thess. iii. 12; 1 Thess. iv. 9–12; Acts xx. 35.

those whose conduct in this respect should not be in harmony with these precepts. "If any man obey not our word by this epistle, note that man and have no company with him, that he may be ashamed. We command you in the name of our Lord Jesus Christ, that ye withdraw yourselves from every brother that walketh disorderly and not after the tradition which he received of us."[1] Now, exclusion from the church brought with it, above all, exclusion from the Lord's Supper, and, consequently, from the repast of charity, which preceded it.[2] It equally brought with it an exclusion from all regular participation in the offerings of the faithful. All the benefits of the Christian communion ceased for him who had banished himself from it by his disorderly conduct. It was permitted to assist him in pressing need, as one would have aided a heathen; but he lost all his rights to the regular charities. The widows, whom the church assisted, were also held to benevolent labors for the community. It was exacted that they should have done good works, practised charity, succored the afflicted, and sought, in a word, every occasion of doing good.[3]

The poor man was, in a still more solemn manner, summoned to respect the rights of his neighbor, and guarded against all the inclinations which might have led him to infringe them. The duty of charity, which, according to St. Paul, is the fulfilling of the law,[4] the

---

[1] 2 Thess. iii. 6, 14.

[2] 1 Cor. v. 9–11. Among the Jews, he who was excluded from the synagogue, was also excluded from the sacred repasts used on festivals and Sabbath days, (Drescher, *De agap.*, p. 30, &c.)

[3] 1 Tim. v. 10.

[4] Rom. xiii. 10.

duty of renunciation, of contempt for the world, was prescribed to the poor as well as to the rich. Far from stimulating his desires, from intensifying his wants, from breaking, or exasperating his spirit by a sad portraiture of his position, far from rendering him morose, or from making him poorer through envy, the apostles preached to him that contentment of mind, which, added to piety, is the greatest gain; they painted to him the love of riches as a source of a crowd of insensate desires, which urged the man to his ruin; they exhorted him to show himself as they did, content in poverty, as in abundance, happy, provided he had wherewith to nourish and clothe himself, and eager, above all things, to secure eternal life.[1] St. James, himself, after those strong reproaches which he addressed to the rich of his day, did not address to the poor other lessons than those of resignation in their sufferings. "Be patient therefore, brethren, unto the coming of the Lord. Grudge not one against another, lest ye be condemned. Take the prophets who have spoken in the name of the Lord, for an example of suffering, affliction, and of patience."[2]

Every time that a new religious doctrine appears in the world, provided that it seems favorable to the ill-favored classes, it inspires them with hopes which too often result in seditious efforts. We have only to recall the revolts of the Peasants, and the excesses of the Anabaptists of the sixteenth century. No doubt, too, that, at the dawn of Christianity, on hearing the liberty and equality of the children of God proclaimed,

---

[1] 1 Tim. vi. 6–12; Phil. iv. 12.

[2] James v. 7–11.

more than one slave, more than one of the oppressed, hoped to break his chains, more than one poor man dreamed of a better division of property here below. The apostles hastened to dissipate these dangerous hopes. It was not equality, it was charity which they brought into the world. They came to abolish no right, but to teach every one to use his own well. They declared, no less expressly than their Master, that they changed nothing in the organization of society, nor in the exterior condition of persons.[1] St. Paul said to the Christians who were bent down under the yoke of Nero, "Let every soul be subject unto the higher powers, let as many servants as are under the yoke count their own masters worthy of all honor, and they that have believing masters, let them not despise them, but rather do them service because they are faithful and beloved."[2] They did not rivet forever the chains of the slave; they exhorted him, on the contrary, to recover his liberty, if he could do so according to law; but, as long as he was not legally enfranchised, they bound him to his duties by a new law, that of affection, of conscience. Let every one remain, before God, in the state in which he was when he was called.[3] Could one disavow more strongly all subversive tendency? could one consecrate more formally the

---

[1] 1 Cor. vii. 24.

[2] Rom. xiii. 1–7; 1 Tim. vi. 1–5. "Christ," says Augustine, on this occasion, "has not made of a slave a freeman; he has made of a bad slave a good slave; he has not said: 'Leave thy master, who is perhaps unjust and impious, whilst thou art just and faithful;' but: 'serve thy master better than ever.'"

[3] Eph. vi. 5–8; 1 Cor. vii. 20–24.

rights of each? Seeing the apostles recognize, sanction, in the name of God, a right so revolting in our eyes, which one man exercised over other men, who would believe that they thought of contesting that which they exercised over things, over inanimate objects?

Let us pause a moment here, and, seizing, in this relation, the spirit of the evangelical preaching, let us see how it conciliated the mutual obligations which spring from property; how, over all established rights, it spread a religious idea, which at the same time consecrated its inviolability and regulated its use.

The earth is the Lord's, and the fullness thereof.[1] Such is, upon this subject, the starting point of the gospel. God is the author, consequently the Master of all good things; and, as such, He is the warranter to those to whom He dispenses them, but, in return, He prescribes certain conditions to them. He says to the rich, These goods, which thy ancestors have left to thee, or which thou hast acquired by thy labor, are inviolable; no one of thy fellows has a right to claim them from thee. But from whom do these goods come to thee? Who has directed events so as to make thee possessor? Who has caused thy ancestors and thyself to prosper? To whom art thou indebted for the faculties thou dost enjoy? Who has preserved thy forces, thy health, and kept thee from a thousand accidents that mar the prosperity of so many others? Apollos had planted, thou hast watered; but who hath given thee increase? It is I, saith the Eternal, and if

---

[1] 1 Cor. x. 26; *Cfr.* Levit. xxv. 23; Psalm xxiv. 1.

I have done it, to what end and for whom have I done it? In granting thee much beyond what is necessary for thy wants, have I wished only to furnish an aliment to thy sensuality and thy caprices? Have I, in giving thee privileges, lost all remembrance of thy brothers? Hast thou by thyself any title to my preference? Have I renounced that universal providence which extends even to the birds of the air and to the lilies of the field? In manifesting myself as thy benefactor, have I ceased to be the common father of all men? No; thy conscience and thy heart tell it thee; above all, that heart, in which I have made to shine a ray of my goodness, that heart, which, in spite of thee, is softened by the sufferings of thy brothers. That which I have given to thee, I have given also to thee for the love of them; that which I might have accorded to them directly, I have preferred to have pass by thy hands, I have chosen thee to be the steward unto them, the dispensator of my favors. The less thou art responsible to them for the use of the property which thou hast received, the more thou art responsible to me.[1] Thou art free, without doubt, to employ it for

[1] This distinction between the civil and religious law corresponds to that which lawyers establish between the *perfect* or *positive* law which is the province of law proper, and to which legal actions in court, or legal sanctions or enforcements are attached, and the *imperfect* law, which is exclusively of the domain of the conscience. The latter is the only one which Troplong admits for the poor in regard to the rich, (Esprit democr., du Code civil; Séances de l'académie des sciences morales, 1850, Vol. VII., p. 312–318; Vol. VIII., p. 51–62, Cousin, *Justice et charité*, p. 49.) De Gérando has established the same distinction, but in a less precise manner,

thyself alone, but I am free, also, to withhold the inheritance a thousand times more precious, which I have reserved for thee, and, if thou hast frustrated thy brothers in this life, to frustrate thee, likewise, in the life to come.

It is thus that the gospel consecrates, at the same time, the rights and the conditions of property, in deriving them from the same principle. God gave it; this is at the same time the foundation of the rights of the rich and of their obligations; or, rather, before this great fact disappears all other right but that of God, and duties alone remain for men, the duty of each one to respect the advantages which God has given to his brothers, the duty of sharing with them what he himself has received.[1]

---

and which might easily give place to error. (De la bienf. publique, Vol. I., p. 463–472.)

One may compare, in this respect, the duty of benevolence to that of forgiveness, and generally to all those of which love is the principle. Neither law nor men can require any thing from me towards him who offends me; but God makes Himself his lawyer in my heart; He reminds me of my own offences, His own forgiveness, the brotherly bonds which unite me to the offender, His paternal views towards me by suffering the injury to be done, and, in the name of a superior law, of which He is the only arbiter and the only guarantee, He says to me: "If ye do not forgive, neither will your Father which is in heaven forgive your trespasses." In the same manner the rich owes nothing to the poor, from whom he has received nothing; but he owes all to God, from whom he has received every thing, and who, in compensation of so many graces, asks him for a little of his superfluities for his disinherited brethren.

[1] 1 Peter iv. 10.

CHAPTER III.

CHARITY IN THE SECOND AND THIRD CENTURIES.

THE principles which we have just seen established in the time of the apostles, were constantly those of the church in the two centuries which follow.

There was, doubtless, more than one attempt to introduce different maxims into it. The same theosophic schools which sought, at this epoch, to introduce into Christianity dogmatic elements the most foreign to its essence — some the dualism, others the pantheism of the East — attempted to introduce, also, the moral principles corresponding to these two tendencies, and which Clement of Alexandria has characterized with as much justice as precision. "The Gnostic sects," says he,[1] "are all exposed to these two dangers; either a culpable indifference as to morals, or an extravagant abstinence, founded upon the impious hatred of the creation." These, opposing to the Principle of Good, the Creator of the invisible world, a Principle of Evil, to which they attributed the creation of the material world, considered all enjoyment of terrestrial blessings as a concession to this evil principle. Those, identifying God and the universe, and making consequently everything proceed from God — evil as well as good — saw in a licentious and disordered promiscuousness the sub-

[1] Clem. Alex., Strom., lib. III. c. v.; Vol. I. p. 529. (Oxon. 1715.)

limity of wisdom. To deny one's self everything, or to indulge in everything—such were the two excesses between which the Gnostic sects were divided; and these two excesses resulted equally in the negation of property. In effect, we see individual property combated, under these two heads, on the one hand by the dualist sects, the Marcionites and the Manicheans,[1] and on the other by the pantheistic sects of the Carpocratians[2], the Prodicians, the false Basilidians—so many branches of the Egyptian gnosticism.

But the church always repelled such maxims. Lactantius puts among the number of capital errors which the ignorance of the true God caused Plato to commit, the absolute community recommended by this philosopher. "An odious system," he says, "in whatever concerns women; more tolerable, but still unjust, in whatever concerns property, since it favors the idle and extravagant at the expense of the industrious and

[1] "Marcio," says Clement of Alexandria, "in hatred to the work of the demiurge (Creator), would not allow anybody to possess anything as his own." (Strom. III. 4; Vol. 1. p. 522.)

[2] Clem. Alex., ibid., c. 1, 2, p. 510, etc.; Matter, *Hist. du gnost.*, Vol. II. p. 274, 289, 293. Epiphanes, son and successor of Carpocrates, published, about the year 125 of our era, a book with this title, "*On Justice*," in which he defined that virtue as a community with equality, and he consistently supported the community of goods and women. In the Cyrenaïc Libya, two inscriptions have been found—one Grecian, the other Phœnician—originating in the same sect. "The source of justice," says the one, is to live happily in common." And the other, "A community of goods and of women, such is the source of the divine justice and perfect peace of those whom Zoroaster and Pythagoras, those illustrious hierophantes, elected from the midst of the blind multitude to live in common." See those inscriptions in Matter's work

sober man."[1] Clement of Alexandria, after having, in his *Stromatas*, opposed to the false gnostic, imbued with the reveries of the East, the true gnostic, an imitator of Jesus and instructed in the holy doctrine of the apostles, attempts, in another treatise, to prove the legitimacy of the possession, and of the use of the goods of this world, and to reject the exaggerations which, in this respect, they pretended to support from the authority of Jesus Christ. "The words of Jesus to the rich young man should not be understood materially, but in their profound and intimate sense; 'Sell that which thou hast,' the Saviour said. This is to say — what? To cast away his wealth? No; but to renounce the false ideas which he formed of it, his excessive love for it, his avarice, and his disquiet. The Son of God here gives a new precept. He does not demand, then, what others had asked before, but something greater and more divine; that is, to purify our heart from its vices and to extirpate radically from it all that is estranged from Him. Already some philosophers have been seen to renounce their wealth, but at the same time to increase the vices and troubles of their souls — to become proud and contemptuous of the esteem of other men. How could the Saviour advise that which is fitted to ruin us still more than to save us? Is it not better to preserve an honest

on Gnosticism (Vol. II. p. 290; Vol. III., plates), and in the "Theolog. Studien and Kritiken," von 1833, where they are accompanied with the observations of Kopp and Raoul Rochette, (pp. 334, 335.)

[1] Lactant., *Epit. inst. div.*, c. 38, Opp. Gœtting., 1736, 12mo., p. 864.

mediocrity and to share it with those who are indigent? How share our goods with others, if we have none? Is it not to be inconsistent with the order of Jesus, 'Make to yourselves friends of your riches?' It is not well, then, to reject goods which can be useful to a neighbor; they are instruments of which it is necessary to make good use. They are destined to serve and not to command. They have not in themselves anything good or bad. When, then, it is ordered to sell them, that only means that it is necessary to renounce the passions and the troubles which they engender."[1] Certainly, we do not think that this sense was exactly that of the words of Jesus. We have seen that, knowing the empire of wealth over the heart of the young man who questioned him, the Saviour had really advised him to make the sacrifice of it. But if the interpretation of Clement was inexact in this particular case, it was right in general; and the at least tacit approbation which it received from the contemporaneous church proves how far it was from condemning or denying individual property.

Cyprian and Origen, nourished in more ascetic sentiments than Clement, adhere more to the letter of the exhortation of Jesus. "Let those," says Origen, "who, to elude the rigor of it, under the pretext of human feebleness, have had recourse to allegory, recall the example of the Theban Crates, who sold all his goods and gave them to the people, saying, 'Crates, this day gives liberty to Crates.' If he did

---

[1] Clem. Alex., *quis dives salvus*, c. 3, 11–14; Opp., Vol. II., pp. 337, 241, etc.

that for pagan philosophy, of how much more is he capable who looks to evangelical perfection!" And, to show the possibility of this relinquishment, he recalls the history in the first chapters of St. Luke. So Cyprian, in his sermon upon alms.[1] But both of them soon show, by the considerations in which they proceed to indulge, that they regard this sacrifice as a virtue — as not of precept, but of advice — as a work not obligatory, but only the more meritorious inasmuch as it supposes a higher degree of renunciation and of love. They praise Zaccheus, who, however, had preserved a part of his wealth — Abraham, who, while practising hospitality, was rich in lands and in slaves.[2] Origen himself explains to Celsus "that Jesus, when declaring that it is difficult for the rich to enter into the kingdom of God, does not mean to praise all the poor, nor to condemn all the rich; but only those who allow themselves to be corrupted by their riches, and cannot support their burden. Riches are good, says he, as often as they are used for doing good."[3]

The church of that time, then, recognised unanimously the legitimacy of wealth, not only in a civil

---

[1] Orig., *Comment. in Matth.*, XV. 15. (Orig. Opp., Ed. Delarue. Paris, 1740; Vol. III., p. 672); Cyprian, *De oper. et eleem.* Opp., Paris, 1842, 8; p. 478.

[2] Cyprian., *ibid.*, p. 478.

[3] Orig., *ibid.*, c. 16, etc., p. 674; *Cont. Cels.*, VI. 16, Vol. I. p. 642. Hermas seems to represent riches as an obstacle to salvation, but only as far as they divert the rich from God's worship, and prevent him from setting persecutions at defiance for Him. (Herman., *Past.*, lib. I. vis. 3, c. 6.)

but also in a Christian point of view. It considered wealth as the inviolable property of those to whom God had dispensed it; and alms, consequently, as a sacrifice entirely free and voluntary, which no one save the Author of all good things had the right to exact. Though charged to recall to all their religious obligations, it did not feel permitted, in this respect, to exercise the least constraint or to intimate any commandment. Justin Martyr says, "our rich give *when they wish*, and *what they wish*." "Each one of us," says Tertullian, "presents his modest offering once a month, or when he wishes, *if he wishes*, and if he can; for *no one is constrained*. Every one does it *voluntarily*."[1] Irenæus expresses with force this character

[1] Just. Mart., *Apol.*, II. p. 98, 99 (Opp., Paris, 1615, fol.); Tertull., (*Apol.*, c. 39, Opp., Paris, 1842, 8vo., pp. 73, 74); Const. Apost., II. 36 (Ap. Coteler, Vol. I. p. 249). These remarkable declarations suffice to refute the consequences which some have drawn from other passages of Justin and Tertullian. When the latter says soon after, "Itaque animo animâque miscemur, *nihil de rei communicatione dubitamus; omnia indiscreta* sunt apud nos præter uxores" (*ub. sup.*, p. 74), and when Justin Martyr says (*ub. sup.*, p. 61), "We, who loved before all the goods of the earth, now we *put in common* (εις κοινὸν φερομεν), and *give a part* of it to all the poor (κοινωνοῦμεν)," it is evident that they do not mean to speak of an absolute community, which would exclude any property, consequently any gift—with much more reason any voluntary gift—but only of a community of interest and affection, that lead them to contribute with all their power to the relief of their brethren, "Animo animâque miscemur." (Stickel and Bogenhard, *ub. sup.*, p. 104; Poetz, *Comment.*, etc., p. 113, not.) It is in the same sense that we must understand those words of Barnabas' epistles, evidently borrowed from the first chapters of the Acts: Κοινωνήσεις ἐν πᾶσι τῷ πλησίον σου, οὐκ ἐρεῖς ἴδια. ("Thou shalt put

of spontaneity which distinguishes Christian from Jewish alms, and which, according to him, constitutes its high superiority. "There were," says he, "sacrifices and offerings among the Jewish people; so there are in the church, but with this difference, that there it was slaves who offered them, here it is free men. The Jews were bound to the regular payment of tithes; the Christians, enfranchised by Jesus, consecrate all their property to the use of the Lord, giving freely and heartily still more than the Jews, because they have greater hopes."[1] It belonged, then, to no one among the Christians to claim alms as a debt;[2] the poor were to wait with patience and submission for the generosity of their brethren, and testify their gratitude, first of all, to God the author

---

all in common with thy neighbors, and thou shalt not say that anything belongs to thee of thine own.") Barnab., *Ep.*, c. 19. In Patr. Apost., (Opp., 8vo., Tubing, 1842, p. 39.) As to the passage of Lucian, which, in his narration of the death of Peregrinus (c. 12), seems to assert that at his time Christians considered all things as common among themselves, besides that this assertion would be completely denied by history, many interpreters, instead of κοινὰ, read κενὰ ἡγοῦνται, which agrees better with the context, showing the contempt of the Christians of that time for terrestrial goods. (Augusti. *Lehrbuch der Christlichen Archæol,*, Vol. I., p. 50.) But the word κοινὰ may also be understood in the vague meaning just above mentioned.

[1] Iren., *De hæres.*, IV. 34. These words sufficiently explain the precept of *giving all*, which Irenæus seems to express somewhere else in a more absolute manner. (*Ibid.*, c. 27.)

[2] The priest Valens, whom the Philippians had excluded from their communion, is designated in Polycarp's epistle by the epithet of πλεονέκτης, avaricious. (Polyc., *Ep. ad Phil.*, c. 11, 12.) But his avarice was that of Judas; it had brought him to misuse, in

of all these favors, and then to their brothers, as for a kindness which each one had a right to withhold. "Let not slaves ask to be redeemed from the treasury of the church, for fear that they be found slaves of cupidity. Let them resign themselves, rather, to their state, and serve, with still greater zeal, for the glory of God."[1] "Let the poor," says Hermas, "render to God prayer and thanksgivings for the rich."[2] The apostolic constitutions, the first six books of which contained the usages and regulations in vigor in the church up to the epoch of Constantine, likewise recommend to widows and orphans to receive with reverence the aid accorded to them, and to render thanks for it to God; they advise that the bishop make known to the poor the names of their benefactors, in order that they may pray for them by name. As for widows "envious and speaking evil, who, in place of invoking the benedictions of God on their benefactors and their bishop, were inquiring as to what others had received, and were complaining of the injustice of the distributors of alms," they are treated as "evil souls who belong not to Christ."[3] The same constitutions prescribed assistance to every poor man, not according to his expectations, but in proportion to his true needs, (of which the bishops and deacons were declared sole

---

concert with his wife, the money of the church. (Hœfele, *Patr. App. Opp.*, p. 201, note.)

[1] Ignat., *Ep. ad Polyc.*, c. 4 (*ub. sup.*, p. 179.)

[2] Herm., *Pastor*, III., simil. 2 (*Patr. App. Opp.*, Ed. Hœfele, p. 291; *Cfr.* Clem. Rom., 1 *Ep. ad Cor.*, c. 38 (*Ibid.* p. 83.)

[3] Const. apost., IV. 5.; III. 4, 12–14 (in Coteler, *Patr. apost.* Amstelod., 1724, p. 296, 279, 288, &c.)

judges), and in the most proper manner to make sure his temporal and moral good.[1] "And you, the youth of the church," they added, "work with assiduity to provide for your needs, and give yourself up in all holiness to your work. God hates the lazy. Those then who are poor from the faults of their conduct, from drunkenness, or debauchery, do not merit aid; they are not worthy even of being members of the church."[2] "Wo," says Saint Clement of Alexandria, "to those who have and who, nevertheless, from hypocrisy and meanness of spirit, consent to receive from their brethren."[3]

Thus stimulating the efforts of the poor, thus recalling to him, in so express a manner, the inviolable respect due to rights and to property, the teachers of the church could, all the more advantageously, preach to the rich the spirit of devotedness and of sacrifice, which they did, not by dryly reproducing the recommendations of the apostles, as a lesson well conned, but with a copiousness and warmth of expression proper to them, and which, nevertheless, allies itself almost always with an entire fidelity to their models.

Like them, it is to the great principle of the unity of God and his universal love for men that they associate the principle of human fraternity and the love due from man to man.

"I have just explained what is due to God," says Lactantius, "I will now tell what is due to man, though these two duties fundamentally form but one, since

[1] *Ibid.*, II., 27, 28; IV. 2, l. c., p. 243, 295.

[2] *Ibid.*, II. 4, 63; l. c., p. 217, 274.

[3] Clem. Alex., *Fragm. comm. in Matth.* v. 42.

man is the image of God. God, in creating man in a state of nakedness and feebleness, for which he has compensated him with .the gift of reason, has given him, besides, those sentiments of sympathy which induce him to love and to seek for his equals, and to demand of them and to lend to them, by turns, a support against all dangers. A sacred bond, which we could not break without criminality, and, in some sort, without parricide; for, if we all derive our origin from the same man, whom God formed with his own hands, we are relatives even by that, and not only we ought to abstain from doing harm to one another, which is avowed by the philosophers, but we ought to be always ready to do good to one another; we owe subsistence to the poor and succor to the afflicted."[1] Origen says, "We are all, by nature, neighbors to each other; but by deeds of charity, he who can do good becomes more particularly the neighbor of the poor. Charity always tends, then, to God, from whom is its origin, and regards our neighbor, whose nature we partake. Thus, this mutual affection, due to each other, though it admits of degrees and should be proportionate to the dignity and diverse merits of our brethren, ought also to embrace all men, even to our very enemies,—and those in the bonds of iniquity, since the rights of relationship, which unite us to them, exist no less."[2] "Do good to all men," said Hermas; give to all the poor with simplicity of heart; for God

---

[1] Lactant., *Instit. div.*, VI. 10, p. 531, &c.

[2] Orig., in *Cant. Cant.*, prolog. et lib. III., Vol. III. p. 29 et 73. *Cfr.* Hom. 34 in Luc., *ibid.*, p. 972, &c.

wills that we should give of our goods to all.[1] Cyprian said, "Let us be, by our liberality, imitators of that of our Heavenly Father, who bestoweth equally unto all, the sun, the rain, and all common blessings."[2] It is by following this order, in imitating God in his inexhaustible bounty, in borrowing of him this amiable attribute, that the Christians could the better unite themselves to him, and testify to him, at the same time, their admiration and their gratitude. "Who can sufficiently praise," said Saint Clemens Romanus, "this bond of the love of God? Who can worthily celebrate its beauty, its magnificence? Who can say to what height it raises us in inviting us to Him?"[3] "When faith shall have revealed to thee," says, in his style full of emotion, the author of the Epistle to Diognetus, the greatness of the love of God for man, what love wilt thou not feel, in turn, for Him who hath first loved thee? And if thou lovest Him, thou wilt become the imitator of his goodness. And be not surprised that man can imitate God. In effect, he can if he will; not in seeking riches and sway, not in crushing his inferiors with the weight of his power; for the greatness of God does not consist in these things, and this would not be to imitate him; but in loading himself with the burdens of his brothers, in making his inferiors share all the advantages which he enjoys, in participating of the gifts of Providence with the poor, he becomes divine to those whom he relieves, and is truly the imitator of the Most High."[4]

---

[1] Herm., *Past.*, lib. II., mand. 2, l. c., p. 265.

[2] Cyprian, *de Op. et eleem.*, Opp., p. 491.

[3] Clem. Rom., 1 *Ep. ad Cor.*, c. 49, l. c., p. 95.

[4] Epist. ad Diogn., c. 10, Opp. Patr. Ap., p. 236, &c.

But, if such are the natural ties of relationship which united men together, and the mutual obligations resulting from them, how much more close and fraternal, according to the church, are those which established among the disciples of Christ their community of faith, of worship, of vocation and of hope!"[1] "If, in spite of your harshness to us," said Tertullian, in his Apology to the Pagans, "we are your brothers by nature, our common mother, by how much more just title ought those who have recognised in God one common Father to be called brothers; they who participate in one spirit of sanctity, and who, from the same ignorance, have attained the same truth and the same light."[2] So, to the sentiment of the natural blessings of God, was united, to excite their mutual charity, the sentiment of the blessings of grace. Redeemed, at the price of the blood of Christ, from the slavery of sin and death, and not able to pay him the price of their ransom, they were to repay it to those whose low condition, out of charity, he had chosen, in whose humble livery he had been clad, with whom, in short, he had, in some sort, identified himself, regarding what was done for them as done for himself.[3] Each Christian

---

[1] Minuc. Fel., *Octav.*, c. 31, p. 207, Ed. Lindn., 1760, 12mo.

[2] Tertull. Apol., c. 39, p. 74, &c.

[3] Hence it happened that, according to Ignatius, the Docetes, who believed that they exalted the dignity of Jesus by denying the reality of his coming in the flesh, his sufferings and death, were strangers as much to the feelings of charity, as to those of Christian piety. They were not able to imitate a devotion which they disregarded. He said: "Ignorant as they are of the grace of Jesus Christ, who has come to save us, they have no compassion either for the widow, or for the orphan, or for the captive, or for those

must see, in his poor brothers, an image of Christ suffering for him, and endeavor, in his turn, to comfort him in them. "Yes," said Cyprian to those who recommended to him the deliverance of the Numidian prisoners, "if charity did not lead us to redeem them, yet we ought to see in them so many temples of God taken by the barbarians, or rather Christ himself made prisoner, and to redeem him who hath redeemed us with his blood." [1] What! Jesus had given his life for them, and they should give nothing for the love of him, they would not make for him who had saved them the least of the sacrifices which so many made for the enemy of their salvation! "What shame for you," eloquently exclaims Cyprian, "and what ignominy for your Redeemer, when, on the last day the dæmon, accompanied by his servants, shall advance towards Jesus Christ and dare to say to him: 'As for me, I have endured neither outrages nor rods for these; I have not shed my blood nor suffered for them the punishment of the cross, I have not redeemed them at the cost of my life, I had not, either, a celestial kingdom to promise to them, no paradise, no glorious immortality; and yet see what presents they have made to me, what zeal, what devotion they have displayed in my service! And you, show me the treasures which these Christians, to whom you have given your law, to whom you have promised celestial goods

---

who suffer from thirst and hunger." Ignat. c. 6; p. 172. Or else, absorbed by the vain metaphysical speculations in which they made religion to consist, they neglected sanctification and good works.

[1] Cyprian, *Ep.*, LX., p. 202.

in exchange for those that are perishable, have exchanged for your blessings.'"[1]

However, were they ignorant that it was only thus that they could, according to the church, appropriate to themselves the favors of redemption? "After baptism," said Cyprian, "we would have no resource to expiate our continual faults, if the divine compassion had not taught us works of justice and pity, as a way of safety, and alms as a means of washing out the stains of our vices."[2] "To give to him who is hungry something to eat, to clothe him that is naked, to open our houses to strangers and to those without a resting-place, to lend our assistance to orphans and to widows, to redeem captives, to visit and nurse the sick, to provide for the burial of the dead, this," Lactantius said, "is the sacrifice truly agreeable to God, who is appeased by the piety of his children far more than by the blood of victims,"[3] and who, as Justin Martyr said, "does not ask that we should consume by fire the things which he has created for our subsistence, but that we should use them for ourselves and for the indigent."[4]

But when the objector asked of Lactantius, Shall I go and dissipate thus the riches painfully amassed by my toil or by that of my ancestors, and see myself reduced to have recourse to the charity of my brothers? "Pusillanimous man!" he answered, "thou fearest poverty, then, that poverty which your philosophers

---

[1] Cypr., *De opp. et eleem.*, p. 488.
[2] *Ibid.*, p. 473; *Cfr. Ep.* LII., p. 149.
[3] Lactant., *Epit. Instit. div.*, c. 65.
[4] Just. Mart., *Apol.*, II. p. 60.

have praised as the most tranquil of conditions! What thou fearest is, on the contrary, a refuge from all disquietudes. Dost thou not know, then, to how many hazards wealth exposes thee, too happy if it does not cause thy death! Loaded with the booty which excites the envy of thy own kin, thou goest in the midst of snares. Why dost thou hesitate to put in a secure place that which a thief, a proscriptive decree, or the hand of the enemy, will strip from thee perhaps, and to trust thy treasures with God, with whom thou hast neither thieves, nor rust, nor tyrants to fear? He who is rich in God is never poor. Besides you are not told to diminish or dissipate your patrimony, but only to consecrate to a better use what thou wouldst consecrate to things of nothingness. On that, with which thou wouldst nourish wild beasts for the circus, nourish the poor, redeem captives; out of that with which thou wouldst acquire wretches for the sword, provide for the sepulture of the dead. From thy perishable goods make unto God a noble sacrifice, to obtain, in return, an eternal reward."[1] "A grand and sublime deed," exclaims Cyprian, "to constitute God our debtor."[2] "A marvellous exchange," says Hermas, "is that which is established between the rich and the poor! The rich gives to the poor what

[1] Lactant., *Inst. div.*, VI. 12, p. 548–550.

[2] Cyprian, *De opp. et eleem.*, p. 492. *De habit. virg.*, p. 352. "When," says Clement, "you draw water out of a well sustained by springs, the water is soon as abundant as before. Likewise the fund of alms is renewed soon after it has been employed; its source is inexhaustible, for it is the blessing of the Lord." (Clem. Alex., *Pædag.*, III. 7.)

he needs, and the poor, in turn, enriches him by his prayers. Thus the vine embellishes with its branches and enriches with its fruit the elm on which it leans."[1] "O rich man," adds Clement of Alexandria, "wilt thou not conclude so precious a bargain? Thou whose salvation is each day compromitted by so many creatures, raise for thy safety an inoffensive and pacific army of old men, pious orphans, and meek widows, select spirits who conceal their nobility from the eyes of men, wish to be holy without parade, and are here below as if in exile, waiting for the day that is to unite them to God. Such are the guardians which you need. No one is idle, no one is useless; one will pray for thy salvation, another will sympathize with thy pains, another will sigh for thee in the bosom of God; as many poor relieved, so many advocates for thee, so many intercessors for thee before the sovereign judge."[2] "Ah!" says Cyprian, "what shall be thy glory and thy joy, in the last day, when the Master, reviewing his people, will give to thy merits and thy deeds the promised recompense, goods eternal and celestial for temporal and terrestrial goods, and will open to thee the kingdom of heaven!"[3]

These eloquent exhortations, of which the pre-

---

[1] Herm., *Past.*, lib. III. *simil.* 2, *ubi sup.*, p. 290, &c.

[2] Clem. Alex., *quis div. salv.*, c. 32–36; *Opp.*, Vol. II. p. 953, &c.

[3] Cyprian, *De opp et eleem.*, p. 491. The day of the eternal retribution was then considered as very near. Barnab., 6, *Epist.* c. 21, l. c. p. 4I. Cyprian, *Ad Demetr.*, p. 434; *De mortal.*, p. 471; *De exhort. ad mart.*, p. 522. Tertull., *De cultu fœmin.*, II. 9; *Opp.*, Vol. I. p. 295, &c., Lactant., *Inst. div.*, VII. 25, &c.; *Opp.*, p. 682, &c., &c. *Poetz, Comment., de vi quam*, &c., p. 36.

ceding citations offer but an imperfect summary, derived a new force from the situation of those to whom they were addressed. Isolated amidst a hostile and persecuting world, they felt so much the more the need of strict union with each other, and of lending a charitable support against all evils.[1] Justin Martyr paints to us the change effected in this respect among the disciples of Jesus. "We all," says he, "who only lived for the goods of this world, this day liberally divide what we have with the poor."[2] Tertullian shows us, in his turn, the house of each Christian and his table and his granaries hospitably opened to all the brethren, and Christian women eager to carry aid to the poor in all places, and to visit the most humble roofs.[3]

But though these individual alms may have then formed the largest part of the gifts distributed by charity, they are naturally less known to us than the deeds of collective benevolence. Consequently these last we have carefully to retrace.

The letter of Pliny to the Emperor Trajan proves the maintenance of the *agapæ*, or repasts of charity, in the churches of Asia Minor.[4] A crowd of other witnesses testifies also to the preservation of this usage in most of the Christian communities, and at the same time gives us precious details concerning

---

[1] Poetz., *ibid.*, p. 108. Vulliemin, *Mœurs des Chrétiens*, c. 2, p. 17, etc.

[2] Just. Mart., *Apol.*, II. p. 61.

[3] Tertull., *ad uxor.*, II. 4.

[4] Plin., *Epp.*, X. 97.

the spirit which continued to preside over it.[1] The apostolic constitutions recommend to those who wish to invite aged women to their love-feasts, to invite, in preference, those whom the deacons would point out to them as the most indigent.[2] "The name, even, of these repasts," says Tertullian, "makes known their destination. By their means we relieve our poor, not as you nourish your parasites, in selling to them their subsistence at the price of a thousand insults, but as beings worthy of all regard and of all honor, whose humility only recommends them more particularly to the eyes of the Eternal. There is nothing immodest; it is only after having prayed that they sit down to the table; they only eat sufficient to appease their hunger, and only speak in recalling to mind that they are heard of God; they mingle with these pious entertainments the reading of God's word and songs in His praise; and they separate, not to run to debauchery, but to return each one to his regular and peaceful life."[3] That at times, according to the testimony of Clement of Alexandria, and of Tertullian himself, having become Montanist,[4] the pompous vanity of some of the rich introduced preparations which altered the primitive simplicity and gravity of these repasts, we cannot deny; but it

[1] *Const. Apost.*, II. 28. Minuc. Fel. *Octav.*, c. 9, p. 58; c. 31, p. 205. Tertull., *Apol.*, c. 39; Opp. p. 75; *De Bapt.*, c. 9, p. 414. *Epist. ad Diogn.*, c. 5 (*ubi sup.*), p. 229. Lucian, *De Mort. Peregr.*, c. 12 (Opp., Vol. III. p. 335). Drescher, *De Agapis*, p. 32–37

[2] Constit. ap., II. 28 (Ap. Coteler., p. 243).

[3] Tert., Apol., c. 39, p. 75.

[4] Clem. Alex., *Pædag.*, II. 1; Tert., *De jejun. adv. Psych.*, c. 17.

appears that these reproaches applied rather to the funeral suppers, too faithfully imitated from the mortuary repasts of the pagans;[1] as for the others, the satirist Lucian himself recognizes their pious and charitable purpose.[2]

However, at the epoch of which we speak, the feast of charity was not celebrated every day, and the eucharist itself, especially since the second century, was not regularly accompanied by it.[3] But even in this case the interest of the poor was not forgotten. The care of furnishing the bread and wine for the Lord's Supper was in general left to the faithful, and the usage was to offer upon the altar far more than was necessary for the celebration of the sacrament; the surplus, reserved for the sustenance of the clergy and the poor, was distributed to the latter by the deacons. The names of those offering were inscribed on the diptychs and read aloud in the prayer of conse-

---

[1] Raoul-Rochette, *Antiq. Chr. des Catacombes* (Mém. de l'Acad. des Inscrip., Vol. XIII. p. 132–137). One might suppose, too, that that misuse was more frequent in the agapæ separated from or preceded by the eucharist. The guests, not being checked by the solemnity of the sacrament, by which this feast was usually terminated, allowed themselves to be more easily overcome by the attractions of good cheer.

[2] Lucian, *ub. sup.* He designates them under the title of δεῖπνα ποικίλα, and mentions chiefly the agapæ that Christians celebrated in prisons in behalf of the confessors of the faith who were confined within.

[3] Drescher., l. c. p. 20. Thus Justin Martyr has described the ceremony of the eucharist on the Lord's day, without mentioning the agapæ. *Apol.*, II. p. 98.

cration. This gift, which bore the name of *sacrifice*,[1] replaced, in some sort, the victims offered by the Jews at their festivals. It was particularly abundant when made in behalf of a friend or relative, whose funeral was commemorated,[2] and above all at the anniversary of the death, or as they then said, of the birth of the martyrs.[3] The ideas of Christianity and of charity were so closely united in the minds of the faithful, that they did not believe that they could celebrate the memory of a Christian without acquitting themselves, in his name, of some deed of benevolence.

Independently of these offerings, made for the eucharist or for the agapæ, by the richest of the community, the usage was that each of the faithful should remit to the deacon or the bishop, every week or every month, an offering proportioned to his means, to be distributed to the poor.[4] The Apostolic Constitutions say, "If God has freed you from the yoke of the ceremonial law, he has not exempted you from the contributions to be paid to the priests,

---

[1] Προςφορὰ, θυσία, *oblatio, sacrificium*. The bread which composed this offering was sometimes in such a quantity that the altar was overwhelmed with it, as it is said in some orations. Fleury, *Mœurs des Juifs et des Chrétiens*, part. III. § 9. The communicants themselves lay also an offering upon the altar. *Conc. Eliberit.*, can. 28.

[2] *Oblationes pro defunctis*. Tertull., *De coron. mil.*, c. 3; *De monog.*, c. 10; *De exhort. cast.*, c. 11. Cyprian, *Ep.* LXVI.; *Opp.*, p. 231.

[3] *Natalitia martyrum*.

[4] Just. Mart., *Apol.*, II. pp. 60, 93. Tert., *Apol.*, c. 39, p. 74. *Const. Apost.*, II. 25, 35 (*ubi sup.*), p. 238–248, etc.

nor from benevolence, to be exerted towards the poor. Love, then, thy neighbor as thyself. .. Give what is needful to the poor. Do not appear empty before the priests, but offer thy gifts voluntarily; send to the *corban* what thou canst."[1] These constitutions even mention first fruits and tithes, which many Christians continued, according to the Jewish usage, to raise on their crops for the support of the needy.[2]

When these resources did not suffice, and some new and pressing need was felt, or there was some great misfortune to relieve, they had recourse to general collections, when each one gave of the products of his toil;[3] those who had nothing were invited to fast and to give to their brethren what they thus retrenched from their ordinary fare.[4] Sometimes the whole community was invited to observe this fast.[5]

Finally, many gifts were made on solemn occasions, when the church, for example, received new proselytes.

---

[1] *Const. Apost.*, II. 36 (*ub. sup.*, p. 248, etc.); Thomassin, anc. et nouv. disc. de l'Eglise; Paris, 1679, fol., Vol. I. p. 336.

[2] *Const. Apost.*, II. 25. 27, 34. Origen even maintained that on this point the precept of the ancient law had rather been confirmed than abolished by the Gospel (Orig. *Hom.*, XVII. in *Jos.*, Vol. II. p. 438, etc.); but the nature of the obligation was different, and we do not see any sanction, even ecclesiastical, directed against those who departed from it. Moreover, Origen here rather mentions the offerings intended for the support of clergy.

[3] Thomassin (*ub. sup.*, p. 333; Cyprian, *Ep.*, LX. p. 203, c. 3; Orig., Hom., X.; *De Levit.* Opp., Vol. II. p. 246.

[4] *Const. Apost.*, V. (*ub. sup.*, p. 304; Herm., *Past.*, lib. III. sim. 5.

[5] Tertull., *De jejun.*, c. 13.

Cyprian, at his baptism, sold for the benefit of the poor all his real estate, and even his gardens which he possessed near Carthage.[1] Gregory Thaumaturgus, when he wished to go into solitary life, renounced all his property.[2] Many Evangelists, when departing for their missions, distributed their fortunes to the poor.[3] Marcion, in his zeal as neophyte, had given to the church one hundred thousand *sestertii*, which were restored to him when he was excommunicated.[4]

We are far, assuredly, from pretending that this charity never suffered an eclipse. It had, even in the time of the apostles;[5] it abated with still greater reason, when the first fervor began to cool, and less severe trials were imposed on the new proselytes. Those times when the church enjoyed the most calmness without, were rarely those in which she displayed the most virtue within. With zeal, union and charity relaxed; the spirit of sacrifice, less called upon by circumstances, languished; the care of private interests began to prevail over the general interest. In the period of peace which preceded the persecution of Decius, more than one of the faithful, as St Cyprian tells, forgot the example of the primitive church, allowed the love of wealth to take possession of their hearts, and closed them against the inspirations of charity, and, thinking no longer of anything but to augment their patrimo-

---

[1] *Cypriani vita*; Cypr. *Opp.* p. 1.

[2] Greg. Nyss., *De vit. Greg. Thaum.*, Opp. 1562, p. 334.

[3] Euseb., *Hist. Eccl.*, III. 37; Ed. Vales.

[4] Tert., *Adv. Marc.*, IV. 4; *De Præsc. hær.*, c. 30.

[5] John, *Rev.* II. 4, Stikel and Bogenh., *De morib. prim. Christ.*, p. 142–144.

nies, they had recourse to fraud and usury to succeed.[1] The same afflicting symptoms were renewed before the persecution of Diocletian, according to Eusebius.[2] But these egotistic dispositions, let us hasten to add, were then rarely those of the majority; and, even in the days when Christian charity was the least active, the largesses which it inspired still formed a striking contrast with the inveterate selfishness of the pagan world.

Though each one was free to give directly to the poor, the product of the regular contributions of the faithful, as of the collections made among them, were ordinarily put into the common fund.[3] At this epoch, besides, the church accumulated little. Always threatened with the rapine of the pagans, counting always, besides, upon the charity of its members, it provided largely for the present need, leaving "to the future the care of what concerned it." After the torture and death of Sixtus I., Lawrence, his deacon, foreseeing his own martyrdom, also, and the pillage of his church, assembled all the poor that he could find in Rome, and distributed to them its treasures, without sparing even the sacred vases, which he sold to assist them. The prefect of Rome, informed of this liberality, and not doubting that the Christians had in reserve still considerably more goods, ordered the deacon to deliver them to him. St. Lawrence asked three days; at the end of this term, he showed to the Prefect, drawn up

---

[1] Cyprian, *De laps.* p. 364, etc.; *De opp. et eleem.*, p. 482, etc.

[2] Euseb., *Hist eccles.*, VIII. 1.

[3] Just. Mart., *Apol.* II. p. 98, etc., *Const. Apost.*, II. 27, III. 4, (*ubi supra*, p. 243, 279.)

before the church, the blind, the lame, the maimed, and the wretched of all kinds, whom he nourished, saying to him: "behold my treasures; profit by them for Rome, for the Emperor, and for yourself." This noble answer was taken for an insolent subterfuge, and caused the holy deacon to be condemned to perish upon the glowing embers.[1]

The bishop, as chief of the church, was charged with the administration of its revenue.[2] Ordinarily he divided it into three equal parts; one for the support of the ministers of worship, a second for the expenses of the worship itself, and the third for the relief of the unfortunate. This was distributed daily and at the domicil of the deacons, under the inspection of the bishop,[3] either to those who had need of some temporary succor, or to those whose position, age, or infirmities, left no other habitual resource than the alms of the church. In order to avoid all intrusion and all fraud, their names were inscribed in a special register, to which, later, was given the name of *matriculus*, or

[1] Ambros., *De off. min.*, II. 28; Prud., *Peri Steph.*, hym. 2.

[2] *Const Apost.*, II. 27; III. 4.

[3] Cyprian's letters and the canons of the Elib. concil., make mention of some bishops or deacons who misused the deposits of offerings to make usurious loans, or to contract fraudulent bargains (Cypr., *Ep.* 42, p. 131. Conc. Elib. can., 18, 20.) Thus, the Deacon Nicostratus was convicted of having taken away the money of the poor. But Gibbon, c. 15, acknowledges, himself, that those abuses of trust could not have been very frequent, as long as the offerings of the Christians were free and voluntary; and there were bishops who, far from becoming rich at the expense of the public treasure, supplied its deficiency by giving their own part for the relief of the poor. This was done, among others, by Cyprian during his exile (*Ep.* 36, p. 106.)

ecclesiastical canon. The deacons had there to indicate the age, sex, profession, and position of each person to be helped, and, for this purpose, to inform himself of these things most circumstantially and most exactly.[1]

In the first rank of those assisted by the church, at this epoch, were, naturally, the generous confessors who expiated their fidelity by confiscation, exile, or chains. The Apostolic Constitutions particularly recommend them to the charity of the faithful.[2] St. Cyprian, a fugitive himself, for this cause, invited his clergy not to let them want anything in their prison, and to assist the poor, who, having remained firm in the faith, were persecuted for the name of Christ.[3] Each one was eager to protect them in their flight, to receive them in his house, to carry them food, to tender succor to them, to assist them before their judges, to render them the last services at the final hour. The cruel edicts of Decius, of Diocletian, and of Licinius,[4] could not prevent it. It was thus that Origen, Justin, Theodotus,[5] Anastasia, and so many others, exposed themselves to the implacable hatred of the pagans, and devoted themselves, in advance, to martyrdom.[6] Are

---

[1] Cyprian, *Ep.* 38, *Opp.*, p. 108. "Vos vicarios misi, ut . . . ætates et conditiones et merita discerneretis." The apocryphal work of the Acts of Peter, alludes to this matriculation. (*Epit. de gestis Petr.*, c. 151; ap. Cotel. *Patr. ap.*, Vol. I., p. 799.)

[2] *Const. Apost.*, V. I.; *ubi supra*, p. 304.

[3] Cyprian, *Ep.* 37; *Opp.* p. 107.

[4] Euseb., *De vitâ Const.*, I. 54.

[5] Theodotus' hotel, was, says his biographer, in times of peace, the place of meeting for the Christians, and in times of persecutions, their place of refuge. Bolland., *Acta Sanctor.*, ad 18th May, p. 152.

[6] Euseb. *Hist Eccles.*, VI. 3; Baillet, *Vie des Saints*, 25th Dec., p. 308.

we to see in this charity, so heroic, only the ardor of party spirit? Let us admit for a moment that this sole motive acted upon the Christians; let us admit even, with Lucian, that at times it rendered them dupes to false appearances;[1] happy humanity, when union, mutual devotion, party spirit, if it is preferred to call it thus, will no longer be wholly on the side of the wicked; when the friends of a good cause shall know how to understand, to aid and to sustain each other, when love of goodness will find somewhat of the encouragements which hardihood for evil finds!

After the confessors of the faith, the principal objects of Christian charity were those families whom the exile, captivity, or martyrdom of their heads left without support. Nothing, assuredly, more natural and just. "It was necessary," said Lactantius, "that the Christians, fully assured as to the fortune of these pledges which they left after them, might, without regret, brave death for the cause of truth and justice."[2] We see Origen, after the death of his father, and the confiscation of his patrimony, received in the house of a Christian dame, who provided generously for his education.[3] The ascetic Seleucus, before being himself called to seal his faith by martyrdom, devoted himself wholly to the service of the widows and orphans of confessors, and was to them both protector

[1] Lucian, *De mort. Peregr.*, c. 12, 13, 16.

[2] Lactant., *Inst. div.*, VI. 12, p. 546.

[3] Euseb., *Hist. eccles.* VI. 2. Felicity, a short time before her martyrdom, having been delivered of a daughter, a Christian woman brought her up, as her own child. Fleury, *Hist. ecclés.*, V. 17.

and father.[1] In all the churches a large portion was allowed to them from the common treasury.

Besides, all the poor or sick widows over sixty years of age, or even younger when they did not marry and still lived with propriety, were, by the same title, and on the same conditions as in the days of the apostles, inscribed upon the roll of those assisted by the church.[2] So, too, with the children of those deprived of their parents. When no private person offered to take care of them, they were recommended to the bishop, who was to be a father to them, and had to watch over their conduct and education. "Bishops," say the Apostolic Constitutions, "take care of the orphans, see that they need nothing, give the young man the means of learning a trade to earn his living by, and furnish him the tools necessary for his business, that he may support himself. As to the orphan girl, nourish her till she is marriageable, when you may give her in wedlock to some brother."[3] But more frequently, however, the young girls, whose poverty placed them under the guardianship of the church, far from being destined to marriage, were, on the contrary, encouraged to a perpetual celibacy, and upon this condition were inscribed on the roll for ecclesiastical aid;[4] they

---

[1] Euseb., *Hist eccles.*, lib. *De martyr. Palæst.*, c. 11.

[2] Paetz, *Comm. de vi rel. christ.*, p. 113; Ignat.; *ad Polyc.*, c. 4, (Hæfele, *Opp. pat. ap.*, p. 179;) Const. Ap., III. 1–12, (*ubi supra*, p. 274–288.)

[3] *Const. Ap.* IV. 2, p. 295.

[4] Παρθένους τὰς ἀναγεγραμμένας ἐν τῷ τῶν ἐκκλησιῶν κάνονι, Socr., *Hist. eccles.*, I. 17.

formed a sort of clerical order,[1] to live like the priests at the altar.[2]

Exposed children were almost in every respect

[1] Δι' ἔνδειαν ἐν τοῖς κληροῖς τεταγμένας: Thus they are designated by Sozomen (*Hist. eccles.*, V. 5.) The apostolic constitutions assign to them a similar rank, by assimilating them as well as widows, deacons, and readers, to the Levites of the old covenant (*Const. Apost.*, II. 25, p. 241.)

[2] Never did the church give herself up to the exaggerated asceticism of the dualists, who condemned marriage in as far as it was instituted by the principle of evil to perpetuate a creation impure and malignant. But though maintaining against them the legitimacy and sanctity of marriage (Paul, 1 Cor. vii. 28; 1 Tim. iv. 1–5; Clem. Alex. *Strom.* III., 3, 6, 7, 13, &c.), she nevertheless, as early as that time, preferred celibacy. Now, with Paul, she wished in difficult circumstances, to spare for her members the trouble and the afflictions of the flesh, and thus turn them more completely to the things of the Lord (1 Cor. vii. 7–26, 32–34;) then, with Tertullian, Cyprian, Origen, and the most of the Fathers, she flattered herself with raising them to a higher perfection; then, again, jealous for herself of the consideration which the ascetic Jews and heathens drew upon themselves, she wished to vie with them in the palm of abstinence, she wanted to have her glorious train of virgins and of the continent. And, who knows, but in those praises of celibacy, there were no ideas similar to those, which in our days, have preoccupied the economists, and which very certainly, in those times contributed to bring into credit ascetic sects. Is it without reflection that Clement of Alexandria and Lactantius said: "it was better not to marry, when not able to support one's children, than to be led to become with them homicidal." (Clem. Al., *Strom.*, II. 18, Vol. I. p. 477; Lact. VI. 20, § 25.) And when, later, St. Jerome said to the adversaries of a religious celibacy: "The world is full, the earth cannot longer contain us. . . . The field is sowed but to be reaped. . . every day war and sickness destroy us," (*Hieron.*, *adv. Helvid.* Opp. ed. Ben., Vol. IV. part 2, p. 143,) do we not think we hear one of the apostles of the *princi-*

assimilated to the poor orphans.[1] When they were presented to the church, she entrusted their primary education, under the inspection of the bishops, to the widows and consecrated virgins;[2] gave them a trade; instructed them in the faith, and, whilst pagan barbarism peopled with them its *ergastula*, its schools of gladiators, its places of prostitution, the church recruited with them the fold of Jesus Christ. It is by this kind of proselytism, the most honorable of all, that, at all times and even in our day, she establishes herself most firmly among the heathens.[3]

---

ple of population? Thus it seems then that upon assisting poor widows and virgins, as long as they devoted themselves to continence, the church wanted to prevent them from seeking in marriage a dangerous support, perfidious resources, to save them from an alternative of misery and crime, of sparing herself and society from an increase of burdens, and of solving, finally, by abstinence and charity, the terrible problem which the heathen world solved by exposure and infanticide. (Tert. *Apol.*, c. 9; Minuc. Fel., *Octav.*, c. 30; Athenag., *Legat.*, p. 33, *ad calc. opp. Just. Mart.*, Lact., *Inst. div.*, VI. 20, &c., &c.)

But let us say that such considerations never overcame higher interests; never did the fear of favoring an increase of population induce her to refuse an assistance to those wanting it: she never punished by abandonment the faults of improvidence. Thus mothers fallen into indigence by the charges of a too large family, were like others recommended to the charity of Christians (*Const. Ap.*, II. 4.)

[1] Tertullian comprehends them evidently in the category of the "pueri parentibus destituti," who, at his time, were assisted by the church, (*Apol.* c. 39.)

[2] Terme et Montf., *Hist. des Enf. trouvés*, p. 74.

[3] The missionaries, in the diverse heathen countries, especially in China, are chiefly engaged with seeking out and bringing up exposed children.

She placed, moreover, among the number that were assisted by her, the old men, the infirm, those who were sick and destitute of other aid, and, in general, all those who were not capable of working, whilst she only granted a supplement to persons in strength, whose labor was not sufficient to support their families.[1]

Cornelius, a bishop of Rome, tells us that towards the middle of the third century, his church sustained ordinarily, besides a numerous clergy, "more than fifteen hundred poor, such as widows and persons afflicted with different evils."[2] The other churches, doubtless, assisted a proportionate number. But if, to the evils which are the ordinary lot of humanity, were added some extraordinary and public calamity, the spirit of charity, increasing with the evil, coped with these new requirements. In the third century, following the long wars of Gallienus and the famine which they had caused, a contagious malady broke out in Alexandria. Struck repeatedly with so many scourges, the pagans gave themselves up to that blind and stupid fear, which, in a rude multitude, excludes all other thought than that of danger. Inhuman by the excess of fear, they "repelled from their houses," says Dionysius of Alexandria, "those who began to be attacked by it; deserted their most intimate friends; threw the victims, still breathing, upon

[1] It is what we may conclude from the 38th epistle of St. Cyprian, ed. in 8vo., p. 108.

[2] Cornel., *Ep.* (ap. Euseb., *Hist. eccl.*, VI. 43). Pope Urban I. affirmed that at his time not one of the Christians at Rome was reduced to beggary. (Arnold, *Erste Liebe*, Leipz., 1732, p. 456.)

the public square, and gave the dead bodies, without burial, to the dogs, vainly hoping thus to escape from the attacks of the evil. The Christians, on the contrary, seeing in this scourge, as in all the evils of life, a trial sent from on high to exercise their patience and fortify their faith, regarded it with serenity and met it with courage. Possessed of an ardent charity, forgetful of all solicitude for themselves, a crowd of them attended day and night and nursed the sick for the love of Jesus. The priests, the deacons, the laymen, and among them the most distinguished of the company, died victims of the contagion, joyful in sacrificing their lives for their friends and brothers. Others, pressing in their arms the saints who had just expired, closed their eyes, carried them upon their shoulders, washed them, enveloped them in shrouds, till, struck in turn, they received from the surviving the same service."[1] Some years before, under the reign of Gallus, the pest of Corinth had brought out a similar contrast between the Christians and pagans. "While these latter," says Portius, the deacon, "possessed by fear and avarice, were only occupied in avoiding all contact with the sick, and with securing for themselves the spoils of the dead, the bishop Cyprian confined himself to his flock, whose dangers he shared, and succeeded, by his pathetic exhortations, in sustaining the confidence and exciting the devotedness of the faithful."[2] "All," adds his bio-

---

[1] Dyon. Alex. Ep. (*ap.* Euseb., *Hist. eccl.*, VII. 22).

[2] At that time he pronounced his sermon on *Mortality* a masterpiece of Christian eloquence. "Is it not necessary, my beloved brethren, that this plague, which seems to us but a messenger of

grapher, "felt themselves animated to follow him and to sacrifice themselves with him, by the charity which is due to brothers and to the members of Christ. The employments were immediately allotted, according to the condition and resources of each one. Those who could not give money, did more, in giving themselves to take care of the sick. These pious deeds of charity continued during the whole of the plague, which still raged at the death of Cyprian.[1]

Another occasion had already offered itself to the illustrious bishop to put to trial the charity of his flock, in a calamity, which, in a certain sense, did not affect him. In the year 253, the Barbarians, making incursions into some of the cities of Numidia, had carried away a crowd of Christians of both sexes, who suffered among them all the horrors of captivity. The Numidian bishops, not in a condition to pay the ransom of these prisoners, addressed themselves to the metropolitan bishop. An offer was never received more gratefully than was this demand for help. "Blessings upon you," Cyprian answered them, "for having shown to us a fertile field where we can sow seed which must yield to us an abundant harvest. Here are a hundred thousand *sestertii*,[2] which I have collected among the clergy and people of this church over which I preside. And if new perils threaten you, we are ready to send to you new assistance.

---

death, tries the dispositions of every one of us, makes known if healthy people attend the sick, if parents love each other, if masters pity the pains of their servants? . . . (*Cypr.*, *Opp.*, p. 466.)

[1] Pontii, *Vit. Cyprian.;* Cypr., *Ep. ad Demetr.*, p. 433.

[2] About 3250 dollars.

We only ask of you, in return, the tribute of your prayers."[1]

But it was not alone in the circle of a single city, in the extent of a single province, that these wonders of charity were displayed. We have seen that, since the time of St. Paul, Christian benevolence knew no distances. The churches, established all over the extent of the Roman world, sustained between themselves relations the most fraternal and affectionate. Every Christian, into whatever country he went, provided he was furnished with a recommendation which made him known as such, was sure to find among his brethren the services and assistance of hospitality.[2] Every suffering church was assisted by her sister churches. Distances seemed to approach each other, mountains to bow down, seas to contract, in order to favor this commerce of kindness, which extended from one end of the empire to the other. "What Christian," wrote Clement of Rome, to the faithful of Corinth, "has not admired the magnificence of your hospitality? You were always more prompt to give than to receive; no favor embarrassed you; you were constantly ready for all kinds of good works."[3] Later, the church of Rome received the

---

[1] Cyprian, *Ep.* 60, p. 203, *seq.*

[2] *Const. Ap.*, II. 58; Poetz, *Comment. de vi rel. chr.*, pp. 109, 112; Vulliemin, *Mœurs des Chrétiens*, c. 2, p. 18. Cyprian, on recommending to his clergy to provide in his absence for the wants of the poor, does not except strangers, and wishes that care may be taken of them, from out of his own portion (Cypr., *Ep.*, 36, p. 106). The Apostolic Constitutions recommend likewise not to neglect strangers in their distributions (Lib. II. c. 36).

[3] Clem. Rom., *Ep.* 1, *ad Cor.*, c. 1, 2.

same testimony from that of Corinth. "For a long time," Dionysius, bishop of that city, wrote to pope Soter, "you have been accustomed to load all the brethren with favors, and to assist all the churches in their wants, in whatever place they may have been established. You thus follow faithfully the traditions of your fathers."[1]

In view of a charity so impartial, so forgetful of all diversity of place and origin, so entirely a stranger to all the considerations which elsewhere arrested its activity, in view of these Christians, of every country, who mutually loved and aided each other like brothers, the common pagans were stupefied and almost scandalized. A union so intimate between those who did not know each other must conceal some vast conspiracy against the rest of mankind, some secret pact, stronger than any oath, menacing all social order; that they should know each other thus without having seen each other before, these Christians must have carried some magical sign upon them. "See," said they, "how they love each other; how they treat each other mutually as brothers and sisters, and are ready to die the one for the other." And, to

---

[1] Dyonis. Cor., *Ep.* (*ap.* Euseb., *Hist. eccles.*, IV. 23). Lucian pays unintentionally the most beautiful testimony of that mutual charity among churches. "When Peregrinus," says he, "had been put into prison as a Christian, deputies came over from Asia to comfort and to help him. For it is incredible to see the ardor with which the people of that religion help each other in their wants. They spare nothing. Their first legislator has put into their heads that they are all brethren. . . ." (Lucian, *de morte Peregr.*, c. 13.)

that stupid crowd, this was the most serious of all their complaints.[1] "It is true," Tertullian answered them, "this fraternal love has something surprising for you, who only know how to hate each other and to attempt each other's lives. Our fraternity astonishes you, because it permits no bloody tragedy among us, and we consider ourselves as brothers in the community of those same interests which with you so often break the ties of fraternal love. But when you see in it the proof of a common and culpable hatred against you, the sign of a conspiracy plotted against the human race, you forget that you are yourselves the objects of our charity, and that Christian love embraces you also, and with you the whole world, which is, to our eyes, but one vast republic. You forget that, notwithstanding your persecutions, far from conspiring against you, as our numbers would perhaps furnish us with the means of doing, we pray for you and do good to you; that, if we give nothing for your gods, we do give for your poor, and that our charity spreads more alms in your streets than the offerings presented by your religion in your temples."[2]

In effect, Christian charity, though more intimate, without doubt, among the Christians, knew how to rise above differences in worship, and to exert itself for the love of God even towards those who slighted and blasphemed it. The Jews themselves, on entering into the church, laid aside their exclusive and

---

[1] Tert., *Apol.*, c. 39, p. 74; Minuc. Fel., *Octav.*, c. 9, § 2; Orig., *Cont. Cels.*, I. c. 1, p. 319.

[2] Tert., *Apol.*, c. 37–39, 42, Vol. I. p. 71–75, 79, 80.

inhuman prejudices.[1] "Our religion," said in concert Justin Martyr, Athanagoras, and Theophilus of Antioch, "prescribes to us to love not only our own, but also strangers, and even our enemies."[2] "If all have affection for their friends," says Tertullian, "it only belongs to Christians to love those by whom they are hated."[3]

During the pest at Carthage just mentioned, while the pagans, not knowing to whom they should attribute the evils which they suffered, had the cowardice to accuse the Christians of them, and made of them a pretext for new outrages against them,[4] Cyprian exhorted his flock to render good for evil to those madmen. "If we do good only to those who do good to us," said he, "what do we more than pagans and the publicans? But if we are the children of God, who sends the rain upon the just and upon the unjust, let us prove it by our deeds in blessing those who curse us, and doing good to those who persecute us." "The Christians of Carthage yielded to this appeal," adds Pontius, "and the abundance of their gifts was such that all had a part of them, strangers as well as the followers of the faith."[5]

Under the tyrant and persecutor Maximin, Alexandria was a prey to a pest and a famine, the lament-

---

[1] Stickel and Bogenhard, *Comment.*, p. 76.

[2] Just. Mart., *Apol.*, II. pp. 61, 62; Athenag., *Legat. ubi sup.*, p. 12; Theoph., *ad Autol.*, p. 126 (*ad calc.* Just. Mart., *Opp.*, Par. 1615, fol.).

[3] Tert., *ad Scap.*, c. 1, p. 151.

[4] Cyprian, *ad Demet.*, Opp. p. 433.

[5] Pont., *De vita Cyp.*

able details of which Eusebius has transmitted to us.[1] "The rich pagans, frightened by the crowd of beggars, after having scattered much alms for some time, fearing at last to see themselves reduced to mendicity, took refuge in an inexorable hardheartedness. The two scourges redoubled at the same time in intensity, groans and complaints were heard through the whole city; it was not rare to see two or three corpses borne at the same time from the same house. On this occasion the Christians alone gave proofs of a charity truly heroic. Although they had, like those of Carthage, to complain of persecutions recently excited against them, forgetful in so great a calamity of the injustice of their adversaries, some devoted themselves to the burial of the dead, with which the streets were encumbered;[2] others, assembling upon the públic squares the unfortunate suffering with hunger, distributed bread to all without distinction; so that their enemies themselves did not hesitate to recognize that it was they alone who sincerely served the

---

[1] Euseb., *Hist. Eccles.*, IX. 8.

[2] The church very early placed the free sepulture of the dead among the number of acts of charity which she recommended. Independently of the reasons of immediate utility, which may in this respect strike every mind, she saw a high suitableness in having the creature formed in the image of God respected even in its mortal remains, and its body decently given back to the earth from which it had been taken. Lactantius forcibly combats those who considered such cares as superfluous (*Inst. div.*, VI. 12). A part of the offerings of the faithful was devoted to it; and as early as the third century a kind of minor order, set apart for that office, was consecrated by the name of *copaitæ*, grave-diggers.

Divinity; and all the country resounded with their praises."[1]

Perhaps it was more easy, in those times, to rise above the differences of belief and of nationality, than to shake off the prejudices of condition and of birth, to find brothers to be aided and relieved among the followers of another worship, than in those slaves whom the law, custom, and philosophy itself, placed below humanity. But the same Gospel which said to the Christians, "There is neither Greek nor Jew, Barbarian nor Scythian," said to them also, There is neither citizen nor stranger, "bond nor free."[2] Through the apparent degradation of the man condemned to serve, it showed to them, by the eyes of faith, the dignity of the man come, like them, from the hand of God, formed in His image, and called, like them, to his knowledge and salvation.[3] In the bosom of the pagan city, where man only counted as a member of that city, and where the debasement of two-thirds of humanity served to sustain the dignity of the other third, Christianity came to found a new city in the image of the celestial Jerusalem, where rank was marked only by virtue, where the slave found himself sometimes the superior, at least the equal, according to faith, of those to whom, according

---

[1] Euseb., *Hist. eccles.*, IX. 8.

[2] Paul, Col. iii. 11.

[3] Acts xvii. 26; Eph. iv. 4, etc., etc.; Tschirner, *De Dignitate hom., per rel. chr. adserta* (*Opusc.* Lpz., 1829, p. 51, *sq.*; 66, *sq.*). "There is among us no distinction of persons," say both Tertullian and Lactantius; "Christian justice makes equal in our eyes all such as bear the name of men."

to the world, he was a slave. Between the Christian master and slave was no religious distinction; they came into the same sanctuary to invoke the same God, to pray, to sing together, to participate in the same mysteries, to sit at the same table, to drink of the same cup, and to take part in the same feast. How should this community of worship not have profoundly modified their mutual relations?[1] How could the master have continued to see in his slave that *thing* which the Roman law permitted him to *use* and to *abuse?* Also, whatever might still be the force of habit and of manners, there were rarely seen in the Christian houses those masters, still less those pitiless mistresses, such as Seneca and Juvenal have painted to us; the slave, there, had to fear neither the cross, nor tortures, nor abandonment in sickness, nor to be thrown off in his old age; he had not to fear that he should be sold for the amphitheatre or for some one of those infamous occupations which the church reproved, and from which she struggled, at every price, to rescue her children.[2]

---

[1] Vulliemin, *Mœurs des Chrétiens,* p. 34–38.

[2] There was an anathema not only against those who devoted their slaves to the profession of gladiators, but also against those who encouraged by their presence inhuman exhibitions (Tschirner, *ubi sup.*, p. 68). The church admitted, generally, in her bosom no one having a profession contrary to Christian sanctity; she excommunicated gladiators, mimes, and actors, and did not receive them before they had taken a more honorable way of living. An actor of Carthage having pretended to remain in the church without ceasing to teach his art, under pretext that he needed it to subsist, Cyprian insisted upon his renouncing it, engaging him to have himself inscribed upon the roll of assisted persons until

Finally a devoted and faithful slave always had, in a Christian house, the hope of recovering his liberty. It was not rare, without doubt, to see Pagans enfranchise their slaves; some even did it from motives of gratitude or attachment; but ordinarily necessity, caprice, vanity, often even the most sordid calculations alone presided over the emancipation of slaves,[1] and these miserable creatures, cast almost without resource into the midst of a society whose free labor found so little encouragement and employment, hardly used their liberty except to do evil, and went for the most part to increase the crowd of proletarians and of beggars,[2] so that it is not astonishing if the emperors had attempted, though without success, to limit, by their laws, the right of enfranchising. As to the church, when she encouraged it, it was not as an interest, but as a favor; she exhorted the masters to liberate the slave as often as he was in a state to support himself.[3]

---

had provided for him in another way, and, in case the church was overloaded, he offered to furnish him with food and clothing himself. (Cyprian, *Ep. ad Euchrat.*, p. 205.)

[1] Wallon, *De l'esclavage*, Vol. II. p. 406, etc.; Moreau-Christ., *Du problème de la misère*, t. I. p. 83–85; Dureau de la Malle, *ubi sup.*, Vol. II. pp. 223, 310; Gothofr., in *Cod. Theod.*, Vol. V. p. 245. Many masters at Rome liberated their slaves, to share with them, as patrons, the product of public distributions.

[2] De Champagny, *Les Césars*, Vol. IV. p. 58, *sq.* Libanius shows us free laborers more the slaves of the fear of starvation, than the slaves were of their masters (Liban., *De Servit.*, Opp., Vol. II. p. 651, etc.).

[3] It sometimes happened that the church herself paid for the ransom; she did it especially for Christian slaves or captives submitted to heathen or barbarian masters. She consecrated to it

But the enfranchisement was not an abandonment; the Christian remained the *patron*, in the best sense of that word, of those whom he had ceased to be the master of, and, in case of misfortune, the freed man found an almost sure resource in the aid of his brothers. The church, which, by its moral influence, had worked to render him worthy of liberty, continued to protect him after he had attained it. The emancipation of slaves at this day, would be less difficult and less dangerous if it was always done in this spirit.[1]

Now let us sum up the facts which we have just enumerated; let us recapitulate the works of Christian

---

the product of collections, or the treasure of the community. "Out of the legitimate work of the faithful," say the Apostolic Constitutions, "deliver the saints, redeem the slaves, the captives, etc." (IV. 9, *ubi sup.*, p. 300). Ignatius alludes likewise to the redeemed slaves at the expense of the community (απο τοῦ κοινοῦ, *Ep. ad Polyc.*, c. 4). Finally, Clement of Rome speaks of Christians who carrried devotion so far as to sell themselves to redeem others from slavery (I. *Ep. ad Cor.* c. 55, *ubi sup.*, p. 100).

[1] The church has been thus unjustly accused of having, by the imprudence of her emancipations of slaves, caused the plague of pauperism. Manumission had been used with much less discretion at other epochs of Roman society. The one hundred thousand freedmen who, as early as from 240 to 210 previous to our era had been admitted to the privilege of citizenship, the slaves liberated *en masse* by the alternating politics of Marius and Sylla, the thousands of them who under the republic were daily liberated, either by will, to do honor to the funeral of their master, or by necessity, there being no food for them, or by revenge, to defeat the eagerness of creditors; all those freedmen, finally, who in Cicero's times were in a majority in the urban and rural tribes of Rome, formed elements much more threatening to the social well-being than were subsequently those freed by charity. (Morean-Christophe, *Du probl. de la misère*, Vol. I. p. 80, etc.)

charity during these three centuries, those gifts which it caused to circulate from man to man, from church to church, those numerous lists of the poor who were relieved; of widows, orphans, and old men who were assisted, of the sick that were comforted, the captives redeemed, the slaves withdrawn from an unjust captivity; let us recall those famines appeased, those public scourges partly prevented, and we will judge, without doubt, that it was not in vain that Christian charity had appeared in the world. In the midst of those Roman cities, which, by the side of an extravagant luxury covered incalculable miseries, there arose so many oases, communities, not opulent, indeed, but where no one at least wanted for necessities, and where all the evils of indigence were, if not removed, at least relieved.

What unheard-of wisdom, then, one will think, had presided over the organization of these communities! To remove far from them a scourge against which modern science struggles in vain, what skill was not necessary to the founders of the church, what profound study must they not have made of the conditions of the material well-being of societies!

We have seen, however, that their efforts, in general, had altogether another aim. Occupied, above all, with the spiritual salvation which Jesus had come to bring to men, they wrought for the future world much more than for the present, for the interests of the soul far more than for the wants of the body, and for eternity far more than for time.

But it was precisely from this thought of eternity that the first Christians derived the remedies against the evils of the present life; the rich, the spirit of disinterestedness which made them sacrifice perishable goods, without regret, for their brothers, in exchange for goods imperishable; the poor, the spirit of resignation, which made them limit in this life their desires, their wants, and to support, in the expectation of an eternal happiness, transient privations; all, in short, derived from it the spirit of charity, which they eagerly assumed as one of the first conditions of salvation, and which made of their society a body strictly one, a phalanx impenetrable to the evils of want.

This is all the art of the first Christians. This the whole secret of Jesus and his apostles; they secured the present interests of humanity so much the better, that, above all, they laid up for themselves future treasures. The church, founded by them for the spiritual salvation of man, found itself in that, so much the better adapted to his temporal needs; so true is it, that in order to govern this world well, the point of support must be out of this world, and that it is only by regenerating souls and tempering them with the thought of heaven, that the happiness of societies can be secured. "Godliness," says St. Paul, "is profitable unto all things, having the promise of the life that now is and of that which is to come;" but it is because it has the promises of the future life that it has also those of the present, according to the words of Jesus: "Seek ye first the kingdom of God and his righteousness; and all these things shall be added unto you."[1]

[1] "The more vigorous and extensive the social movement shall be," says Guizot, "the less will politics be sufficient to divert mankind in commotion; it requires for that purpose a higher

Besides, the effects of charity extended far beyond the bosom of the society which had proclaimed it. Its principles began, though slowly, to penetrate even into pagan society itself, and to enter into public opinion, and thence to exert a real influence even upon the legislation and administration of the Empire. It is this that we have now to show.

CHAPTER IV.

THE INDIRECT INFLUENCE OF CHARITY ON ROMAN LAW IN THE FIRST THREE CENTURIES.

DURING the period of the Roman Law which it is agreed to call the philosophical, extending from Cicero to Constantine, this law underwent an internal revolution which had the effect of tempering its primitive rigor and of bringing it nearer to the maxims of equity.[1]

This was at first the work of conquest and of philosophy. At the same time that conquest mingled together different people, and confounded races, brought conquerors and conquered in contact, old and new subjects, and forced reciprocal considerations on

power than an earthly one; longer prospects than those of this life; it requires God and eternity." (*De la rel. dans la soc. moderne, Revue franç.*, Vol. V. p. 10.)

[1] Giraud, *Eléments du droit romain.*, p. 338; Troplong. *Infl. du Christ., sur le droit civ. des Romains*, p. 47, etc.

them all, Philosophy, the interpreter of these new relations, introduced new forms and larger and more genial principles of law, which, adopted by the Jurists, insensibly mitigated the ancient rudeness of the Roman laws.[1] But from the unanimous confession of the historians of the Roman Law, nothing contributed so much to bring it near to the maxims of natural right and of equity as the silent but active influence of the rising Church. Jurisprudence was modified by philosophy, but the philosophy was impregnated unconsciously with the principles of charity. From the bosom of the church, where they had been proclaimed for the first time, these principles, like beneficent emanations, spread themselves farther and farther, entered into the current of opinion, penetrated those hearts best prepared to receive them, imposed themselves by their reasonableness upon the intelligence of philosophers, and, from their minds, passed into their discourses, into their writings, and hence into the Pagan society, of which these distinguished men were considered as the oracles.[2] It is, indeed, impossible not to recognize the progress which moral philosophy had made since the time of Cicero.

As to Cicero, everything, almost, reduces itself to the just and the honest. To injure no one, to work

---

[1] Naudet, *Secours publics*, *ubi sup.*, p. 83.

[2] Troplong, *ubi sup.*; Villemain, *De la philos. stoïque et du Christ.*, (Nouv. Mélanges, p. 276, etc.) "What in Christian law corresponds to the intimate feelings of man, had taken a secret influence before those dogmas had triumphed over idolatrous opinions, and the heathen world, hard and corrupt, was insensibly converted to humanity before it was to religion."

for the common welfare, which, according to him, was, above all, that of the family and native country; such, in his view, was almost the whole of morality. Only rarely, and by momentary elevation, did he rise to the general nótion of humanity.[1] Seneca appears to us more explicit and more abundant upon this point. "Philosophy," he says, "teaches us to adore the gods, to love man; to revere the empire of the former, to recognise our relationship with the latter. Man should be a sacred thing to man.[2] We are members, only, of one great body. Nature in engendering us all, has made us all relatives to each other, and has made a law of mutual love for us all."[3] "All men," said Epictetus, "are brothers by nature, inasmuch as they are sons of Jupiter." An ancient had said, "Our slaves are our enemies; let us leave them no respite; they must sleep or they must work!" And Cicero himself when relating the cruel deed of the Prætor Domitius towards a Sicilian slave, had not dared to express either blame or praise.[4] Now, it is not only the Platonic Plutarch who revolts at the barbarous maxims of the masters of ancient times; the Stoic, also, softens and grows human. "Live with thy inferior," says Seneca, "as thou wouldst have thy superior live with thee." "Who would dare to limit his liberality to those who wear the *toga?* Nature commands us to be useful to men, whether they are slaves or free, ingenuous or freed; all are citizens of the same country. Wherever man is, there good may be done."

---

[1] Cicer., *De off.*, 1, 10, III. 17; Troplong, *De l'esp. dém. du code civil.*
[2] Senec., *Ep.*, 90. [3] *Ibid., ib.*, 95.
[4] Cicer., 2 in *Verr.*, V. 3.

Besides, he calls to mind that, "the slaves have the same origin as their masters; that, if they are enslaved as to the body, as to the soul they are free; that they are our enemies only because we make them so;" and he calls his own, "his humble friends."[1]

What a change in a few years! How had Stoicism been transformed since Cato![2] How had it become superior in clemency, in humanity, to Platonism itself, which, in the time of Cicero, especially, was vain of its great pre-eminence in this regard! Must we not recognise here, the indirect, but evident influence of Christianity? Why not see, in these new maxims of Seneca and Epictetus, a reflection of those of St. Paul, with whom the first was, if not, as many have believed, in literary intercourse, at least in a communication of ideas, and whose doctrines and writings were probably known to both of them?[3] "Epictetus," says M. Villemain, "was not a Christian, but the imprint of Christianity was already upon the world."[4]

Now, what such men as Seneca and Epictetus said, was of authority for their contemporaries and their posterity. Stoicism, such as they had modified it, was, in particular, the most accredited system of philosophy with the jurisconsults of the first three centuries.[5] It

---

[1] Senec., *De irâ*, III. 31; *De vit. beat.*, XXIV. 2; *De benef.*, III. 28; *ep.* 47.

[2] Troplong, *Influence*, etc., p. 54; Villemain, *ubi sup.*, p. 278.

[3] On this subject see particulars in Troplong, *ubi sup.*, p. 71–79; see also Schœll, *Hist. de la littér.*, *rom.* (Panckoucke, *Œuvres de Sénèque*, Vol. VII. p. 551).

[4] Villemain, *De la phil. stoïque.*, p. 279.

[5] Troplong, *ubi sup.*, p. 54.

was after Seneca that Florentinus and Ulpian said, "Nature has established a certain relationship between us. All men are equal as to natural right; by the same natural right, all men are born free. Slavery is an institution of the law of nations, by which one man is submitted, contrary to nature, to the dominion of another."[1] Julius Paulus, a jurisconsult of the time of Severus and Caracalla, assimilates, as did the Christian authors, infanticide and exposure to any other murder.[2] All the enlightened jurisconsults were penetrated with the same maxims. The emperors themselves, guided and counselled by them, were, after their example, penetrated with the same opinions; and they introduced these into their laws. Like Ulpian, who, while bringing Christians to the cross, spoke their language, which he believed to be that of stoicism,[3] the emperors, while persecuting Christianity, practised Christianity without knowing it.[4]

If it is probable that policy alone determined Tiberius,[5] as it had Augustus, to open a bank for gratuitous loans in favor of any who could give double security,[6] dictated to Claudius the decree which enjoined upon patrons to furnish to those they had enfranchised food

---

[1] Troplong, *ubi sup.*, pp. 81, 82.

[2] Terme, *Hist. des enf. trouv.*, p. 62. [3] Troplong, *ibid.*, p. 79.

[4] "A singular fact in the world's history," says Villemain, "the judge and the victims had almost the same language." *Ibid.* p. 286.

[5] It is hardly possible, indeed, to attribute any other motive to a prince whose maxim was that the duty of a good shepherd is *to shear his lambs.*

[6] Naudet, *Des sec. publ. chez les Rom.* (Acad. des inscr., Vol. XIII. p. 86).

and clothing, and caused, under Nero, those distributions, so dear to the Roman populace, to be multiplied;[1] and if vanity and caprice were without doubt of much influence in the favors with which Adrian loaded some provinces, some other ameliorations introduced into the Roman administration will appear to us as more directly emanating from Christian principles. It was probably under their inspiration that, after the end of the first century, a real mitigation in the lot of slaves was introduced.[2] It would be difficult, in effect, to assign another cause for this change. The epoch had not yet come when the scarcity of this kind of merchandise would oblige the masters to spare it; it was, on the contrary, in its greatest abundance. However, we see already many efficacious measures taken for the amelioration of slavery. Claudius declared free those slaves whom their masters had exposed, during their sickness, on the island of the Tiber, according to the ancient usage.[3] Under the reign of Nero, a magistrate was commissioned to receive their complaints against the cruelties of their masters. Adrian took from these latter the right of life and death, prohibited the *ergastula*, only suffered to be put to the rack such slaves as should be found near the place where their master had been killed, forbid them to be sold for prostitution, or the combats of the amphitheatre, without the consent of the judge. Antoninus Pius punished as a murderer whoever put them to death without grave motives. Mar-

---

[1] Le Bas, *Hist. rom.*, Vol. II. p. 212.

[2] Troplong, *ubi sup.*, p. 82, etc. [3] Sueton. *Claud.*, c. 25.

cus Aurelius, during his reign, abolished, or at least disarmed the combats of gladiators.[1] Trajan established as a principle that an infant born in legitimate wedlock of free parents did not lose its liberty by having been exposed.[2] This same prince, partly from humanity, partly from the motive of public utility which had already determined Augustus,[3] caused the names of five thousand children to be added to the frumentary list; for the provinces he established a fund in favor of poor children whose parents would consent to bring them up; and this institution was extended by Adrian, Antoninus, and Marcus Aurelius.[4] After Pertinax, when the exhaustion of the treasury hindered the continuance of these allowances, they were in some places supplied by private gifts. Many of them bequeathed money to their cities or to their municipalities for the instruction or sustenance of children and the support of the aged.[5]

---

[1] Spartian., *Adrian.*, c. 18; Wallon, *Hist. de l'esclav.*, Vol. III. p. 60–65; Hegewisch, *Epoq. de l'hist. rom., la plus heureuse*, etc., Paris, 1834, p. 240; Villemain, *ubi sup.*, p. 280.

[2] Plin., *Ep.*, X. 71, 72.

[3] In order to increase the free population, reduced beyond measure during the civil wars, Augustus had given 2000 sestertii for the support of every child that the parents would bring up, and admitted to the *congiarium* the children below eleven years.

[4] Naudet, *Secours publ.*, loc. cit. p. 76–78. They called *pueri alimentarii* children thus raised at the expense of the public treasure; "*Ulpians*," those raised in virtue of the edict of Trajan; "*Faustinians*," the young girls assisted by Marcus Aurelius, in honor of his wife, Faustina. They estimate at 660,000 dollars the funds created by Trajan. (See the two edicts of this prince in Hegewisch, *Essai sur l'époque*, etc., p. 186.)

[5] Naudet, *ubi sup.*, p. 78.

11

Up to the time of Adrian, the property of those condemned for State crimes was entirely confiscated; Adrian adjudged one-half of it to their children; and even, on a particular occasion, he restored it all to them.[1]

To Antoninus Pius is attributed a boundless benevolence. Marcus Aurelius considered this virtue as the ideal of moral perfection, and he raised to it a temple on the Capitol.[2] He was accustomed to say: "As a Roman, I have Rome for my country; as a man, I have the world." He has left in his writings many maxims evidently marked with the Christian spirit,[3] and to which his administration generally conformed; in his efforts to repress the abandonment of infants, he seems, like Julius Paulus, to have deferred to the urgent protestations of Athenagoras.[4] Pertinax, in order to reduce the imposts, himself submitted to honorable privations.[5] Alexander Severus, the Emperor of these times who most fully recognized the enlightenment and virtues which he owed to Christianity, who placed Jesus among the number of the objects of his worship, and caused one of the maxims of evange-

---

[1] Hegewisch, *loc. cit.*, p. 119.

[2] Dio. Cassius, LXXI. p. 34; "Beneficentiæ deditus, cui templum ædificavit in Capitolio, quamque proprio quodam atque inaudito antè nomine nuncupavit."

[3] "Thou wilt love men," says he, "if thou happenest to think that thou art their brother, that it is by ignorance that they commit faults, and that in a short time thou wilt be all dead." (Villemain, *de la Phil. st.*, *ubi sup.*, p. 279.)

[4] Athenag., Legat. (*ad. calc. Just. Mart. Opp.* 1686, p. 38); Villemain, *ubi sup.*, p. 290.

[5] Le Bas, *ubi sup.*, p. 277.

lical charity to be engraved upon the walls of his palace, exercised towards his subjects a liberality, sometimes hardly judicious, it is true, but often as extensive as it was appropriate. He opened free schools for the children of poor families, and made to the poor loans of money necessary to buy land, at a very low rate of interest or gratuitously. He protected foundlings, even if born in servitude, and guarded the liberty of the free-born child who had been sold by its parents.[1] Diocletian also made laws to hinder the sale of children,[2] and to maintain the liberty of insolvent debtors; so much was the indirect influence of the church felt even by the princes who persecuted it![3]

Let those, then, who boast that they possess secrets important for the happiness of humanity cease, when they are not successful, from attributing it to the ill-will of those in power; let them refer it to their own impatience, or to the inopportuneness of their reforms. It is not right that the whole of society should be experimented on continually; it has the right to exact of those who aspire to regenerate it, a preliminary and sufficient trial of their systems; and, in truth, it has never to fear this trial. Every idea truly salutary, and which answers to a real profound need, makes its own way in the world. It is sufficient that those who adopt it have faith in it, and labor to realise it among themselves. From this centre, however contracted, it

---

[1] Naudet, *loc. cit.*, p. 87; de Gérando, *de la Bienf. publ.*, Vol. II. p. 138.

[2] Terme et Montfalc., *Hist. des Enfants trouvés*, p. 63.

[3] Troplong, *Infl. du chr.*, p. 76–79.

soon radiates and spreads; the good it produces is its best apology; and, opinion once for it, it soon has power on its side also.

Thus the church proceeded in the first centuries. She did not come to overthrow the old form of society,[1] she only claimed for herself the right of existing; she changed nothing in the old relations, but, by the side of them, created new ones; she prescribed new virtues, subjected her members to new duties, made within herself the reforms which she proposed to the world, and, for the rest, awaited the natural and spontaneous progress of opinion. Her expectation was not deceived. Feeble, abandoned, persecuted as she then was, she however caused her influence to be felt afar off, and to reform even the legislation in the name of which she was oppressed.

But her charity prepared other triumphs for her. Though in extending her gifts she wished only to conform to a divine order, though it in no way accorded with her views to pay for conversions, to buy proselytes, yet it was impossible that this spirit of benevolence should not powerfully aid her exterior progress. The standard of charity ever rallies the poor and feeble; the unfortunate takes voluntarily for guide the hand which comforts him, the arm which sustains him. We read in Saint Epiphanius that Manes, wishing to spread his errors in Mesopotamia, found the surest way to succeed in uniting with himself a man distinguished in that country for his extreme charity.[2] The

[1] Guizot, *Rev. franc.*, Vol. V. p. 13.

[2] Epiph., *Cont. hær.*, II., part 2; Hær. 66, p. 280 (Basil, 1560).

success which Manes sought in this way, was secured habitually by the church without design. In a social state so oppressive, every advantage ought to be for a religion which preached and practised benevolence; the unfortunate naturally crowded where they were sure of finding aid and support.[1] For this cause and others of a more elevated order, the number of Christians increased from day to day, and we approach the moment when a prince, who assuredly did not want political foresight, believed that he could, without danger, and even with advantage, associate the church with his empire.

The adoption of the Church by the State, under Constantine, would necessarily modify, in many respects, the influence of charity in the Roman world. Formerly, limited within a society not authorized by the laws, it only acted as a private virtue. It was only in an indirect manner that its principles had commenced to penetrate legislation. Now the State will lend its concurrence to the Church; it will, itself, proclaim the principles of charity, professing to take it for its guide in its administration and in its laws. Charity will no longer be solely a private virtue, but a public virtue also. On its part, the Church, which till then had preached it, above all, in a religious sense, will exult now to employ it in the service of the State; and, less pressing perhaps than formerly upon

---

[1] This fact is admitted by both friends and foes of the church. Chrys., hom., 11, in *Act.*, c. 3; hom. in *Philem.*, c. 3; Julian., *Ep. ad Arsac.*, Gibbon, *Decline*, c. 15.

the intimate sentiments of charity, it will recommend more urgently its manifestations and its acts.

Here then opens for us in the history of Christian charity a new period, which it imports so much the more to distinguish from the preceding, as it coincides with the epoch of the greatest disasters of the Empire, and consequently of the most terrible ravages of poverty.

To this sad picture we must now turn our attention.

SECOND BOOK.

INFLUENCE OF CHARITY FROM THE COMMENCEMENT OF THE FOURTH TO THE END OF THE SIXTH CENTURY.

CHAPTER FIRST.

AGGRAVATION OF MISERY IN THE ROMAN WORLD.

At all times, industry and commerce were despised at Rome; the only sources of riches appreciated there were agriculture and conquest.[1]

So long as most of the citizens were at the same time proprietors and cultivators, and so long as they had been occupied abroad only by short expeditions, agriculture had flourished among them; the space of seven acres was judged sufficient, at that epoch, for the sustenance of a family. But later, when more distant expeditions detained them with the armies, those of them who had no slaves to replace them in their absence were obliged to leave their lands fallow; and, at their return, instead of the momentary plenty which booty had secured to them in the camps, they only found destitution and straitened circumstances in

---

[1] Cicer., *De offic.*, I. 42; Dureau de la Malle, *Econ. pol. des Rom.*, Vol. II. p. 366, etc.; Blanqui, *Hist. de l'écon. polit.*, Vol. I. p. 68, etc.

their homes. Pressed with debts which their poverty forced them to contract, not in a condition to pay the usurious interest which accumulated from year to year, in order to get relief they sold their estates, or were ejected from them.[1] It was soon the same with that portion of the conquered lands which the State had allotted to these soldiers as an indemnity, and which besides was always very small.[2] The greatest part of these lands were, in effect, sold to the rich, who were alone capable of managing them advantageously. Still oftener, by favor of the credit which they enjoyed with the magistrates, these lands were adjudged to the rich for a small rent on an emphyteutic lease, which finished by converting itself into a strict property, exempt from all charge.[3] In vain from time to time was it attempted to recover these usurped domains; for, the agrarian law was at one time eluded, at another openly violated; the poor themselves, in whose behalf it had been promulgated, were often the first to abandon distant lands which they could not turn to profit, and to which they preferred the resources and amusements of the capital.[4]

Besides, at this epoch of despotism, the rich proprietors had a thousand means of aggrandizing them-

---

[1] Naudet, *Sec. publ.*, *ubi sup.*, pp. 9, 10.

[2] Sismondi, *Etudes sur l'écon. pol.*, Vol. II. p. 23.

[3] Naudet, *ubi sup.*, p. 3, etc.

[4] Dureau, *ubi sup.*, pp. 430, 493. This historian, who highly approves the agrarian law, as being destined to repair a notorious injustice and to increase the middle and free class, which formed the real strength of the state, acknowledges at the same time that it was the people that, by its want of ardor in making use of that law, annihilated its benefit.

selves at the expense of their neighbors. "Some," says St. Chrysostom, "feigning false claims, and presenting a long list of credits, which they pretended to date from their fathers and grandfathers, recovered a house of one, and a field of another, and a slave of a third."[1] Others used all the resources of chicanery. "His neighbor's trees cast too much shade, his house was open to vagrants." Hence a thousand quarrels till he was ousted. The unfortunate supported everything for fear of calling something worse upon himself. Some, according to St. Basil, without any formality, would plough and sow the field of another; blows for him who resisted, injurious accusations against him who complained; the prison, slavery, then sycophants at hand to institute a criminal action against him.[2] "The history of Naboth is old," says St. Ambrose, "and yet it is repeated every day; there is more than one Achab; every day a new one is born; every day some Naboth is forced to quit his estate, followed by his sad family and his wife in tears, for the rich wish to possess, alone, all the earth."[3] Sometimes the poor man himself, to secure a true or pretended protection against the efforts of those who pil-

---

[1] Chrys., hom., 13, in 1 *Cor.*, c. 5, Vol. X. p. 116; hom., 22, in *Gen.*, c. 6, Vol. IV. p. 203, etc.

[2] Basil. Magn., hom. *in div.*, c. 5; Opp., Vol. II. p. 57; Cf. Greg. Naz., *Carm.*, I. 28; Opp. Ed. Ben., Vol. II. p. 547; Salvian., *De gub. Dei*, lib. IV. pp. 188, 234; V. p. 274; see, for similar particulars, in Libanius, Orat. 10, *in Jul. nec.* Opp. fol., Vol. II. p. 293.

[3] Ambros., *De Nab.*, c. 1, Opp. 8, Vol. II. p. 323, etc.; Salvian., *De gub. Dei*, lib. IV. V., Opp. Vol. I. pp. 188, 290; Cf. Horat. *Od.* II. 18, 23, etc.

laged, or against the exactions of the imperial treasury, alienated his property or his liberty.[1] Thus, because of misery and vexations, real estate concentrated itself more and more within a few families; the vast domains, which, in the times of the Gracchi, already gave occasion for so many complaints, were more and more extended every day, especially since the reign of the Antonines;[2] and in the fourth century they already passed all bounds. The half of the Roman possessions in Africa, according to Pliny, was owned by six proprietors, when Nero brought them to death,[3] and elsewhere several hundred miles were travelled without leaving the domains of a certain patrician or of a certain consul.

Now, upon these immense domains, what was the condition of the population which cultivated them? Alas, as wretched as possible! The rich Romans hardly ever retained any one upon their lands, except the debtors whom they had ejected, and whose persons, attached by a *lien*, (nexus),[4] according to the ex-

---

[1] Greg. Naz., *ubi sup.;* Salv., *De gub. Dei,* lib. V.; Gothofr., *in Cod. Theod.,* Vol. IV. p. 173, *De patroc. vicor.*

[2] Dureau, *ubi sup.,* Vol. II. p. 228–230.

[3] Plin., XVIII. 6.

[4] *Nexus.* The debtor unable to pay within thirty days, was placed at the creditor's disposal, and compelled to labor to the amount of his debt; he might, for this purpose, be loaded with chains weighing fifty pounds, and confined at his creditor's. After a new delay, the latter might sell him as a slave (Moreau de Jonnès, *Stat. des peuples anc.,* Vol. II. p. 402). "Slavery for debts," says Troplong, "was for centuries the leprosy of Rome." (See particulars entered into by the same on this subject, *Séances de l'ac. des sc. mor. and pol.,* 2d series, Vol. I. p. 218, *seq.*

pression then used, answered for the rest of their debt; they arbitrarily employed these wretches, thus delivered to their mercy, and accorded to them, in return for a crushing toil, only a meagre subsistence or a pitiful salary.[1] "Upon them, bent down all their lives to their toil, they impose," says St. Chrysostom, "insupportable burdens, and treat them like beasts, without respite; never do they give them the least portion of the harvests which they lock up in their granaries, and they leave them at the end of a fine season as miserable as they were at its commencement."[2]

Soon, however, the large proprietors preferred the work of slaves, very numerous at that epoch, to that of men whom the military service threatened each instant to take from them. "The fields," says Moreau de Jonnès, "were covered with chained laborers, marked on the brow with a hot iron, the head half shaved."[3] As to the free cultivators, whom these slaves replaced, some came to Rome, to seek their subsistence in the public distributions, or in the suite of some rich patron; others, those who were not Roman citizens, wandered sadly in the provinces, where their families perished in inaction and misery.[4]

But the value of the labor of slaves for all work

---

[1] Muller, *Comm. de genio et mor., ævi. Theod.*, p. 19, *seq.* According to Naudet, the greatest part of those wretched creatures lived upon ten cents a day (*Sec. publ., ubi sup.*, p. 11).

[2] Chrysost., hom. 61, *in Matth.*, c. 3, Vol. VII. p. 614.

[3] Moreau de Jonnès, *Econ. dom. des Rom.* (*Journal des Econ.*, Vol. III. p. 70).

[4] Dureau, *ubi sup.*, Vol. II. p. 278, *seq.*

which demands a little intelligence and activity of mind, is well understood. Sismondi observes, that agriculture has never prospered among the ancients except where the slaves were still in feeble proportion and only associated with their masters in their work.[1] When slaves had everywhere been introduced as substitutes of free workmen, the large proprietors, recognizing then that their lands brought them in less than before, had recourse to another expedient. They converted their fields and their vineyards into pastures, where they raised stock under the keeping of only a few servants. This speculation, without doubt advantageous to them, it so economizing labor, finished by ruining and depopulating the country; and the desolation and sterility, which, in the time of Pliny, the *latifundia* had already caused in Italy, was now seen to extend over almost all the Roman empire.[2]

While the resources of agriculture were thus reduced almost to nothing, what became of those of conquest?

Let us observe, in the first place, that conquest, such as the Romans understood it, was the universal impoverishment or rather ruin of the subjects of Rome for the profit of one dominant city, which, after having put them under contribution by its generals and its legions, finished by despoiling them by its veterans,

---

[1] De Sismondi, *Etud. sur l'écon. pol.*, Vol. I. p. 407; Dureau, Vol. II. p. 230; Moreau de Jonnès, *Stat. des peuples anc.*, Vol. II. p. 451.

[2] Dureau, *ubi sup.*, Vol. II. p. 223; de Sismondi, *ubi sup.*, Vol. II. p. 23, *seq.* All that precedes is resumed in a compact and striking passage of Appian (*De bell. civ.*, lib. I., Opp. fol. 1592, p. 353, *seq.*). "Res in contrarium quam putârunt," etc.

its publicans, and, above all, by its prætors and its proconsuls. All the wealth which an active commerce and industrious toil had, during so many centuries, amassed in the cities of the east and south, came, under a thousand names, under a thousand forms, and by all means just and unjust, to accumulate in Rome.[1] But the majority did not profit by it. Some gratifications to the army, some distributions of provisions to the poor citizens, from time to time some pecuniary largesses, dissipated in a day of debauch, were all that came directly to the people from the pillage of the nations;[2] the rest engulfed itself in the treasury of the emperor, and in that of some families, richer by themselves than all the people together.[3]

The evil would have been less, if from this centre these riches, distributed by productive and intelligent expenditure, circulating by channels wisely provided, had nourished the prosperity of the capital and of the provinces. Inequality of conditions is not of itself a

[1] Cicer., *pro leg. Man.*, c. 22, 23; Dezobry, *Rome sous Aug.*, lett. 76, 77; de Champagny, *les Césars*, Vol. II. p. 166, *seq.;* Vol. IV. p. 206; Le Bas, *Hist. rom.*, Vol. II. pp. 97, 109, etc. Let us remember, among others, the exactions of Cassius and Antonius in Asia. It is thought that, within the twelve years that elapsed between Scipio's return and the end of Antiochus' war, more than three hundred millions of francs were brought to Rome, as well in contributions of war, as in precious metals plundered by the generals. The sack of Carthage, alone, produced five hundred millions (Moreau Christophe., *Du probl. de la misère*, Vol. I. p. 93, *seq.*, 188, *seq.; du Droit à l'oisiveté*, p. 43. For particulars, see Moreau de Jonnès, *Stat. des peuples anc.*, Vol. II. p. 530).

[2] Naudet, *Sec. publ.*, *loc. cit.*, p. 6.

[3] Moreau de Jonnès, *Statist.*, Vol. II. p. 532.

source of misery; on the contrary, like the graduated levels on the globe, it is, in the plan of Providence, a source of abundance and fertility. There is an employment of opulence which may be a thousand times more profitable to the poorer classes, than would be the most equal partition. But, it is true, such is not the ordinary fruit of wealth amassed by injustice. That of the rich at Rome hardly profited aught but vice and laziness. Instead of enriching labor, it ruined it by usury.[1] Instead of causing useful citizens to prosper, it only served to nourish, for the vanity of a master, devouring troops of slaves and clients, it made the degrading professions of comedians, buffoons, and parasites to flourish, paid for shows for the people, and furnished means for the profuse liberalities of a triumph, or for the giddy joys of a day of installation. To the refined if not productive luxury of monuments and of the fine arts, had succeeded the material and ruinous luxury of furniture, equipages, and expensive frivolities,[2] and soon the corruptive luxury of the table, and brutal pleasures. In the time of the Republic, the wife of a rich Roman was seen to expend seven millions for one ornament;[3] in the fourth century there might still be seen, according to the expression of a Father of the Church, the subsistence of several families suspended at the ear or from the neck of a

---

[1] Moreau de Jonnès, *Statist.*, Vol. II. p. 533, *seq.*

[2] Ammon. Marcell., *Rer. gest.*, XIV. 6; XXVIII. 4; Dezobry, *ubi sup.*, I. p. 205, etc.; de Champagny, *ubi sup.*, III. pp. 43, 44; IV. p. 45–49.

[3] Naudet, *ubi sup.*, p. 11.

matron;[1] entire fortunes were seen absorbed by the expenses of one splendid repast, of one horse-race, or of one combat of gladiators.[2] All for the egotism and for the sensuality, the pride or the vanity of the few; nothing for the real well-being of the many.

Besides, to reanimate the activity of the provinces by the means of luxury, to permit them by industry to regain in detail that which Rome had taken from them, there was necessary to them a confidence, a security which despotism did not permit them to enjoy. A prey to the avarice of governors, to the rapacity of the farmers of the revenue, they had lost courage to work and produce; the more they were pressed, the less was drawn from them; the riches devoured in Rome were not renewed; commerce did not repair a suffering agriculture; the fertility of one country supplied but slowly and with difficulty the barrenness of another. Hence, in bad years, the frightful famines which the avidity of monopolizers speculated upon.[3] Hence, even in ordinary years, an excessive and ever-increasing dearness, which Diocle-

---

[1] Chrysost., *hom.* 89 in *Matth.*, c. 4, Vol. VII. p. 836.

[2] Basil. Magn., III. p. 46. See in Gregory of Nyssa the description of the unbounded luxury of the rich in his time (*Orat.* I., *de amand. paup.*). They relate that Symmachus' son's installation in the prætorship cost his father ten millions of francs, and that the Senator Maximus, on a similar occasion, doubled that sum. Moreau de Jon., *Econ. dom. des Rom.* (*Journ. des Econ.*, Vol. III. p. 61).

[3] Liban., orat. 10, *in Jul. nec.*, Opp. fol., Vol. II. p. 306; Chrys., hom. 39, in *Cor.*, c. 8, Vol. X. p. 375; Basil., hom., *in illud: de struam*, etc., c. 5, Opp., II. p. 47; Greg. Naz., *Carm.* I. 2, 28; Vol. II. p. 549, etc.

tian essayed in vain to arrest by his celebrated *Maximum*.[1] All the rigors with which he surrounded it were powerless; the famine increased to such a point that to disembarrass himself of beggars, it is said, he had a great number of them drowned.[2] His successors, less barbarous, but subject to the same difficulties, expelled from Rome, on the least appearance of famine, not only the foreigners, but the Italians,[3] "the sons of those whose tribute nourished Rome," says St. Ambrose, "at the risk of exposing themselves to die of hunger."[4] "Thus," says Moreau de Jonnès, "the treasures which the Romans had acquired by their conquests were to them what the mines of America were to the Spaniards; they sextupled the price of things, and caused culture to be abandoned for courses of pillage in distant countries."[5] And, let us boldly add, in causing the ruin of those countries, they prepared that of Rome itself.

Finally, the resources of conquest were far from being indefinite. Rome had, long since, derived from them all that they could furnish. After having extended its domination, in all ways, even to the limits of

---

[1] Lactant., *De morte persec.*, c. 7, Opp., p. 937; Le Bas, *Hist. rom.* II., append., p. 518, *seq.* M. Moreau Jonnès shows, by that edict, that substance was at that time by half, and certain necessary objects ten or twenty times dearer than they are to-day in France, though merchants were losing, and hence ceased importing them. (*Journal des Econ.*, III. p. 42.)

[2] Lactant., *De morte persec.*

[3] Amm. Marcell., XIV. 6, p. 27; Liban., *Antiochic.*, Opp. fol. II. p. 366; *Cf.* Symmach., *Relat.* (*ap. Ambros. Epp.*)

[4] Ambros., *De off. min.*, III. 6, Vol. VII. p. 356.

[5] Moreau de Jonn., *ubi sup.*, p. 70.

the civilized world, after having carried off the wealth of the polished nations of Greece and the East, she now found herself confronted with barbarous nations, among which there was nothing to pillage, but which were already disposed, themselves, to pillage and treat Rome as she had, for so long a time, treated the vanquished.

It was no longer for her to increase her booty, but to defend it; and how could she defend it, since now what formerly constituted the force of the Roman armies, the middle class, had almost entirely disappeared?[1] In time of danger, Rome armed the slaves, but the slaves defended the territory still worse than they cultivated it. Auxiliaries were then enrolled; but to pay those four hundred thousand strangers, who on all sides were to hold in check the enemies of the empire, it was necessary to triple and quadruple the imposts.[2] All groaned under the scourge of the exactions of the imperial treasury, and the extortions of the soldiery. The decurions, charged at their own risk with levying the taxes, and responsible for the sum fixed by the law, abandoned their property to escape from their duty.[3] The debtors of the fisc, not in a condition to pay their arrears, left of themselves their desert lands,[4] and became beggars. The burden then fell upon the *Coloni* attached to the glebe, and upon a small number of free country people whom the tyranny of the rich culti-

---

[1] Dureau, *ubi sup.*, II. p. 280.

[2] Moreau de Jonn., *ubi sup.*, p. 65; *Stat.* II. p. 521, *et seq.*; Le Bas, *hist. rom.*, II. p. 375; Dureau, II. p. 353, *seq.*; 493.

[3] Theodoret., *Ep.* 43; *Opp.*, Vol. III. p. 928.

[4] Peyron, *fragm. cod. Theod.*, p. 150, 153–156; Lactant., *De morte persec.*, c. 7, 936; Salvian., *de gub. Dei.* V., Vol. I. p. 290.

vators had spared.[1] If they could not pay, they were thrown into the State prisons; they were scourged with the whip, and subjected to tortures,[2] from which they often did not escape except at the price of the honor of their wives, or of the liberty of their children.[3] A great number, to escape from the impost, fled among the barbarians,[4] or, becoming barbarians themselves, under the name of *Bagaudi*, they devastated the provinces of the empire, and retook by pillage what an oppressive administration had taken from them.[5] How paint the misery which then desolated the empire? Fathers were seen selling their children for bread. The public places and avenues of the city swarmed with beggars.[6] "Go," said St. John Chrysostom, to a friend who complained of his misfortunes, "go and visit the porches of our public baths, where so many unfortunate ones, stretched upon straw or upon filth, some even without clothing, trembling with

---

[1] Theodoret., *ubi sup.;* Salvian., *ubi sup.*, p. 284; Liban., *Basilic.*, Opp., Vol. II. p. 147.

[2] Le Bas, *Hist. Rom.*, II. p. 377.

[3] Liban., *Basilic.*, p. 146, *seq.*, Salv., *ubi sup.*, p. 292, *seq.*

[4] *Cod. Theod.*, XI. 1, *De annon. et trib.*, I. 7, ann. 361, *seq.* From the reign of Theodosius, the condition of proprietors had become so intolerable, and the abandoned lands so numerous, that they were left to the first occupant, on the condition of a two years' possession. Giraud., *Elem. de Droit Rom.*, I. p. 373.

[5] Salvian., *ubi sup.*, p. 278–80.

[6] Cod. Theod., XIV. 8, l. 1; Greg. Nyss., *Orat.* 1, *de paup. am.* (*in Orthodoxogr.*, p. 1781). Chrysostom calculated that at Antioch a tenth part of the population was absolutely without resources, and lived upon alms from day to day (Hom. 66, *in Matth.*, c. 3, VII. p. 657).

cold, tormented with pain or with hunger, seek to move the passers by with the spectacle of their wo."[1] Palladius draws a still more heart-rending picture of the beggars, lying under the porticoes of Ancyra, the unhappy wives of whom were sometimes delivered in the open air, in the midst of a rigorous season.[2]

To these evils, which had existed for a long time, but which were aggravated from day to day, were added, since the fourth century, others still more terrible.

We have said that every power which only knows how to grow and become rich at the expense of others, necessarily and inevitably devotes itself to destruction; the term of its progress is the commencement of its ruin. From the day that it ceases to inspire terror, it sees resentments and vengeance fall upon itself; from the moment when it has the world no longer for its slave, it has it wholly for its enemy. The Roman empire had to undergo to its very end the consequences of its fatal policy. Its provinces, depeopled of free men interested in their defence, guarded by malcontent or ill-paid mercenaries, remained open on all sides to barbarians. The inhabitants themselves, far from repelling them, called them into the heart of the empire; "For," says Salvian, "their dearest wish was not to remain under the domination of Rome."[3] Then began those terrible invasions, which continued, without interruption, from the death of

---

[1] Chrysostom, *ad Stagir.*, III. 13, Vol. I. p. 223.

[2] Palladii, *Hist. Laus*, c. 115, p. 205; Paris, 1570.

[3] Salvian., *ubi sup.*, p. 290; de Sismondi, *Etudes sur l'écon. pol.*, Vol. I. p. 94.

Theodosius, bringing with each new flood of barbarians all scourges at once. In the west, nought was to be seen but cities destroyed, provinces ravaged, plains depeopled, and opulent families ruined and wandering from one end of the empire to another, or led away into captivity. For example, let us limit ourselves to Italy. Let us consider at the time of St. Ambrose, Bologna, Modena, Piacenza, and all the country around reduced to a desert; at the time of Pope Gelasius, Æmilia, Tuscany, almost destitute of inhabitants; later, under Pope Gregory, all the population of Italy fleeing before the Lombards. Let us consider, above all, the fate of Rome, blockaded, famished, ransacked, pillaged finally by Alaric, hardly preserved from the hordes of Attila, taken and retaken five times under Justinian, and at each time treated with redoubled cruelty, its senatorial families cut down by the sword, and the rest of its inhabitants almost destroyed by a long famine.[1]

It is evident that all this arose from having, from its origin, despised the true and legitimate sources of the wealth of nations, discouraged free labor, sacrificed commerce, industry, agriculture itself, to war and conquest; it was for having sought in injustice and violence the sources of her prosperity and grandeur, that Rome had at last come to the depths of misery. A memorable lesson for those States which can still profit by it!

---

[1] Gibbon, *Decline*, etc., c. 36, ad fin.; de Sismondi, *ibid.*; c. 10, pp. 161, 199, 211 (ed. 8vo., maj.); Pelag. I., *Epist.* 15 (*in* Labbe concil. coll., Vol. V. p. 802).

As for the Roman empire, having gone down for so many centuries upon this fatal descent, it was no longer possible for it to remount it. Its catastrophe was imminent. All that could be done for its subjects was to break, to weaken the shocks; the evil was without remedy. All that could be hoped was, to find some palliatives for it.

And firstly, as one of the principal causes of the wretchedness was the abuse which the rich and great made of their power, it was necessary, as far as possible, to protect the feeble against these oppressors.

Then, everywhere where the misery was felt, not being able to oppose to it the only efficacious remedy, that is, the resources of a free and fruitful labor, it was necessary at least to do all to alleviate the evils and privations which it brought in its train.

Such was the double task which Christian charity had to fulfil from the fourth century. Let us examine in what manner it undertook the task and how far it succeeded in it.

CHAPTER II.

CHARITABLE INTERVENTION OF THE CHURCH IN FAVOR OF THE OPPRESSED.

So many authors have occupied themselves with the influence of Christianity in mitigating slavery, and many in so learned and profound a way, that, after them, it would be superfluous to enter upon long details. We will only recall the principles of the church in this regard.

"The doctrines of the church," says Wallon, "must conduct to the abolition of slavery. But the apostles had not exacted it, and the Fathers of the church were not in a better condition to accomplish it; for, after as before the public establishment of the faith, it was always, even under the Christian emperors, the old society, bound by all its habits to slavery. More than one law was necessary in order to change such a state of things; the change was a revolution, and to accomplish it effectually, it was not the slave which it seemed urgent to take from the master, but, above all, it was necessary to wean the master from slavery by the sentiment of the dignity of man. Now, the task was long; and, besides, there was another, more grave and more pressing; namely, the enfranchisement of souls from the yoke of sin."[1] So that the church abstained from exciting the slaves and from seeking their emancipation, for fear that their efforts after temporal liberty would turn their eyes from a spiritual liberty of a higher price. "Why," said St. Chrysostom, "did the apostle leave slavery to exist? To the end that you might learn the excellence of the liberty of the soul; for, even as it needed a prodigy to preserve intact the bodies of the three children in the fiery furnace, so there is less of grandeur and of marvellousness in suppressing slavery than in showing that there is liberty even in its bosom."[2]

---

[1] Wallon, *Hist. de l'escl.*, Vol. III. p. 318.

[2] *Ibid.*, p. 335; Chrysost., in *Genes. serm.*, 5, c. 1; Opp., IV. p. 666.

The masters then, could, without ceasing to be Christians, keep their slaves.[1] The priests themselves and the bishops had some, which they often enfranchised only at their death, like St. Gregory, of Nazianzen,[2] or like St. Augustine and the clergy of Hippo, when they voluntarily renounced individual property and decided to live in a community.[3] This did not hinder the church from encouraging the enfranchisements. "As our Redeemer," said St. Gregory the Great, (in emancipating two slaves belonging to his church,) "put on human nature to break the bonds that held us captive, and to restore us to our original liberty, it is salutary to restore liberty, by emancipation, to those whom national laws subject to servitude."[4] Chrysostom condemns the unbridled luxury shown in keeping slaves. He would have preferred that the masters should only keep the number strictly necessary for their service, and have trades taught to the others, that they might gain their living, so that they might ultimately be set free. "This," said he, "is what might truly be called charity."[5]

---

[1] The church formally condemned the Eustachians of Cappadocia, who denied the character of a Christian to any owner of slaves, and the Circoncelliones of Africa, who excited slaves to rebellion. Concil. Gangr., can. 3 (Labbe *concil.*, Vol. II. p. 415). Chrysostom proves, by Paul's example, that people ought to forbear to take slaves from their masters, for fear of causing Christianity to be cursed as at enmity with established civil relations. (Chrys., *in Ep., ad Philem., argum.*, Vol. II. p. 773.)

[2] Greg. Naz., *Testament.*, Opp., Vol. II. p. 202, *seq.*

[3] August., *de vit. et mor. cleric.*, Serm. 355, c. 2; Serm. 356, c. 3, 7, Vol. XXI. pp. 349, 357.

[4] Gregor. Magn., *Ep.* VI. 12; Opp., Par. 1705, Vol. II. p. 800.

[5] Chrys., Hom. 40, *in* 1 *Cor.*, c. 5, Vol. X. p. 385.

But the church recommended to them, before all and always, sentiments of fraternity which would make them treat their slaves as, in their place, they would have desired to be treated by them. Whilst the pagan Libanius exhausts his rhetoric to prove that the slaves are more free and happy than their masters,[1] the Fathers of the church show to the masters the sad condition of their slaves, exhort them to spare them from all excessive work, all inhuman treatment, to show them, on every occasion, sympathy, mildness, and a truly paternal commiseration, even in indispensable punishments.

Similar recommendations abound in their discourses and writings.[2] They do not admit the poor excuses of the masters. "They are vicious," they said; "it is an insubordinate and lazy race, inclined to lying, thieving, and all vices." But what made them so, if it was not the harshness and the pernicious examples of their masters?[3] And what other means were there to correct them, but to take care of their souls and to use more of humanity towards them?[4] "Your female servants are intolerable, you say, if they are let alone. True, but there are other means of correcting them than with the whip. Kindness will succeed better than fear. They are inclined to drunkenness; take

[1] Liban., *De servit. orat.*, Vol. II. p. 649–651.

[2] See Wallon, *loc. cit.*, p. 343–349; Chrys., *in Ep. ad Phil.*, Vol. II. p. 775.

[3] Chrysostom speaks with indignation of the rapine, violence, and infamous disorders of manners to which slaves were compelled by some masters. (Chrys., *in Ep. ad Phil.*, hom. 1, c. 2, Vol. XI. p. 777.)

[4] Salvian., *De gub. Dei*, IV. p. 182.

from them the occasions for getting drunk: to libertinism; marry them off: to theft; watch them. If this slave has faith, she is your sister in Christ. Has she not a soul like you? Has she not been honored of the Lord? Does she not sit at the same table? Has she not, with you, an illustrious origin? She has vices, you say; have free women not vices too? And yet, the Gospel would have their husbands support them."[1]

The example of the holy did still more good than their precepts. Noble Christian dames, Paula, Fabiola, attempted, by a touching familiarity, to edify the souls of those whom fortune had subjected to them.[2] "Lea," says St Jerome, "resembled less a mistress in the midst of her slaves, than a servant in the midst of her companions, so much did she bend to their condition by her sympathy and goodness; she was also respected and cherished by the most of them."[3] Synesius, the bishop, demands in recovery a slave who had fled. "It is not one of mine," he adds, "for I treat them so that they love me much more as a master of their choice, than they fear me as a ruler imposed on them by the law."[4] Such masters were well situated to preach compassion and clemency unto others. We see, then, St. Basil thank Callisthenes, who, at his instance, had spared two slaves, whom he had sworn to deliver up to punishment.[5] Finally, when recom-

---

[1] Chrys., hom. 15, *in Ephes.*, c. 3, Vol. XI. p. 112, *seq.*

[2] Hieron., *Ep.* 86, *Epit. Paul,*, Opp. IV. part 2, p. 670.

[3] *Ibid., ad Marcell. de exitu Leæ.*, Ep. 20, *ubi sup.*, p. 52.

[4] Synes., *Ep.* 144, Opp. Paris, 1632, p. 281.

[5] Basil., *Ep.* 73; Opp., Ben., III. p. 167.

mendations and prayers were useless, the church opened to the oppressed or threatened slave the refuge of a sanctuary, and, whilst this asylum protected him from the first transports of the rage of his master, the bishop went to implore, and very often obtained his pardon.

Again, it was the interest of this unfortunate class that animated the church in its efforts for the abolition of the combats of gladiators. What fervor of charity glowed in the monk Telemachus, when, having arrived at Rome at the moment when these cruel sports were celebrated, he threw himself into the middle of the arena to separate the combatants, and perished, a victim of the fury of the people! But his blood was fruitful as that of the martyrs, and the law of Honorius was its worthy price.[1]

The church equally surrounded with its protection the unhappy *coloni* attached to the glebe.

"Pay to the hireling his just wages," said St. Ambrose; "despise not the poor who consumes for thee his life in toil, for it is to deprive him of life to refuse the subsistence due to him. Remember that thou art also a hireling on earth, and give to the hireling that thou mayest, in thy turn, ask of the Lord."[2] St. Augustine, learning that some poor *coloni* were obliged to pay to their masters the double of what they legitimately owed, complained for them to the magistrate

---

[1] Prudent., *in Symmach.* II. 11, 21; Theodoret., *Hist. eccles.*, V. 26. In the year 404, Honorius abolished entirely the contests of gladiators. Gothofr., *in Cod. Theod.*, Vol. V. p. 398.

[2] Ambros., *De Tobiâ*, c. 24, § 92; Opp., Vol. II. p. 412; Cf. Chrys., hom. 61, *in Matth.*, c. 3, 4, Vol. VII. p. 614–616.

of their province, and rendered him responsible for all the violence that might be used against them.[1] Maysimas, a Syrian monk, upon the same subject, addressed remonstrances to the governor Letoius.[2] The Pope, St. Gregory, is informed that the *coloni* of the Roman Church in Sicily are trampled upon by his agents, that they exact more grain of them than is right, that many of them, who were born free, have been claimed as slaves; he writes instantly to the sub-deacons of Sicily, that they should have an eye to these abuses, and preserve the *coloni* of the church from all injustice and oppression.[3]

After the condition of the slaves and the *coloni*, there were none more miserable than the small free proprietors, whom the great, under a thousand pretexts, and by a thousand odious means, spoiled of their estates. And with what courage did the church defend them against these privileged thieves! "O thou, who, to rob the poor, dost bring unjust suits against him, transport thyself in thought before the Supreme Tribunal, without a defender who will plead for thee against these unfortunate creatures whom thou hast made thy victims. O rich man! of what use to thee are thy magnificent constructions? Even after the death of their possessor they utter an accusing voice. Each one, regarding them, exclaims, 'What tears they have cost! How many orphans stripped to the last, how many widows reduced to despair!' 'What, again

---

[1] Aug., *Ep.* 247, *ad Romul.*, c. 1, *seq.*, Vol. XLI. p. 368.

[2] Theodoret., *Relig. hist.*, c. 14; Opp., Vol. III. p. 842.

[3] Gregor. Magn., *Epp.* 1, 42, 53 (Labbe, *Conc.*, Vol. V. pp. 1055, 1064).

declaiming against the rich,' says one to me. Yes, as you are against the poor. Against the plunderers? Yes, like you against those whose property you plunder. Until you cease to devour the poor, I will not cease to cry out against you. Touch not my lamb if you do not wish me to defend it."[1]

The barbarity of usurers was treated no less gently.[2] St. Ambrose describes them to us as enticing their victim, at one time by the attraction of pleasure, at another by that of a few days' relief, entangling him by perfidious advances, strangling him by invisible ties, which they draw tighter and tighter, till they could despoil him at their leisure.[3] He paints the despair of a father of family under the talons of one of these vultures, who constrains him to alienate his estate and to sell even his own children. "I have seen," says he, "a lamentable spectacle; children sold at auction to pay the debt of their father, heirs of his disasters, who should have been heirs to his goods. And the creditor, far from blushing at such a sale,

---

[1] Basil., *Hom. in divit.*, c. 6; Opp., Vol. II. p. 58; Chrysost., *in Genes.*, hom. 30, c. 2; *in Ps.*, 48, Vol. IV. p. 296; Vol. V. pp. 507, 523; Ambr., *De Nabuth.;* Greg. Naz., *Carm.*, lib. I., § 2, c. 28; Salv., *De gub. Dei*, IV., Vol. I. pp. 188, 234.

[2] "Is there anything more cruel," says Chrysostom, "than to take advantage of the poverty of one's neighbor, and under the mask of kindness, to plunge him into an abyss? The poor does not come to thee in order to be deprived of the little he has, but to be relieved of his poverty; and thou, feigning to help him, thou hastenest his ruin." Chrys., *Cur. in Pentec.*, hom. c. 1, Vol. III. p. 32; Cf. *in Matth.*, hom. 5, c. 5; hom. 56, c. 5, Vol. VII. pp. 82, 573, etc.

[3] Ambros., *De Tobiâ*, c. 3, *seq.*, Vol. II. p. 364, *seq.*

urged its conclusion. 'They have been nourished with my money,' he said, 'let their services now reimburse the advances I have made.' O, the insatiable rapacity of the usurer, worthy of Satan, of whom he is the faithful image!"[1] The rate of interest was so high among the Romans, that to lend on legal terms with the firm resolution of being paid, was, in some sort, to resolve in advance on the ruin of the borrower. So that the Fathers of the church saw scarcely any difference between lending on interest and on usury, and renewed, in this respect, the prescriptions of the Old Testament.[2] They wished that, while refusing to the intemperate, to the gamester, to the voluptuary, what would only serve to feed their passions, the miseries of the poor should be relieved gratuitously. But while preaching humanity to creditors, they respected their rights; and when they could not obtain a forbearance from them, or an equitable reduction, they sometimes aided a debtor to pay,[3] and even did not fear to engage themselves personally for them. St. Augustine wrote one day to his flock to assist him in reimbursing seventeen *solidi* of gold. Having nothing wherewith to pay the debt of a poor person

---

[1] Ambros., *De Tobiâ*, c. 8, 9, p. 375, *seq.*

[2] *Ibid.*, *ib.*, c. 2, 14, p. 364, 386, *seq.* The doctrine of the Fathers on this matter served as a basis to the civil and religious legislation of the Middle Ages, which prohibits any interest, but which, by this prohibition, ended only in augmenting the scourge of usury.

[3] Gregory the Great orders Anthimus, his deacon, to pay in part the debts of Maurus, and to obtain from creditors, if he could, to discharge him for the remnant. *Epp.*, VII. 37 (Labbe, *Conc.*, Vol. V. p. 1328.)

who had applied to him, he had borrowed the sum necessary, and, as he could not return it, he found himself on the point of being prosecuted. It was necessary for the church and clergy of Hippo to disengage him by means of a collection.[1]

The more elevated was the condition of the creditor, the more profound was the misery of the debtor, which found so much the more sympathy among these generous instruments of charity. The writings of the Fathers are full of their supplications in favor of private persons, of cities or of provinces crushed beneath the weight of imposts. It is St. Basil who prays the governors and the assessors of taxes of Cappadocia, at one time to spare an old man burdened with children; at another to lighten the burthen that weighs upon Cæsarea; here to exempt from the oath peasants subject to the tax; there, to accord a respite in the levy of the impost for the military equipment; elsewhere, to discharge from *curial* offices the grandson of an old man who found himself improperly subject to them; and elsewhere again, to diminish the taxes which overwhelmed the peasants of the Taurus.[2] It is Theodoret, Bishop of Cyrus, who writes to the Patrician, Areobinde, in favor of the agriculturists visited the preceding year by a famine,[3] and who addresses letters

[1] August., *Ep.* 268; Opp., Vol. XLI. p. 422.

[2] Basil., *Epp.* 36, 37, 75, 76, 83–85, 110, etc.; Opp.,.Vol. III. pp. 114, 170, 171, 176–178, etc.

[3] Theodoret., *Ep.* 23; Opp. Vol. III. p. 917. "Have mercy," says he to him, "on those poor who have worked so much and gained so little. Let the sterility of the year before you, by the compassion you will use towards them, be the occasion of an abundant spiritual crop."

upon letters to influential personages, to the empress herself, for the inhabitants of his diocese, of which, on false reports, they had augmented the imposts.[1] Presented with warmth by men whose devotedness was known, whose characters were venerated, whose eloquence had the gift of persuasion,[2] these reclamations were almost always favorably received. St. Basil and St. Gregory accompanied with their benedictions the governors whom they had more than once implored, and whose clemency they had experienced.[3] Paul, Bishop of the Novatians of Constantinople, put so much fervor in his supplications for the debtors of the fisc, that he almost always obtained their freedom.[4] St. Epiphanius, Bishop of Pavia, obtained from Odoacer an exemption from imposts, for five years, for that city, which had been burned and pillaged by the Heruli; he caused the Ligurians, who had been doubly taxed, to be relieved, and obtained from Gondebald the redemption of the prisoners taken by Theodoric.[5]

When the faithful were oppressed by the powerful, when subaltern tyrants, magistrates, governors, and proconsuls trampled under them, without pity, the provinces the administration of which had been confided

---

[1] Theodoret., *Ep.* 42, 43; *ibid.*, p. 926–928.

[2] Greg. of Naz., upon terminating his discourse to Julian, an assessor of taxes, reminds him of that love for eloquence, which had always excited in him generous emotions of the heart. (Orat. 19, c. 16; Opp., Vol. II. p. 374.)

[3] Basil., *Ep.* 327, Vol. III. p. 450; Greg. Naz., *Ep.* 146, Opp., Vol. II. p. 123.

[4] Socrat., *Hist. eccl.*, VII. 17.

[5] Baillet, *Vies des Saints*, Jan. 21st, p. 270.

to them, it was, again, the charity of the Christian ministers which protected these victims of caprice. At one time, like St. Ambrose, like Pope Celestin, like Domitian, Bishop of Melitenus, like St. Germain, Bishop of Auxerre, like St. Marcel, Archimandrite at Constantinople, they turned to profit their credit at the court, to introduce there the complaints of the poor and the griefs of the provinces;[1] at another, like St. Gregory and St. Basil, addressing themselves directly to the oppressors, they sought by their severe and yet pathetic remonstrances, to recall them to themselves. "I should fail in the regard which I owe to you and to the importance of your office," said St. Gregory to the Governor Olympius, just ready to chastise the city of Nazianzen, "if I neglected to give you the advice which your interest and that of the people under your administration require. Besides, if God has confided the government of this city to you,

[1] *Vita Sanct.*, *Ambros.*, Cœlestin, *Ep.* 12, *ad Theodos.*, jun. (ap. Labb., *Concil.* Vol. II. p. 1629); Baillet, *ubi sup.*, Jan. 10th, p. 120, and Dec. 29th, p. 409. The intercession of bishops in behalf of the oppressed was considered so precious, that, for this purpose only, they were allowed to visit the court or the camp. *Conc. Sardic.*, c. 7 (Labbe, *Conc.*, Vol. II. p. 632, *seq.*). "They reproach us," says Augustine, "with visiting the great; do not you know that your own concerns compel us to do so against our own will? . . . It is for your sake that we beg for audiences, . . . that we face affronts and refusals, and that we often withdraw with a sad heart." Aug., *Serm.*, 302, c. 17, Vol. XXI. p. 67. The fifth Council of Carthage, in 399, resolved to beg the emperors to appoint "cum episcoporum provisione," *defenders of the poor*, to aid the church in maintaining the latter against the vexations of the powerful. Can. 9 (Labbe, *Conc.*, Vol. II. p. 1217); Bingham, *Orig.*, *eccles.*, III. 11, § 2.

yet as a Christian and a member of the church, he has placed you under our spiritual jurisdiction. I owe an admonition to you, then, and it is this: You hold your power of God; use it as He uses it, for the good of men, and not like Satan, who uses power for their injury. It is by mercy and goodness that you will become like to God, and that you will merit, yourselves, the title of godly upon earth. Others seek to acquire this exalted title by great deeds of devotedness; you, to obtain it, only need clemency. Pardon, that you may be pardoned. Shall I have succeeded in interesting you, you, who more than once have deigned to listen to me with some kindness? Shall I dare, in default of any request, to present to you my whitened hairs and this long series of years passed in the exercise of the ministry? Should I add something still? Well, I present Jesus Christ to you, his sufferings, his cross, the nails that pierced him, the blood which he shed for you, his table where we all commune. I leave you, at last, in presence of God and his angels, with this people which joins in with my supplications. You have in heaven a Master who will judge you as you will have judged your inferiors."[1]

If exhortations and remonstrances remained without effect, the church still persisted. At the risk of turning upon herself the fury of the powerful, she adopted the cause of the feeble, received their goods on deposit, defended them as her own,[2] opened her

[1] Greg. Naz., *Orat.* 17; *Ep.* 141, Opp., Vol. I. p. 322–326, Vol. II. p. 118. On another occasion, he uses the same language with James, Prefect of Cappadocia. *Ep.* 207, Vol. II. p. 174.

[2] August., *Ep.* 252, Vol. XLI. p. 379; *Serm.* 176, c. 2, Vol. XIX. p. 494.

sanctuaries to the oppressed, and, in case of need, resisted the oppressor. St. Ambrose insists much with his clergy upon the protection due to the rights of widows and orphans, and calls to mind how often he has himself sustained, for this sacred cause, the assaults of the great.[1] The first Council of Macon ordained, under pain of excommunication, that widows and orphans should not be brought to judgment before having given notice to the bishop or archbishop, in order that he might have the opportunity of giving to them a defender. The same Council declared that the great and the people of the king, who arbitrarily drove the poor from their houses or their lands, should be anathematized.[2] They were not satisfied with simple threats. Indignant at the cruelties of Andronicus, who, in order to tyrannize more easily over the inhabitants of Ptolemaïs had suppressed the right of asylum, St. Synesius, after having charitably but without success warned this wicked governor, hesitated no longer to hurl the anathema against him. "Let no one," wrote he to the bishops of Libya, "call Andronicus, who has been a scourge to all the Pentapolis, a Christian. Let no sanctuary be opened to him nor to

---

[1] Ambros., *De off. min.*, II., 21, 29, Vol. VII. pp. 314, 330–332. He quotes a fact of this kind that had just happened in the church of Pavia.

[2] *Conc. Matisc.*, ann. 585, can. 12, 14 (*ap.* Labbe, *conc.*, Vol. V. p. 985). So, too, the second council of Tours, in 567, pronounced excommunication against the judges and the powerful men who oppressed the poor, and who, in spite of the advice of the bishops, refused to amend themselves. (Can. 26, *ibid.*, p. 865.)

his; let no priest dwell under the same roof with him, or sit at the same table."[1]

Even the imperial power itself did not overawe these courageous interpreters of charity. When the empress Eudoxia, profiting by a tyrannical law, wished to have adjudged to her the vines of some poor widows, for which she offered, it is true, to pay the price, she found Chrysostom on her path, who, without troubling himself either about the law of the emperor, or the anger of the empress, dared to resist this act of usurpation.[2] Is there need to recall here his intercession and that of Flavian in favor of revolted and repentant Antioch?[3] In vain did Libanius attribute to himself the safety of the city of his birth; it is sufficient to compare his cold declamation with the eloquent words of his rival,[4] it is sufficient, above all, to read the answer of Theodosius, in order to judge which one, the prelate or the rhetorician, had had the glory of bending him. "What merit," says the emperor, "is there in me, who am but a man, for abandoning my vengeance against other men, when the Lord of the Universe, who had taken upon Himself, for our sakes, the form of a servant, and who had done only good to man, has implored his Father for those who crucified him?"[5] St. Ambrose would have had apparently the same success with Theodosius, if he had known in advance of the

---

[1] Synes., *Ep.* 58; Opp., p. 201.

[2] Baron., *Annal. ad ann.*, 401, Vol. V. p. 142.

[3] Theodor., *Hist. eccles.*, V., 20; Sozomen., VII., 23.

[4] Liban., *Orat.*, 12, *ad Theod.*, Vol. II. p. 389, *seq.*; Chrys., *ad pop. Ant.*, hom. 21, Opp., Vol. II. p. 217, *seq.*

[5] Chrys., *ibid.*, p. 223.

chastisement reserved for Thessalonica. Unfortunately the crime had been consummated when the bishop intervened; but, at least, by his courageous anathema, he avenged the rights of outraged humanity and obtained an edict which guarded the monarch for the future against the precipitancy of his own fury.[1]

Thus, the principles of the church regarding political power did not differ from its principles regarding property. In establishing that the superior powers came from God, in insisting upon the submission due to them for this cause, she did not conlude that their authority might be exerted in an arbitrary manner, but, on the contrary, proceeding from a divine source, it ought to be employed according to the spirit of God himself, and for the good of His children.[2] "The ruler," says St. Paul, "is a minister of God to thee for good."[3] This was all the politics of the gospel, but, how elevated and rich! What notion more salutary could be given of power, to render it dear to those who were submitted to it and to regulate its use among those who wielded it? The sincere love of rulers for those whom they govern in the name of the Father of men, a love which, according to St. Augustine, is reconcilable with the most severe duties of justice,[4] the re-

---

[1] Sozom., *Hist. eccles.*, VII., 25; Theodoret., V., 18.

[2] "Though ordained by God to serve as instruments for His providence, malignant powers are not the less odious and cursed to his eyes." Syn., *Ep.* 57, *adv. Andron.*, Opp., p. 191.

[3] Rom. xiii. 4.

[4] "Jesus Christ," says Augustine, "prohibits not the vengeance necessary for the correction of the sinner, for it is an instrument of compassion, and prevents not such as take it from bearing personally many wrongs. But there is no man proper to that sort

spect and confidence of people for those whom the Sovereign Master has invested with his power; these two sentiments, which cannot exist the one without the other, but which are developed and fortified by each other, when once they shall have been profoundly impressed upon the heart, will they not become the surest guaranty of the happiness and tranquillity of States?

CHAPTER THIRD.

EXHORTATIONS OF THE CHURCH IN BEHALF OF ALMS.

To protect the oppressed, whom the law left without defence, to sustain the rights of widows and of orphans, by a benevolent intercession to obtain alleviations for people overwhelmed with imposts, milder treatment for *coloni* and slaves, and respite for unfortunate debtors, to deliver up usurers to the opprobrium of opinion, to trouble the usurpers of the property of the poor in their unjust possessions, to save the innocent, whose ruin would have brought on that of their families, finally to combat, by pacific means, that unchecked despotism, which, from the heights of society, weighed upon all classes, and principally upon the inferior ranks, this was, without doubt, to weaken some of the causes and to lessen some of the evils of

of vengeance except the one who knows how to overcome hatred by the power of his charity." (August., *Serm. dom. in mont.*, I., 20, Vol. XIV. p. 190.)

poverty, but it was not to destroy poverty itself. Its roots were too deep for any one to hope to reach them. It penetrated at all points a society in decay, an empire ready to fall. The dulness or rather the almost total absence of commerce and industry, the decline of agriculture and of all the arts, the wars and invasions, these are the sources of a flood of evils which charity could neither turn aside nor prevent, and which, therefore, it could only endeavor, with so much greater ardor, to assuage.

We are to see, then, the church turn its principal efforts to this. From this moment benevolence, especially under the form of alms, takes a place in the scale of Christian duties which it had never had before. It is no longer only as a manifestation of fraternal love that the Christian orators recommend it, but it is, above all, as a palliative to the miseries which desolated their flocks. We would be pleased to cite entire their admirable pleas in favor of the poor. Let us here reproduce the principal arguments. This is the only way to show the wholly new importance which they had attached to this duty, and to characterize the spirit in which they preached it. There are few subjects upon which the ancient Christian eloquence in the fourth century exerted itself more.[1] Perhaps our readers will be pleased if we gather some traits of it here, and cite some of those profound maxims, some of those pathetic passages, those true and striking pictures, which, after so many centuries, and in spite of the less happy passions here and there mingled with them, have still the secret to soften and to move us.

---

[1] Villemain, *Tableau de l'éloq. chr.*, pp. 131, 181.

One winter's day, as Chrysostom crossed the streets of Antioch, to go to the cathedral, he met upon his way a multitude of poor and beggars, more numerous than common, whose aspect saddened him profoundly. On his arrival it was impossible for him to confer with his audience on any other subject, and, after having caused the sixteenth chapter of the first epistle to the Corinthians to be read: "My brothers," said he, "I want to acquit myself of an embassy just and necessary, as well as honorable for you. Those who send me are the poor of your city; my titles are neither the popular votes, nor the decrees of a senate, but the lamentable spectacle which has just struck my eyes. In coming here, across the public squares and the streets near the church, I have seen lying on the corners a crowd of wretched men, some crippled, others deprived of sight, others covered with ulcers, and showing hideous undressed wounds. A witness of so many miseries, I would believe myself the most inhuman being if I did not expose them to you, especially to-day and at this period of the year. For, if it becomes us at all times to remind ourselves of the compassion which we owe to our brothers, we who have at all times need of the compassion of God, never is it necessary to urge alms more than in the rigorous season. In summer, the softness of the temperature brings some relief to the poor. Covered with the rays of the sun, they can better dispense with vestments, they can better lie in the open air and on the naked earth; they need neither wine, nor strengthening aliments; some water and a few vegetables are sufficient for them; it is also the season when most of the workmen, the ploughmen, the sailors, and masons can earn their living; but in winter, when they have need of so many things, work fails and they cannot procure them. To-day, then, if we find no one who can employ them, let us at least seek compassionate souls who will comfort them, and let us enlist for this embassy the great patron of the poor, the Apostle Paul, in commenting on the exhortations which he addressed to the Corinthians."[1]

Chrysostom did not fear to render himself importunate in insisting continually upon this duty. "Each day they will say to me, 'you speak to me of alms.' Yes, without doubt, and I will not cease to speak to you of them. Were you as docile as I could wish, I would speak to you yet again, to hinder you from relaxing. But if you have not arrived midway even, whose is the fault? Is it for the unapt scholar to complain of the repetitions of his master? I groan when I see that neither the experience of things, nor the promises of God, nor the fear of the future, nor our reiterated advice, have any influence over many of you; but I will not cease to warn them until I have succeeded in dissipating this intoxication in which the love of earthly goods keeps them immersed."[2] "I will tell you why we insist," says St. Augustine, to those who reproached him with the same thing, "it is because that each time we go to church or return from it, the poor entreat us to recommend them to your alms, and, receiving nothing, they accuse us of work-

---

[1] Chrysost., *Serm. de eleem.*, Opp., Vol. III. p. 248, *seq.*

[2] *Ibid.*, hom. 88, *in Matth.*, c. 3; hom. 4, *in Genes.*, c. 6; Opp., Vol. VII. p. 829; Vol. IV. p. 21, *seq.*

ing in vain among you. For ourselves, we give what we can, but can we alone satisfy their wants? No, without doubt, and it is for that, even, that we are missionaries among you; you have heard us, applauded us, even. It is well, but these praises augment our responsibility. They are but the leaves of the tree, we expect the fruit."[1]

But, if seeking to penetrate deeper into the thought of these illustrious doctors, we demand of them the grounds of the duty which they preach with so much urgency; like their predecessors, it is to the first source of all obligations, it is to God and his will,[2] manifested in nature and in grace, that they refer us.

They recall the bonds which the Creator has established among men, in stamping upon them all His august image, in calling them all into being from the same blood,[3] in making them feel the evils of each other, and in exposing them all to the same vicissi-

---

[1] August., Serm. 61, *de Script.*, c. 13, Vol. XVIII. p. 235, *seq.*

[2] "The first commandment is a basis to the second," says Bazil, "and by the second we accomplish the first, since God receives our favor in the poor." "We must," says Augustine, "refer all to God; in him and for him we must love all men." Gregory the Great says, likewise, "Whilst most men love their neighbor but for themselves, God commands us to love our friends in Him, and our foes for the sake of Him." Bazil, Reg. *fus. int.* 3, Vol. II. p. 340; Aug., *De doctr. christ.*, I., 22, 26; Vol. IV. pp. 434, 438; *Serm. dom. in mont.*, I., 41, Vol. XIV. p. 169; Greg. Magn., *in Ev.*, hom. 27, Opp., Vol. II. p. 436 (Ed. Basil, 1564).

[3] Chrys., Hom. *de perf. car.*, c. 1, Vol. VI. p. 288. "God having formed the first man, wished that all should be born from him, that we might consider ourselves all as being only one." Cf. Prudent., *in Symmach.*, II. v. 585, *seq.*

tudes; "To love men our equals, made like us, and whom nature herself inclines us to love, what is there difficult in that?" says St. Chrysostom. "God himself has put this sentiment into our souls, for our parents, for all men. By nature we are inclined to pity. We weep over the dead, and we feel for the afflicted. God has wished to show thus how he had at heart the exercise of this duty."[1] "He whom the misery of his brothers," says St. Asterus, "does not touch with compassion, is more cruel than the wild beasts themselves. The wild boars and bulls, it is said, when one of them is killed, raise plaintive cries. The flocks of cranes, when one is taken in a snare, fly about it, crying mournfully. And man, gifted with reason, and to whom God himself has taught goodness, will only be feebly moved by the evils of his brothers!"[2] By the side of this relationship, of this solidarity, which is established among men by their community of nature and of origin, and which God reminds them of, without ceasing, by the mutual sympathy with which he has endowed them, the Fathers have signalised, as one of the principal marks of the will of God, the inequality with which he has shared among them the gifts of mind and of body; so that each one could only find a full satisfaction for his wants in the society of his brethren, and the happiness of each was only assured by the efficacious concert of all. This admirable law, by which God has wished

---

[1] Chrys., *Exp. in Ps.* 5, c. 2, V. p. 30; Hom. 52, *in Matth.* c. 5, Vol. VII. p. 536.

[2] Aster., *in div., et Laz. hom.* (Combefis, Bibl. patr. I. p. 10.

strictly to unite all men, and at the same time to stimulate the activity of each of them, finds eloquent interpreters among the Christian doctors of the fourth century. "See," says Chrysostom, "how many natural bonds God has established among us, and how, by the variety of aptitude which he has given to us, it is so ordered that we should each need the others. As he has given to different countries different kinds of productions, that there may be established among them a continual interchange of good service, so he has allotted to men both temporal and spiritual goods in different degrees, to the end that they should communicate with one another, as St. Paul exhorts them to do."[1]

But, oftener, the doctors of the church, speaking to the Christian sentiments of their brethren, remind them of the new bonds which unite them in the work of grace. Christ, the Brother and Redeemer of them all, Christ, who came to save them at the price of his blood, has marked them all with one seal of regeneration, to be in him but one body. He has established among them a society still more intimate than human society, the church, of which he is the head. Whoever rejects his brothers, rejects Him. Whoever loves them, renders to Him the most sensible proof of his

---

[1] Chrys., hom. 34, *in Cor.*, c. 4, Vol. X. p. 314; hom. *de perf. car.*, c. 1, Vol. VI. p. 288. "We sail," says Gregory of Nyssa, "upon the same ocean, exposed to the same dangers, the same tempests. Whilst thou art navigating, having the wind for thee, give a willing hand to the shipwrecked. Show thyself to him such as thou wouldst find him in thy own perils." Greg. Nyss., *De paup. amand.*, hom. 2, ad fin.

love for Him. So it is no longer only an equal, a brother in nature, whom they should consider in the poor, but an image of their Redeemer, buffeted and crucified for them. Christ,—loved, honored, assisted in the poor,—behold the touching image which the church offers to their regard. St. Martin of Tours, yet a simple soldier and a simple catechumen, having torn his cloak to give a portion to a poor creature pierced with cold, and having undergone the raillery of his companions, saw Jesus Christ in a dream, clad with that part of the cloak and relating to the angels how St. Martin had covered him with it.[1] "A hospitable house," says St. Ephrem, "a house where the poor and the orphans are received, and strangers and travellers, is never deprived of the presence of Christ."[2] "Jesus," says St. Augustine, "though he may have no need of our goods, since he is the Lord of all things, has deigned, nevertheless, to hunger in the poor, to the end that we might be able to prove our gratitude and do something for him. So the rich ought to count him among the number of their children, or as a brother whom they have in heaven, and who has a part in the distribution of their riches. He who nourishes his brother, nourishes Christ himself. Give, then, to him who asks of thee, for it is Christ who asks through him, what he has given to thee Himself, in making Himself poor for thee."[3]

---

[1] Sulpit. Sever., *De vitâ beat. mart.*, c. 3, p. 303, *seq.;* Lpz., 1709, 12mo.

[2] Ephrem, *Sermo. de amor. paup.*, c. 1, Vol. VII. p. 132, Ed. Caillau.

[3] Aug., Serm. 60, *de Script.*, c. 11, Vol. XVIII. p. 225; Serm. 1,

Following this idea, and sustaining it, besides, by some words of the Old or New Testament, the ancient doctors of the church had already represented alms as one of the surest means of moving the Sovereign Judge and effacing the sins of men. Their successors press this motive with still more force and urgency. Less happy than they would have wished, when they essayed to excite a devotedness of heart pure of all egotism, they sought at least to oppose to the vile interest of the moment, an interest of a more exalted kind, pointing to the giving of alms as the surest means of escaping from future chastisements.

This manner of preaching alms, certainly, was not without danger; it was at the risk of habituating the Christians to think only of themselves, even in the good which they did to others, to give to acts a value, a merit, independent of the principle which dictated them; perhaps, even, to harden themselves in sin from the hope of a too easy reconciliation. The doctors of the church understood the danger, and attempted to prevent it. "It is for those who have reformed their lives," says St. Augustine, "that alms are salutary. If you give only to acquire the right of sinning with impunity, you do not, in the poor, feed Jesus Christ, but

---

in Ps., 48; *De discipl. ch.*, c. 3. And in another place: "It is not the hand thou seest that receives thy offering; it is the hand that prescribes thee to give." (Serm. 86, *de Script.*, c. 3.) The same thought is continually expressed in the Fathers. See Chrys., hom. 15, *in Rom.*, c. 6, Vol. IX. p. 601; hom. *in illud: propter*, etc., c. 2, III. p. 196; Hieronym., *ep.* 86, *ad Eustoch.*, Opp. IV., pars 2, p. 679; Leon. Mag., Serm. 1 and 4, *de Collect.*, p. 4 et 5; Serm. 5, p. 6 (Opp. Colon. 1546), etc.

you seek to seduce your Judge."[1] "It is one thing," says St. Gregory the Great, "to give alms for one's sins, and another thing to sin under a promise of giving alms. To believe that it is permitted to sin because we give, to believe that in redeeming our faults we can commit others to be redeemed, is, in giving our effects to God, to give ourselves to the devil."[2] The Fathers particularly denounced the error of those who believed that they could legitimate acquisitions ill obtained, by consecrating a part of them to works of charity. "If you give," says St. Gregory of Nazianzen, "give of thine own, and neither nourish nor clothe the poor with what is not thine."[3] "There are those," says St. Chrysostom, "who, after having pillaged another, believe themselves excused for ten or a hundred farthings, which they distribute. Jewish or rather Satan's alms!"[4] "What does it serve to give to one what thou hast taken from another? It is he whom thou hast injured that thou shouldst aid, in restoring to him four-fold, otherwise you remain a debtor." "Alms given from ill-gotten wealth are a theft and a homicide."[5]

The Fathers sometimes go still further; they would

---

[1] Aug., Serm. 39, *de Script.*, c. 6; Enchirid. ad Laur., I. 20, Vol. XXVI. p. 146.

[2] Gregor. Magn., *Pastor. cur.*, adm. 21, Opp., Vol. I. p. 1288; *Conf.* Salv. *de Avaritiâ*, lib. I., Opp., Vol. II. p. 160, *seq.*

[3] Greg. Naz., *Carm.* I. 28, Opp., Vol. II. p. 560.

[4] Chrys., hom. 85, *in Matth.*, c. 3; *Cf.* Hieron., *Comm. in Ezech.*. XVIII., Vol. III. p. 822.

[5] Chrys., *De verb. Ap: habent,* etc., hom. 3, c. 11, Vol. III. p. 289; *Hom. in Phil. præf.;* c. 3, etc.; *Cf.* Aug., Serm. 178, *de Script.*, c. 4; Isaac, *De contempt. mund.* (in *Orthodoxogr.*, p. 1627).

not have attributed to the material act of giving alms a merit which belongs only to alms given according to God, the true characteristics of which they are careful to define. They would have in those, no mixture of ostentation, or of vain-glory, no desire to bind the conscience of the poor, saying that "he who, from this motive, gives to the poor, is in no better condition than he who gives nothing." They would have love and humility preside over them. "The just Judge, they say, has not only regard for the action, but also for the motives that dictated it."[1] "When the dæmon," says Chrysostom, "sees us nearly saved by some good work, he seeks to make us tarnish it, to annul it by pride. No more than fasting or prayer are alms of any avail if not grounded in humility;" St. Luke observed that, "the first Christians laid their goods at the feet of the apostles, to show with what humility they made alms, not thinking that they conferred a favor, but that they honored themselves in nourishing Christ. True alms are those which are cheerfully made, and when he who gives believes rather that he receives."[2]

---

[1] Theodoret., *Comm. in ep. ad Cor.*, c. 13, § 4, Opp., Vol. III. p. 186.

[2] Chrys., hom. 31, *in Gen.*, c. 1; *De prof. Ev.*, hom., c. 2, Vol. III. p. 301; *De compunct. ad Dem.*, I. 4, Vol. I. p. 129; *in dict. Paul.*, c. 2, Vol. III. p. 243; hom. 13, *in* 2 *Cor.*, c. 3; Ambros., *de off. min.*, I. 30, etc. Augustine is led to ask himself how the precept of giving alms may be reconciled with that of glorifying God by our alms, and he resolves thus this apparent contradiction: "It is one thing to seek God's glory, another to seek ours. Do, without display, deeds which, if known, will turn to the glory of God." (Serm. 148, *de Script.*, c. 11, *seq.*, Vol. XIX. p. 248; Serm. 338, *in dedic. eccl.*, XXI. p. 212.)

But, it must be confessed, if the Fathers of the fourth century applied themselves thus to mark the character and conditions of alms, they insisted oftener on their value and necessity. Wholly occupied with the assistance which an ever-increasing misery demanded, they disquieted themselves less with the spirit with which gifts were made than with their abundance, and did not cease to encourage alms by the perspective of the heavenly recompense promised to them. Alms cover sins, and gain heaven. This they all preached, without exception; it is the theme to which they ceaselessly returned, and which they developed with an incredible fecundity. Among all the works which then passed for meritorious, to this they assigned the first rank. "God has no need of vases of gold, nor of souls of gold," says Chrysostom. "It is well to ornament the churches; but would it not be a derision if Christ should see his house adorned with gold and silver, whilst he Himself remained naked at the door?"[1] "The old law," says St. Augustine, "exacted offerings to God; the King comes in person, he also exacts presents. What? Alms.[2] The field of the Lord is watched by prayer, ploughed by fasting, but seeded by alms.[3] Virginity is nothing without it; it is a flame, but alms are the oil which feeds it; it is that that was wanting to the foolish vir-

[1] Chrys., hom. 50, *in Matth.*, c. 3, 4.

[2] Aug., *Enarr. in Ps.* 44, c. 27, VIII. p. 311.

[3] Leon. Magn., Serm. 2, *de jejun.* Opp., p. 8; *Cf.* Greg. Nyss., *De am. paup.*, *ubi sup.*, p. 1782; Chrys., hom. 4, *in Gen.*, c. 7; hom. 8, 11, etc.; IV. pp. 30, 63, 85; Ambr., *de Nab.*, c. 5, § 19; Basil., *hom. in div.*, c. 3, II. p. 54.

gins whose lamps had gone out, and who were excluded from the festive halls.[1] Martyrdom itself is nothing without charity, and, of itself, it cannot make Christians, while charity, without martyrdom, has made acceptable disciples to the Lord."[2] Alms lighten and take off the burden of sin. "They have wings to cleave the air, cross the firmament, and transport our prayers even before the throne of God, as witness the alms of the centurion Cornelius. Whatever may be thy sins, if thou givest alms, fear not, they outweigh them all in the balance of the Judge."[3] Wealth is a burden which it is necessary to lay aside in order to rise to heaven, and to enter into the strait gate,[4] it is

---

[1] Chrys., *De pœnit.*, hom. 3, c. 2; hom. 50 and 78, *in Matth.*, VII. pp. 519, 751; *Ep.* 1, *ad Olymp.*, etc.; Aug., Serm. 93, *De Scr.*, c. 5.

[2] Chrys., *Hom. de perf. car.*, c. 1, etc.

[3] *Ibid.*, *De pœnit.*, hom. 3, c. 1.

[4] "If we wish," says Gregory of Nyssa, "to raise ourselves to heavenly things, let us disburden ourselves of those of the earth. By what means? The Psalmist answers: 'He hath dispersed, he hath given to the poor; his righteousness endureth for ever.'" (*De beat. ad fin.*, Opp., 1562, p. 45.) "God," says Augustine, "has made you companions on a journey; thou art overloaded, the poor has nothing; share with him thy burden. Thou relievest thyself by aiding him." (Aug., Serm. 61, *De Script.*, c. 12.) And in another place: "The burden of every one is his sins. That of the miser is his avarice; see him, sweating, drudging under his burden. . . . Laziness tells him, sleep; avarice, get up; laziness, rest; avarice, work, cross the seas. . . . Jesus, after having carried thy burden, teaches thee to carry thy own. What is this burden? Faith, hope, and charity. Is it heavy? On the contrary, they are wings to fly to heaven. Wouldst thou take away from a bird his wings, under the pretext that they encumber him?" (Aug., Serm. 164, c. 4, 9.)

a treasure to be gotten out of a besieged city and sent to a place of safety. It is a provision of corn, which rots upon the damp earth, and which it is necessary to store in granaries above. Alms are the favorable wind which drives the ship into port; an exchange wholly to the advantage of the rich; a loan upon a mortgage of the best conditions, a usury upon God himself, "that generous Dealer," as Paulinus calls Him, who, for a penny which he receives, promises to restore a hundred-fold. "God has suffered misery to exist, to give occasion to pity; He has preferred that there should be poor, in order that the rich might have the means of redeeming their sins." In this sense, the poor are called the physicians of souls, the treasures, the jewels of the church, the door-keepers in the kingdom of heaven, our interceders before the celestial throne. As for themselves, moreover, it was added, let them not think that they are deprived of the means of redemption. Each one is rich in his manner, every gift received from God is riches which one can share with his brethren, consequently coin with which he can purchase paradise.[1]

Alms, in a word, practised according to the power and means of each one, are the sure but indispensable

[1] Const. apost., VII. 12 (Cotel. 1, p. 369); Aug., *in Ps.* 48, Serm. 1, c. 9, ep. 122, c. 2; *Serm. de Scr.* 86, c. 1; Serm. 60, c. 7; Serm. 61, c. 12; Serm. 164, c. 4, 7, 9; Cæsarii hom. 15, *init.* 35; hom. 2, *de eleem.*; Chrys., *ad pop. ant.*, hom. 2, c. 7; *De pœnit.*, hom. 3, c. 2; hom. 7, c. 6, 7; hom. 4, *in Gen.*, c. 7, 8; Paulin., *De gazophyl.*, c. 5, 7; Prudent., *Cathemer*, hymn. 7, Opp., p. 215, *seq.*; Greg. Nyss., *De paup. am.* (*ubi sup.*, p. 1782); Aug., *Enarr. in Ps.* 36; Serm. 3, c. 6, *seq.*

passport to a place in the kingdom of heaven, which the Fathers exacted. Chrysostom pathetically transports his listeners to the other side of the tomb, and makes them contemplate the destinies of the rich man and of Lazarus. "Death has come," he says, "and has changed the parts. It has been recognized who was the rich man and who was the poor; the rich man has been proclaimed poor, and Lazarus rich. As upon the stage, each one takes a part, different from his real condition, which he reassumes at night on laying aside his borrowed mask, so the rich man, as soon as night, that is, death, has come, becomes the poorest of men, and sees himself reduced to demand of Lazarus a drop of water. On expelling Adam from Paradise, to increase his punishment God placed him in view of this place of delights. Just so he says to the wicked rich man, 'I have placed the poor Lazarus at thy gate that thou mightest find in him a teacher of virtue, an object for thy charity. Thou hast disdained that means of salvation; let it henceforth be the means of thy punishment.'"[1]

To these exhortations, to these promises, to these menaces, and to a crowd of other motives, the enumeration of which I designedly abridge,[2] the selfishness

---

[1] Chrys., *De Lazar.*, conc. 2, c. 3, 4, Vol. I. p. 731, *seq.*; Greg. Nyss., *De paup. am.*, l. c., p. 1785. "Whilst the rich," says Augustine, "treated himself daintily, it was found very well; but it was thought differently when he was in hell, digesting what he had eaten here below; that is to say, iniquity." *In Ps.* 48, c. 8; *Cf.* Serm. 345, *De Scr.*, c. 1.

[2] The Fathers sometimes represent, as a new motive for giving alms, the interest of the church, amidst infidels. "Let us cease,"

of former times no less than the selfishness of to-day, opposed its cold excuses.

The rich were asked to give of their superfluity; but behold," according to St. Basil, "how they eluded

---

they say, "showing ourselves attached to the world, so as to scandalize even heathens. The more they will be inclined to believe, if they see us imitating our Master's charity, the less they will be, if they see us possessed with the same passions as themselves; loving money like them, and perhaps more; like them, fearing poverty. . . . What success would we not have with them, if we would imitate the charity of the primitive church! there would not be now a single heathen." (Chrys., hom. 11, *in Act.*, c. 3; hom. 7, *in* 1 *Cor.*, c. 6; *in Phil. præf.*, c. 3.) Sometimes, resorting to motives of a lower order, they show in benevolence the only way for the rich to secure for themselves public esteem. (Chrys., *Exp. in Ps.* 48, c. 1, 6; Ambros., *De off. min.* II. 16; Aster., *Hom. adv. avar.*, ap. Combefis, l. c., p. 46.) Sometimes, too, to assist the faith of the feeble, they relate certain marvellous effects then attributed to benevolence; here, for instance, they speak of a granary emptied for the benefit of the poor by a charitable child, and which, upon his praying, is fuller than ever; there, of a bishop who by a miracle finds a sum of twelve scudi, which he had borrowed for the poor. (Greg. Mag., *Dialog.* 1; Opp., Vol. I. p. 1342, *seq.; Cf.* Sozom., Hist. eccles., I. 11, etc.) Chrysostom himself, from the example of Cyprian, seems to attribute the resurrection of Dorcas to the power of alms (Hom. *in illud: propter*, etc., c. 3, Vol. III. p. 196, *seq.; Cf.* Cypr., *De op. et eleem.*, p. 477), and to discover in that virtue a kind of magical efficiency in preventing a violent death and in remedying reverses of fortune. "Some, when robbed," says he, "hasten to call on sorcerers; thou, give alms and relieve the ship as is done in a tempest. Thieves have robbed thee, give Christ the remnant." (Chrys., hom. 3, *in Col.*, c. 6; Paulin., *de Gazophyl.*, c. 10, 11, Opp. p. 34. That monk spoke less ingeniously, but more truly, who advised the afflicted to devote themselves to attending on the sick, saying that nothing better appeased the troubles of the soul than acts of charity.

the precept, behold the artifice suggested by the devil. Wishing to pass off the superfluous for the necessary, they divided it into two parts, one for the present, the other for the future; one for themselves, the other for their children; then they subdivided the first part into two new portions, one for actual usage, the other to remain concealed; the first alone must already exceed the necessary; it must suffice for ornament without, for external pomp, for the conveniences of travelling and the pleasures of the house. They must have chariots for themselves, for their baggage, horses for the turf, for the chase, coachmen, lackeys, slaves of all kinds, palaces, baths in the city, and in the country."[1] In a word, rank to sustain, fatal accidents to be provided for, children to raise and to establish; such were then, as to-day, the pretexts alleged against giving alms. Then came the ordinary complaints of the laziness, the ill-conduct, the effrontery of the poor, and the pretended fear of augmenting their faults by ill-placed favors.

But the Christian orators repelled far from them such pretexts. They did not admit the convenient maxims of our days, that "luxury is the benevolence of the rich, that their vanity and their vices are the resource of the indigent."[2] It did not seem indifferent to them to cause estimable families of cultivators to live upon their estates, or to propagate in the cities

---

[1] Basil., *Hom. in div.*, c. 2, Vol. II. p. 53.

[2] "This is an axiom of a parasite!" exclaims Jos. Droz (*Econ. pol.*, p. 330, *seq.*). "Morality worthy of Escobar!" adds Michel Chevalier (*Revue des Deux-Mondes*, 15 juillet, 1850). "Apicius' temperance would have done more good than his gluttony."

an unhappy and fatal mass of parasites, swindlers, and idle women. Even in point of proper expenses, every use of wealth did not appear to them equally profitable to the poor. Without examining profoundly, as much as has since been done, the problem in its economical point of view, without establishing very clearly the distinction between productive and unproductive expenses, they judged the question from a moral point of view, and this is, perhaps, after all, the soundest way of judging it. Every use of wealth which tended to remove man from God, and from serious thoughts, to nourish in him and in others, after his example, sensual, vain, or selfish inclinations, every expense relating exclusively to self, and which left nothing to relieve the unfortunate, for that, alone, seemed to them worthy of blame; and it was in terms the most energetic that they branded that frivolous and often even extravagant and shameful luxury, which the rich affected to consider as a duty of their position. "Thou sittest at a sumptuous feast," says St. Chrysostom, "when Christ is in need; thou drinkest the wine of Thasos, when he has not a glass of water to quench his thirst. I do not speak to those who invite courtezans to their table; as well speak to unclean beasts. But are you not ashamed, you who nourish dogs, parasites, and vile buffoons at great expense, and who reject Jesus Christ? O woman, of what use is thy gold to thee? To make thee appear beautiful? But thy soul, is it embellished?"[1] "What wilt thou an-

[1] Chrys., hom. 48, *in Matth.;* c. 6, Vol. VII. p. 501, *seq.; in Ps.* 48, c. 6, Vol. V. p. 513, *seq.*, etc.; Basil., Hom. *quod mund.*, etc., c. 8, Vol. II. p. 169. Ambrose distinguishes two sorts of liberalities;

swer to thy Judge," says St. Basil, "thou who clothest thy walls and leavest thy fellows naked, who suffereth thy corn to rot and dost not give of it to the wretched? Let an unhappy one beg before thy door, thou sayest that thou hast nothing to give; but thy hand, that motions him away, glittering with a ring of price, falsifies thy words. How many poor debtors might be liberated, how many houses re-constructed, with that ring! Thy wardrobe would suffice to clothe a whole people, and thou dost not blush to send away the poor naked.[1] All that exceeds need, is useless and superfluous. To wear a shoe larger than the foot does not aid, but encumbers the wearer. Thou wishest to build a splendid mansion; well, but let it be in heaven."[2] St. Asterus laughs at those magistrates who on the first day of January ruined themselves in public repasts, feasts and shows, all for the vain-glory of seeing their names inscribed upon the registers, and who, at the end of all that, only found forgetfulness and sometimes a tragic death; whilst, by giving to the unfortunate, they would have been inscribed upon the book of life.[3]

---

that of the benevolent man, and that of the prodigal. The former clothes the poor and assists the orphan; the other dissipates his patrimony in play and in useless exhibitions destined to captivate popular favor, etc. (*De off. min.*, II. 21, § 109.)

[1] Basil., Hom. *in div.*, c. 4, II. p. 55, *seq.;* Aster., *Hom. in div. et Laz.*, *Hom. de œcon. iniq.;* *Serm. adv. Catend.* (*ubi sup.*, pp. 6, 7, 31, 74); Ambros., *De Nab.*, c. 13, § 56; Greg. Nyss., *De am. paup.*, orat. 1 (*ubi sup.*, p. 1785); Gaudent., Hom. (*in Orthodoxogr.*, p. 1839), etc.

[2] Chrys., *ad pop. ant.*, c. 5, Vol. II. p. 28.

[3] Aster., Serm. *adv. cal.* (Combefis, *loc. cit.*, p. 73–75); *Cf.* Chrys., *Exp. in Ps.*, III. c. 6, Vol. V. p. 285.

"But I hear," says Asterus, "the excuses of the avaricious; it is poverty that they fear. How make sure our subsistence, if we take no care of our goods? Words of the foolish, who have no confidence in the cares of Providence,[1] and yet have imperishable wealth, which will fail them at the first moment. Speak not to me of your treasures; nothing more deceitful; to-day yours, to-morrow another's; to-day with you, to-morrow against you; evil guests, domestic enemies. Why seek riches as necessary? Nothing more necessary, on the contrary, than to believe them not so; poverty in spirit, this is true wealth. We are poor as often as we fear poverty. He who said, 'the Lord hath given, the Lord hath taken away,' all poor as he seemed, was immensely rich; deprived of his gold, but full of his God!"[2]

"If I alone were concerned," answers the avaricious, "I also could despise riches. But ought I not to preserve and amass for my children?" "Your children! The love which the gospel requires of you for them, does not consist in leaving them so much wealth, but in giving them a Christian education. You ask what will remain for them? The blessing of God, acquired by your alms, the capital and the accumulated interest, if that capital is placed in heaven; a perfectly safe contract with a debtor who will return the loan centupled. The riches which you wish to leave them, will serve, perhaps, for their ruin. Besides, is not

---

[1] Aster., *hom. adv. avar.*, *ubi sup.*, p. 61.

[2] Chrys., hom. 2, *ad pop. ant.*, c. 6; hom. 34, *in Cor.*, c. 5; Ambros., *Ep.* 63, §§ 89, 91; August., Serm. 177, *De Scr.*, c. 4.

your soul dearer still than the worldly good of your children? We should not prefer to our own salvation even the person dearest to us."[1]

As to the vices with which the poor were reproached, the Christian orators recognized that, in effect, more than one had drawn his lot upon himself, by his idleness or his disorders. But they did not understand that all the poor should be put on the same footing, and assisted with the same zeal and bounty; they required discretion, that their alms might bear their fruits.[2] St. Ambrose, above all, recommended the poor who were ashamed to make an exhibition of their indigence, and placed in the last class of the unfortunate who required assistance, those whose misery was caused by their disorderly ways. "There often come," says he to his clergy, "healthy beggars, vagabonds who think only of putting the treasury of the poor under contribution, and, for that purpose, use all kinds of disguise. Let the true poor not be sacrificed to knaves, and, if it is not always possible to refuse importunity, let us at least avoid giving too much advantage to impudence." "He," says St. Basil, "who gives to vagabonds and debauchees, throws his money to the dogs." "Give not," said Jerome, "to the false indigent the substance of Christ, which belongs to the truly poor."[3]

---

[1] Salvian., *De avar.*, Opp. II. p. 132, *seq.;* Chrys., *De verb. ap: habentes*, etc., hom. 2, c. 9, *in Ps.* 48, c. 3; hom. 66, *in Matth.*, c. 4 (Opp., III. p. 278; V. p. 522; VII. p. 658); Basil., *Hom. in div.*, c. 7, Vol. II. p. 59.

[2] Greg. Magn., *Pastor. cura*, part 3, adm. 21, Vol. I. p. 1287.

[3] Ambr., *De off. min.*, II. 15, 16; VII. p. 301, 303, *seq.;* Basil., *Ep.* 292; *De eleem.*, orat. 4; Hieron., *ad Paulin.*, *Ep.* 49; IV. p. 566.

But, when the rich alleged, in a general manner, the vices of the poor, to excuse themselves from giving, the ministers of Christ asked them if these reproaches could not often, with better reason, be applied to themselves. "When a poor man is at thy door, wanting bread, do not reproach him with laziness, without thinking that thou art idle too, and that, notwithstanding, God loads thee with favors. When, then, thou sayest, 'I am astonished to see a healthy young man asking for bread,' he could, in turn, say to thee: 'I am astonished to see a healthy man doing nothing that his Master has ordered, living in laziness, and, what is worse, in gross debauchery.'"[1]. Much more; those very vices which we reproach in them, are they not quite often our own work? "Yes, it is our hardness, our avarice, that makes the poor vile, impudent, and false. He has recourse to artful expedients, because, by complaining, moaning and wandering from door to door, he does not find what is even necessary for him. A horrible extremity, to which we reduce him! Miserable creatures are seen driven to blind their children, the misery, the nakedness of whom could not move us. Others are seen, who, weary of lamenting in vain, leave far behind them the jugglers of our public squares, eating old leather, and driving nails into their heads."

"And thou, thou laughest, thou admirest, thou dost encourage this vile profession by thy gifts! What worse would Satan do? And him who only begs of thee, in God's name, thou dost not even regard, but

---

[1] Chrys., hom. 35, *in Matth.*, c. 3.

sendest outraged away. God says to thee, 'give alms and I will give to thee the kingdom of heaven;' thou dost not hear him; Satan shows to thee a head pierced with nails, and thou becomest liberal! And all this takes place at Antioch, at Antioch whose inhabitants first bore the name of Christians!"[1]

Finally, even if all these complaints about the conduct of the poor had been well founded, ought they to have abated the ardor of charity? When so many unfortunate, for want of finding work or assistance, were exposed to die of hunger, was it well to make such a rigorous investigation of their conduct? Was it well, from fear of aiding a spendthrift, to risk leaving the poor, worthy of pity, to suffer? St. Ambrose himself, in spite of his former warnings, cannot forbear taking circumstances into consideration. "Charity," says he, "does not weigh merits so severely; above all, she provides for necessities."[2] In the same sense, Chrysostom says, "Imitate Abraham, who sought out travellers, and who, in the nets spread for them before his house, caught angels unawares. Inquire not too much after the morals of the poor; he has but one title; it is his indigence; ask not more. God discharged thee from all ulterior investigation, which concerns Him alone. If we scrutinise so curiously our fellow-servants, God will do as much with us, for according as we have judged, He will judge us." The father of Gregory of Nazianzen followed this maxim: "He gave," his son tells us, "always with a good

[1] Chrys., hom. 21, *in* 1 *Cor.*, c. 5, 6.

[2] Ambr., *De Nab.*, c. 8, § 40.

heart, even to the least worthy, so as not to risk doing injury to others, remembering, as the Scriptures say, that it is necessary to cast our bread upon the waters."[1] Let us not, in our turn, judge too severely this unreserved liberality. Circumstances might occur which would make it a law for us to imitate it, calamities so general and so profound that no one could be suspected of reaching out the hand without a motive, nor be repulsed without barbarity.

But, in their exhortations in favor of benevolence, the Fathers of this epoch sometimes advanced maxims much more strange, and the apparent opposition of which, to the primitive liberty of Christian alms, as well as to the rights of property, claim from us an attentive examination.

CHAPTER IV.

OPINIONS OF THE CHURCH ON ALMS IN THEIR CONNECTION WITH THE RIGHTS OF PROPERTY.

"To whom do I do wrong," it was objected to Basil, "in keeping what is my own?" "What is *thy own?*" answers the illustrious Bishop; "of whom hast thou received it? Art thou not like him, who, at the theatre, considered as prepared for himself alone all the

---

[1] Chrys., *de Laz.*, conc. 2, c. 5, Vol. I. p. 733–735; hom. 41, *in Gen.*, c. 4; hom., *in illud: ne vidua*, etc.; c. 16, etc.; Greg. Naz., *Orat.* 18, *funeb. in patr.*, c. 20.

places prepared for the public use? Thus, the rich, having the first occupied that which belonged to all, appropriated it exclusively to themselves. In keeping thy fortune to thyself, thou believest that no one is wronged by thee! Who is avaricious, if not he who is not content with his own? Who is the spoiler, if not he who takes from others what belongs to them? On this account, art thou not a miser and a spoiler, thou who dost appropriate to thyself what thou hast received only to distribute? He who steals a coat from another is called a thief; should we not give the same name to him who, being able to cover the nakedness of another, neglects to do it? The bread which thou keepest is his who is hungry, the cloak which thou retainest is his who is naked; the money which thou buryest belongs to the indigent."[1] So Chrysostom says, in speaking of the rich man, "He had, I acknowledge, done no wrong to Lazarus; but he had not shared his goods with him; now this was an act of rapine. As often as we have not given alms, we will be punished like those who despoil others." And elsewhere, "Let us not call the bad rich man happier than the highwayman who conceals in his cave the riches which he has plundered."[2]

---

[1] Basil., *Hom. in illud: destruam*, etc., c. 7; Opp., Vol. II. pp. 49, 50.

[2] Chrys., *De Laz.*, conc. 2, c. 4; conc. 1, c. 12, I. pp. 725, 733. Also (conc. 2, c. 61, p. 736): "Not to give to the poor, is to plunder them and to take their lives; it is to keep back not what belongs to us, but what belongs to them." And in another place: "Let us not be more savage than animals; they have all in common, and you, you often consume the substance of thousands of persons. Is it not shameful, whilst all is common among us, both things

We are not less surprised at reading in the Latin Fathers, passages like the following: "It is right that Jesus calls the riches unjust," says Jerome, "for it is from iniquity that all riches come; one cannot gain but another loses; hence the proverb, 'all the rich are unjust, or heirs of the unjust.'"[1] And St. Ambrose says, "The example of the birds of the air, cited in St. Luke, proves that the cause of poverty is but avarice; for if the birds of the air have always abundantly to live upon, though they neither plough nor sow, it is because no one of them appropriates to its own particular use the fruits given to be the fruits of all. By appropriating to ourselves things as property, we destroy common goods. The earth having been given as an inheritance to all men, no one can call himself the proprietor of what he has violently wrested from the common funds beyond what was necessary for his living. Nature has created the right of community, and it is usurpation that has made property."[2] St. Augustine says, in the same sense, "The superfluity of the rich is what is necessary for the poor. To possess the superfluous is, then, to possess the property of others."[3] "It is necessary," said St. Gregory the Great, "to warn those who give of their wealth, to do it with humility, in recognition that they only dispense

---

of nature and things of grace, not to have the same community of money?" (*Hom. in Ps.* 48, c. 1.)

[1] Hieron., *Ep. ad Hedib. vid.* Opp., IV., part 1, p. 170.

[2] Ambros., *in Evang.* Luc., VII. 124 (*Cf.* Basil., *hom. de siccit.*, c. 8, II. p. 70); *De off. min.*, I. 28, VII. p. 222; *De Nab.*, c. 1, § 2; c. 3, § 11.

[3] August., *Enarr. in Ps.* 147, c. 12.

from God temporal subsidies, which do not belong to them. As to those who neither take from nor give to others, we must warn them that the earth, from which they have been derived, is common to all, and that it lavishes its blessings upon all in common. Let them not, then, believe themselves innocent, who use for themselves alone the bounty which God has made common to all. In giving what is necessary to the poor, we only restore to them that which is theirs, far from giving them that which is ours; we pay a debt of justice rather than do a deed of mercy, and for this reason the sacred writers designate alms by the name of justice."[1]

In spite of all that these declarations present of paradox, and, in some respect, of dangerous matter, we believe it easy to prove, either by the end proposed by their authors, or by the circumstances in which they were pronounced, or, above all, by the general spirit of their teaching, that they do not presuppose any subversive notion of the rights of property.

And first, no one will find these expressions inconsiderate or too severe, when applied to those who ravished the goods of the poor, when, for example, St. Ambrose addressing himself to the imitators of Achab, exclaimed, "How far, O ye rich, will ye extend your insatiable desires? have ye alone the right to dwell upon the earth? The earth was given in common to the rich and to the poor; why do you appropriate it to yourselves alone? It would seem that the poor man does you a wrong when he possesses something

---

[1] Greg. Magn., *Pastor. cura.*, part 3, adm. 21, 22, I. p. 1286–1289.

which would suit your convenience. It would seem that all which is not yours had been ravished from you; that you might not have any neighbors, you would extend your possessions to the confines of the habitable earth."[1] Certainly, it is impossible to see a more formal homage rendered to the right of property which St. Ambrose seemed just now to destroy. To stigmatize the usurper of another's inheritance, to defend the legitimate possessor against him, what was this but the most formal recognition of that right?[2]

As to the avaricious who were guilty neither of extortion, nor of rapine, in order to comprehend the severe epithets which are addressed to them, we must regard the times and the places. These avaricious, to judge of them by the portrait which has been drawn for us, had ears as dull as their hearts were hard. It was necessary to speak loud and clear to be understood by them. They were to be besieged in proportion to their powers of resistance. What advocate of a good cause, when animated with zeal, always measures his words? What vehement preacher, in the warmth of improvisation, never hazards energetic hyperboles? If St. John treated as homicides those who love not

---

[1] Ambros., *De Nab.*, c. 1, § 2; c. 3, §§ 11, 12; Troplong, *Esp. dém. du code civ.* (*ubi sup.*, VIII. p. 65).

[2] Chrysostom frequently addresses these rich usurpers with his invectives. (*Hom. in Ps.* 48, c. 3; hom. 9 *in* 1 *Cor.*, c. 4.) One may observe, in general, that with the Fathers, both Greek and Latin, the words, *avaritia*, πλεονεξία, as their etymology indicates, mean more commonly a greediness, an eagerness for gain, that leads to usurpation and injustice, than the passion for keeping, that produces egotism and hardness.

their neighbor, if St. Paul charged the avaricious with idolatry, if Athanasius, Augustine, and, after them, Bossuet and Massillon treated those as murderers who left their brothers without succor, the preachers of the fourth century could, without much exaggeration, treat them as ravishers. When they expressed themselves thus energetically, there was little danger that the poor, taking them at the word, would forcibly take to themselves what was refused to them. The excesses of despotism were more to be feared then than those of revolt. Besides, far from encouraging it, the Christian orators did all they could to prevent it.[1] In the presence of the rich, they thundered against avarice;[2] before the poor, they thundered against envy and murmuring; to the rich they preached benevolence; to the poor, resignation. They insisted even upon this virtue in a manner that, at first view, one would be tempted to regard as excessive. In exposing man to want, God proposed much less to exercise his patience than to stimulate his activity, and to develop his facul-

[1] It is what de Barante observes to those who, in our days, thought themselves able to indulge in the same language in their writings, and even from the pulpit. "The church," says he, "addressed the rich for the poor, and the apostles of the day address the poor against the rich. The church wishes the rich to be charitable; the latter, on the contrary, excite the poor to sedition." (*Quest. constit.*, Paris, 1849, p. 126. See the same thought expressed by Guizot: *De la relig. dans les soc. mod.*, Revue fr., V. p. 8.)

[2] Chrys., *In Inscr. alt.*, hom. c. 2, Vol. III. p. 52. The words of Gregory the Great, above cited, and extracted from his Pastoral Rule, were likewise addressed to the rich through the medium of the clergy.

ties and his forces. Neither the apathy of the Hindoo, nor the passive submission of the Mussulman, meet, in this respect, the views of Providence. In the ordinary course of things, it is good for the poor man to feel his position, in order to re-act upon it, and to struggle against it; but what avails it to struggle, if he has no hope of prevailing? Now, at the epoch of which we are speaking, all hope of this kind was refused to him; to enrich himself there were before him only illegitimate ways. In preaching to him resignation and patience above all things, the Fathers of the church gave him a new proof of their inviolable respect for that right. There is nothing with them which tends to inflame the cupidity of the poor; nothing, on the contrary, which does not tend to calm their passions, to appease their murmurs, to reconcile them to their condition, and to make them hate sin and injustice above all things. "Poverty and sickness are not evils, but names of evil. Opulence with sin is the most frightful of miseries; better, a hundred times, is sin with misfortune, because then, at least, it finds its remedy."[1] "The example of Lazarus," says Chrysostom, "renders the poor inexcusable who endure their poverty impatiently; he, so unfortunate, lying at the gate of the rich, did not complain or murmur; he did not say, like so many others; 'What is this? Behold an evil man who passes his life in exquisite pleasures, and I am dying of hunger, exposed to his contempt!' No. He did not say this; and what proves it to me, is, that at his death he was carried by angels to Abraham's

[1] Chrys., *ad pop. ant.*, hom. 5, c. 2, Vol. II. p. 61.

bosom. Let us cease then from saying: 'If God had loved him, He would not have suffered him to be poor.' But let us rather call to mind that God chasteneth whom He loveth."[1] "Let not the rich disdain the poor," says Ambrose, "but let not the poor envy the rich;" and, in one of his works, he develops at length the compensations promised to poverty.[2] "Ye rich, give," says St. Augustine, "and you, ye poor, do not steal; ye rich, distribute your goods; ye poor, repress your covetousness, and remember that the great gain is piety with a competency. Seek for necessaries, nothing more."[3] Is this the language of men who wish violently to change the distribution of wealth, and to strike a level across the social system? Far from putting in question the notions of property, everywhere, on the contrary, they consecrated its maxims. They all zealously declare that it is avarice and not wealth that they attack, that riches in themselves are as little always criminal, as poverty is always holy.[4]

---

[1] Chrys., *de Laz.*, conc. 2, c. 1; conc. 1, c. 9, 12, Vol. I. pp. 720, 724, 727; *in Ps.* 4, c. 9, Vol. V. p. 21; *in Philip.*, hom. 2, c. 3, etc.; Basil., *De invidiâ*, c. 1, II. p. 91.

[2] Ambros., Hexaëmer., VI. 51, 52.

[3] August., Serm. 85, *De Script.*, c. 6, XVIII. p. 415.

[4] Chrys., hom. 83, *in Matth.*, c. 4, VII. p. 796. "What I say is not applied to the rich, but to the avaricious, thirsting for riches." (*Cf.* Hom. 9, *in* 1 *Cor.*, c. 4; Salvian., *De avar.*, Opp., II. p. 154; Basil., *Reg. brev. int.* 92, Opp., II. p. 447.) "It is not riches," says Ambrose, "but pride that has been punished in the wicked rich man; otherwise poor Lazarus would not have been carried into the bosom of the rich Abraham. . . . There are beggars full of pride under their rags, and rich men full of humility." (Ambr., *in Ev.* Luc. VIII. 13; *in Ps.* 48, *Enarr.*, c. 6; Aug., Serm. 50, *De Script.*, c. 7, Vol. XVIII. p. 97.) "One thing," says Chrysostom,

All recognise that property is a gift from God, consequently legitimate and good in itself,[1] and when the disciples of Eustathius affected a haughty and systematic contempt for it, as if worldly riches soiled their possessor, when the disciples of Pelagius maintained that the rich can only enter into the kingdom of heaven by selling all that they have, the orthodox doctors rose against this new heresy, and declared that the rich are no more excluded from the kingdom of heaven than the poor, because God does not regard fortunes, but the sentiments and dispositions of the heart.[2]

"is the rich, another is the avaricious. Thou art rich; I have no objection to it; thou art avaricious, this is why I condemn thee." (Chrys., *De Eutrop.*, c. 3, IV. p. 389; *Cf.* Hieron., *in Matth.*, Opp., IV., part I. p. 22.)

[1] "St. Paul," says Chrysostom, "never prohibited men from enriching themselves, he never ordered them to impoverish themselves, to deprive themselves of their riches, but only not to be proud." "Riches are not an evil, if we use them properly. . . . They are called χρήματα, in order that we may use them, and that they may not use us; and κτήματα, in order that we may possess them, and not be possessed by them." (Hom. 2, *ad pop. ant.*, c. 5, II. p. 26; Hom. *in insc. alt.*, c. 2, III. p. 52; *Cf.* Hom. 63 and 74, *in Matth.*, VII. pp. 630, 721, etc.) "When Christ," says Jerome, "declares that we cannot serve God and Mammon, he does not condemn the rich, but the slave of riches." (Comm. in Matth., IV. p. 14; *Conf.* Ambros., *Ep.* 63, § 92.) "Thou hast riches," says Augustine, "I do not blame thee; thy father was rich, he left riches; thou hast by an honest labor increased thy wealth; thy house is full of the fruits of thy labor; there is nothing to be said against that; only do not call them riches, for they are full of poverty." (Aug., Serm. 113, *De Scr.*, c. 4.)

[2] *Concil. Gangrens.* (Ap. Labbe, Vol. II. p. 415). Like Marcion, it was by a principle of dualist asceticism, by the effect of an exaggerated contempt (βδέλυρμα) for the material creation, that

All the Fathers, then, of this epoch, recognised in man the free use of what he possesses.[1] All, consequently, proclaimed the entire independence of alms.[2]

Eustathius condemned the possession of riches, just as he rejected the use of meat and marriage (Socr., *Hist. eccl.*, II. 43; Sozom., III. 14). As for Pelagius, it is possible that they attributed to him an opinion which was not his, for want of comprehending the rather subtle distinction he established between *eternal life* and the *kingdom of heaven*. Be it as it may, Augustine, on refuting him, had the chance of expressing himself very categorically on the legitimacy of riches (Ep. 157, *ad Hilar.*, c. 23–39, XL. p. 263–274). "Upon renouncing our riches to attain perfection," he concludes, "let us not charge with rebellion those who cannot do it, just as, by devoting ourselves to continence, we must not despise those living in marriage. The rich who make good use of their wealth are more precious to the church than those who, for having sold some little patrimonial estate, take occasion from that to trouble her by their bad doctrine."

[1] "The superfluity of the rich," says Augustine, "is the needful to the poor; but, we grant it to thee, make use of thy superfluities, give to the poor what he needs; use precious things, give the poor coarse ones." . . . And somewhere else: "It is not said to the rich, give all. Let them keep all that is necessary, and even more than is necessary." (Aug., Serm. 61, *De Scr.*, c. 12; Serm. 85, c. 5, XVIII. pp. 235, 414; *Cf. Ep.* 130, *ad Prob.*, c. 7, XXXIX. p. 470, etc.) "Let us flee," says Salvian, "too great riches. But I agree to it; keep them, provided you think of the poor on your death-bed." (Salv., *De avar.*, II. p. 258.)

[2] "Thou canst not, like St. Peter, cure the lame," says Chrysostom; "give at least thy gold. . . . I do not compel thee to do so, if thou dost not wish; I would not coerce thee; but I entreat thee to give at least a part to the poor. God could have compelled us to give alms; but he preferred to obtain them from our mere will, in order that there might be a reward. But, alas! whilst we give without hesitation what we are compelled to give by law, we refuse to give what they ask of us as free men. We are at liberty to give or not to give, says Jerome. Ananias and Saphira were punished

They doubtless wished that they might be as abundant as possible; in this respect they addressed to the rich the most serious recommendations;[1] but declared, at the same time, that they would prescribe nothing as to quantity.[2] All, in a word, enter fully into the idea of St. Paul; and the church was so penetrated with these maxims, that it never pronounced excommunication against any one for refusing to give to the poor,[3] and yet, it often thundered its anathemas against rich despoilers and against the powerful who abused their power.

In what sense, then, did the Fathers of this epoch seem sometimes to teach a community of the goods of this world, and deny that the rich was truly the master of what he possessed? Did they understand by this that God has given to all rights over all things, over the land, and the products of labor, as over the water that we drink and the air we breathe? So far from that, it is the contrary that they inculcate: "You

only for having lied to the Holy Ghost." (Chrys., hom. 90, *in Matth.*, c. 4, VII. p. 845; Hom. 9, *in Phil.*, c. 4, XI. p. 269, etc.; Hieron., *Ep. ad Hedib.*, IV. p. 171.

[1] "The Jews," says Augustine, "give the tenth part of their income; and you, when you happen to give only the hundreth, you are pleased with that little! . . . Why do you not propose to yourselves rather the example of Zaccheus, who gave the half of his possessions to the poor? . . . Why do you not lay upon yourself a permanent and fixed tax? Do you want it to be the tenth? well, let it be so, though it be but little."

[2] "Give to the poor anything you wish," says the same Father. (Serm. 61, *De Scr.*, c. 13, XVIII. p. 235; *Conf.* Chrys., *De eleem.*, Vol. III. p. 254–256; Hom. 43, *in* 1 Cor., c. 2, Vol. X. p. 402; Theodoret., *Comm. in Ep.* 1; *ad Cor.*, c. 16, Vol. III. p. 207, *seq.*)

[3] Bingham, *Orig. ecclesiast.*, VII. p. 520.

have not," says St. Augustine, "a common house with the rich, though you have a common heaven, and a common light with him." "God," says Chrysostom, "has not made riches to be in common, wishing by them to furnish us a means of freeing ourselves from sin."[1] And Theodoret shows, in the inequality of fortunes, one of the most striking evidences of the wisdom of Providence.[2] They did not, then, recognize in men common rights in property. According to them, it is the *destination* of property alone that is common. God has created the goods of this world *for the use of all*, but he has *appropriated* them to a few, only. Considered relatively to other men, the rich is, then, truly the master of his goods, in this sense, that no man has the right to dispute them with him, nor to demand of him an account of their use. Considered in relation to God, he is only a depositary, the responsible administrator of these same goods;

---

[1] Aug., Serm. 85, *De Scr.*, c. 6, XVIII. p. 415; Chrys., hom. 2, *ad pop. ant.*, c. 7, II. p. 30.

[2] "See," says he, "how much in this universe the variety of detail contributes to the perfection of the whole. . . . The weakness of man's nature making indispensable for him the concurrence of many diverse arts, the master and the preserver of that universe has given to the one poverty, to the other riches, in order that the latter might provide with his opulence the first materials for the arts, and that the former may use in them their robust and experienced hands. . . . He made them all dependent the one on the other; the rich on the poor, who prepare for them necessities of life; the poor dependent on the rich, who provide them with advances and buy the products of their industry. . . . If all men were equal, who would serve others; plough, plant, practise the rudest and yet the most useful professions?" (Theodoret., *De curâ aff. gr.*, *Serm.* 6, *de Provid.*, p. 94, ed. Sylb.)

from Him he holds them, and to Him he is incessantly accountable for them. He received them for the advantage of his brothers, at the same time that he did for his own. To divert them from this use, to neglect the support of his companions in service, to use for himself alone gifts destined for all, is to render himself culpable towards God of the same prevarication as a faithless superintendent in regard to his master; it is a theft, not according to human law, but according to divine law. Such, evidently, is the spirit of the declarations which follow, and which, compared with those which we have cited in the commencement, leave no doubt regarding the true sense of these. "Share thy goods with thy brothers," it is said in the Apostolic Constitutions, "and call them not thine own, for it is a gift God makes to men in common."[1] "We believe ourselves the possessors of what we enjoy; but nothing of what we have received is ours. Leave then, whoever thou art, this pride of proprietor, and take upon thyself the humble sentiments of a simple administrator. *Our limbs even, our senses are not ours,* for we cannot dispose of them at will, but *only according to the law of God.* For a stronger reason we are but administrators of the things which we have received from God, in whatever manner it may be, whether by last will and testament, marriage, commerce, manufactures, or otherwise; it is always by the will and with the aid of God. Thou art, then, only administrator of them; but in what manner oughtest thou to *administer* them? In giving to him who is

[1] *Const. ap.*, VII. 12, *ubi sup.*, p. 369.

hungry. Doing that, thou wilt be recompensed by the Law-Giver; infringing his law, thou wilt be punished. We all who wish to make our fortune rest sure, then, ought, like the steward of the parable, to make to ourselves friends of that which is not ours, namely, with what belongs to God, and which He lends to us."[1] No other obligation, then, than a religious one; no other creditor than God, no other sanction than a divine one. So Chrysostom says: "God does not accord to us the things of the earth to have them spent in sumptuous garments, in debauchery, and in orgies, but to have them distributed to the needy. And if we do not do it, we are as culpable as *the receiver of the public funds*, who does not distribute them according to the will of the emperor. What the rich possesses is not his, but his fellow-servants'. Let us, then, administer our riches as being strangers to them; let us share them with the poor, the same as, in large houses, the steward is to give an account of *what he has received* and to distribute it *as his master expects*." And elsewhere: "Our goods are not ours, but *they belong to God;* He has wished that we should be the dispensers of them, not the masters, and it is for that, that he gives them to some, and withholds them from others; for art thou of better clay than they, to merit a better share?[2] In the same way St. Basil explains himself

---

[1] Aster., *Hom. de œcon. iniq.* (Combefis, *Biblioth.*, p. 21–30.

[2] Chrys., *De Laz.*, conc. 2, c. 4, 5, Vol. I. p. 733; *Opus imperf. in Matth.*, hom. 12, VI. p. 69; *Cf.* hom. 77, *in Matth.*, c. 4, 5, VII. p. 747; Greg. Nyss.. *Orat.* 1, *de am. paup.*

in numerous declarations, and so do the two Gregories, and Salvian and other Fathers.[1]

Thus whatever was the force, even the exaggeration of some of their expressions, their doctrine is, after all, always the same as that of their predecessors, the same as that of the Gospel; always alms preached as a purely religious duty, as a precept in the name of God, and the observance of which God alone could exact.[2] The

---

[3] Basil., *Hom. in illud: destruam*, etc., c. 2, 7, II. pp. 45, 50. "Let us give unto Cæsar the things which are Cæsar's, and unto God the things that are God's, by giving to the poor." (Greg., *Orat.* 19 *ad Jul.*, c. 11; Opp., Vol. I. p. 370.) "God," says Salvian, "*has lent us* our goods; we are but the possessors of them by a precarious tenure. In His goodness, however, He allows us to consider them as *ours*, in order to add more merit to our works; but, at the same time, in order to prevent pride, He tells us, 'pay thy debt.' In other words, 'Art thou grateful, give as if it was thine; art thou ungrateful, give as if it were not thine.'" (*De avar.*, I. Opp. II. p. 146; *Conf.* Aug., *Serm.* 50, *De Scr.*, c. 1–5, XVIII. p. 93; Gaudent., *De villic. iniq.; Orthodoxog.*, p. 1853. etc.)

This way of looking upon the source of riches gave birth undoubtedly to a grave question: If God trusts the rich with his goods, to share them with the poor, why does he choose so often for his managers spendthrifts, egotists, and voluptuaries, who use them only to satisfy their passions? The Fathers attempt, and often with some profoundness, to justify, in this respect, the ways of Providence. (See Chrys., hom. 75, *in Matth.*, c. 4; Ambros., *De off. min.*, I. 16, § 60, *seq.;* Aug., Serm. 61, *De Scr.*, c. 2, 3; Basil., *Ep.* 236, *ad Amph.*, § 7; Opp., III. p. 364, etc.)

[2] As to the total sacrifice of his goods in behalf of the poor, when they preached it to the rich, it was only as a work of supererogation; it was, in their view, as any other act of asceticism, a virtue, not of divine precept, but of *advice*, and suitable especially for those who wished to leave the world. (Aug., *Ep. ad Hilar.;* Hier., *Ep. ad Hedib.*, Opp., IV. p. 171; *Ep. ad Demetriad.*, p. 792; Theodoret., *Comment. in ep. ad Cor.*, Opp., III. p. 242, etc.)

same bishops who apostrophized so rudely the monopolist and the miser, would have been the first to have defended them against popular injustice or violence, as they defended from sedition the governors, whom they most violently censured for tyranny.

We had it at heart to establish this before pursuing the examination of the effects of charity. It was important to define well the spirit in which it was preached, to restore to it that character of liberty which, in our days, it has been sought to obscure, to show, in fine, that the church, by insisting more than ever on this virtue, by no means thought to drag it within the domain of law, but left it, as formerly, within the sphere of conscience.

The true spirit of Christian charity thus rendered clear, let us continue to enumerate the resources which it offered to the Roman world for the relief of poverty.

CHAPTER V.

RESOURCES FURNISHED BY CHARITY.

When we call to mind the rapid progress made by the church from the fourth century, when we see the number of Christians, still so limited in the time of Constantine, so increase, in less than two centuries, as to form an immense majority, and soon almost the total number of the subjects of the empire, we must not expect to see the resources of Christian benevolence increase in the same proportion. By no means did all those who professed conversion undergo it from the bottom of their hearts; in many respects, never had the church been less Christian than since the Empire itself had been declared Christian,[1] and the instances of rapacity, related to us of so many of the rich, the earnest remonstrances which it brought upon them from the leaders of the church,[2] the confirmation which these reproaches receive from the evidence of so many contemporary authors,[3] sufficiently prove to us the resistance which the pagan spirit opposed too often, still, to the efforts of charity.

Nevertheless, it succeeded, in many cases, in conquering this resistance, and produced works of beneficence sufficiently abundant, sufficiently brilliant, even, to merit our admiration. It is true, no sumptuous marbles inform us of it; the poor, who were the object of it, could not thus testify their gratitude; and the church had not yet forgotten the modesty which ought to be the ornament of charity. Let a magistrate give a splendid festival to the people, let him leave to the members of his municipality wherewith, each year, to celebrate a feast in his honor; a funeral column, a laudatory inscription was charged with eternising the

[1] The most of the ancient and modern authors attest this partial degeneration of Christian manners from the period of Constantine. (See, among others, Chrysost. Hom. 26, *in* 2 *Cor.*, Vol. X. p. 623; Hieron., *in vit. Malch.*, IV., part 1, p. 91; Fleury, *Mœurs des chr.*, 4th part, III. pp. 137, 143, *et seq.*, etc.)

[2] Chrys., *in Gen.*, hom. 4, c. 6; Serm. 5, *in Gen.*, c. 3; hom. 66, *in Matth.*, c. 3; Aug., Serm. 61, *De Scr.*, c. 13, etc.; Salv., *De avar.*, I. p. 128.

[3] See, for instance, Amm. Marc., *Rer. gest.*, XXVIII. 4.

memory of his largesses.[1] Yet hardly the names of one or two benefactors of the poor are found on the ancient Christian inscriptions which have been collected at Rome.[2] But evidence just as worthy of faith, and, above all, from the enemies of the church,[3] leaves no doubt concerning the prodigies of charity. The names of Nebridius, Cæsarius, Paula, Olympias, and Basil, are inscribed in the memory of the church in characters more durable than they would have been on marble or on brass. Besides it is not a vague enumeration of names, nor of scattered traits which here could answer our end. Desirous of presenting to our readers positive documents, and of a useful application,

---

[1] See, among others, the inscription in honor to the augur Severus, and of his son, the pontiff Torasius. (Maio, *Script. rett. coll.*, V. p. 347.)

[2] In Maio's collection we have only found these: An inscription discovered at Rome, in the portico of the church of St. Mary in Cosmedin, tells that Eustathius, a deacon of that church, had given several estates for the use of the deaconship and the support of Christ's poor. On another, found in the church of St. Lawrence, in Tivoli, a military commander is designated as "cultor ecclesiarum et largitor pauperum." A third is the epitaph of two martyrs, who after having given a large part of their goods to the poor, had shed their blood for Christ's sake. (Maio, *ibid.*, pp. 216, 231, 441.)

[3] We could not of course wish to have one more irrecusable nor less suspicious than that of the Emperor Julian. "Why," says he to Arsacius, pontiff at Galatia, "should we not imitate what has made the success of the impious religion of the Christians, their hospitality, their cares for the sepulture of the dead? . . . Is it not shameful for us not to meet any Jew begging, and that the impious Galileans nourish not only their own indigent, but also ours, whilst we leave ours without assistance?" (Julian, *Ep.* ap. Sozom., *Hist. eccles.*, V. 16.)

we will successively retrace the resources furnished by charity, the manner in which the church administered them, and the use which it made of them for the relief of destitution.

The usage always was, at this epoch, among the most zealous Christians, to offer to God, for the church and for the poor, either the first fruits or the tithes of their harvests and of the products of their toil.[1] In order that this sacrifice might be more easy and light to them, in assuming the character of a religious habit, Chrysostom invited them, in imitation of St. Paul, to put aside each Sunday what they could consecrate to alms.[2]

It was equally recommended to the faithful, to bring regularly to the Supper, as far as possible, offerings either in money or in kind, which represented the victims exhibited on the altar under the old covenant, and which, derived from that the name of *oblation* or *sacrifice*. The names of those who offered, recorded in the diptycs of the church, were read aloud by the

---

[1] *Const. apost.*, VII. 29; VIII. 30. (It is well known that the seventh and eighth books of the Constitutions called Apostolic are generally regarded as having been written subsequently to the reign of Constantine, and as representing the government of the Eastern Church in the fourth century.) See likewise several passages in the Fathers, quoted by Augusti, *Christliche archæol.*, I. p. 314, and by Thomassin, *anc. et nouv. dis.*, I. p. 336. Eustathius, bishop of Sebaste, was charged by the Council of Gangres with having appropriated to himself and his family the first fruits and the oblations given to the church (καρποφορίας ἐκκλησιαστικάς). Labbe, *Conc.*, II. p. 414.

[2] Chrys., *De eleem. hom.*, c. 4; Opp., III. p. 252; hom. 43 *in Cor.*, c. 1, X. p. 401.

deacon before communion,[1] and the hope of receiving more abundantly the fruits of the sacrifice of the altar and of the benedictions of the priest, perhaps, also (why not confess it?) the somewhat mundane pleasure of hearing one's name pronounced in the church,[2] concurred in rendering these offerings productive. At the anniversary of the funeral of a relative, and in the commemorative service celebrated at the altar, they made similar offerings, the product of which was especially reserved for the poor.[3] This usage was still sufficiently general for Chrysostom to regret that the faithful did not do as much at each communion in memory of the death of their Saviour.[4] However, he recognized that, at the approaches of the festival, and when the grand anniversaries of the church recalled more vividly the scenes and the blessings of redemption, the liberality of the faithful redoubled with their devotion.[5]

On certain occasions, general and regular collections were also made for the indigent. Such were those which accompanied the fasts prescribed by the church. The idea of making fasting an auxiliary to benevolence was older than Christianity. It is found among the Jews, and even, it is said, among some of the pagans.[6]

---

[1] Hieron., *in Jerem.*, II.; Opp., III. p. 584; Innocent, I., *Ep.* 25, c. 2; Rheinwald, *Kirchl. archæol.*, p. 337, etc.

[2] Hieron., *Comm. in Ezech.*, XVIII., Vol. III. p. 822, etc.; Bingham, *Orig. eccles.*, V. 4, § 1.

[3] *Const. ap.* VIII. 42; Rheinwald, *ubi sup.*, p. 390–392.

[4] Chrys., hom. 27, *in* 1 Cor.; hom. 31, *in* Matth., c. 4.

[5] *Ibid.*, *in Ps.* 145, c. 1.

[6] According to Aristotle, the city of Samos having asked Sparta for assistance, the latter, which had no public treasury, decreed a

The Church was far from neglecting so fruitful a resource, and one which did not leave even to the poorest persons a pretext for refusing their alms. At the opening of the quarterly fasts of Ember days, she invited each Christian to hand to the collector what he would spare in his diet. All the sermons on fasting, preached at this epoch, are, at the same time, sermons of charity as well as acts of thanksgiving; all recalled to mind the favors of God, and the obligations of charity derived therefrom, for themselves; all emulously comment upon these beautiful words of the prophet; "Is not this the fast that I have chosen, to deal thy bread to the hungry?" "God has caused your fields and your vineyards to prosper," says Leo the Great: "He has blessed your toil that you may aid those who have received nothing for theirs; so that they may bless God with you for the fertility of the earth. He has wished that there should be a fast upon this tenth month in order that each one for himself might be more temperate and more liberal to his brothers." [1]

At the opening of Lent, Augustine and Cæsarius, of Arles, likewise exhorted their listeners to consecrate the days of fasting to visiting the sick and the prisoners, and to take care of travellers. "And let us not omit," they added, "to nourish our brethren with what we deprive ourselves of by fasting." [2] The fasting of

fast for men and beasts for four and twenty hours, and handed to the Samians the product of this saving. (Blanqui, *Hist. de l'écon. pol.*, I. p. 37.)

[1] Leo Magn., Opp., p. 9.

[2] Ambr., *De Nab.*, c. 5, § 19; Cæsar., hom. 18 (*in Orthodoxogr.*,

the last week was especially solemnized by deeds of charity.

In times of public calamities, when numerous and pressing wants were felt, the church did not wait for the return of her anniversaries in order to proclaim fastings and solicit collections. Her ministers presented themselves resolutely before the flock, painted with eloquence the misery of the poor, redoubled their pathetic appeals, and, before the emotion which they had called forth was dissipated, they often gathered in abundant aid. During the pontificate of St. Basil, Cæsarea was a prey to a famine such as had not been seen in the memory of man, and which the manœuvres of speculators aggravated still more. Basil, "who could not," says his friend, "cause bread to descend from heaven, was able at least, by his eloquence, to determine the rich to open their granaries; then, like another Joseph, collecting the poor, he fed them each day with bread and other provisions."[1] Without a free and active commerce, the only efficacious preser-

p. 1899). Private and voluntary fastings were also for the most pious Christians a means of multiplying their alms. Sidonius Apollinaris says of Eutropia: "Parcimoniâ et humanitate certantibus, non minus se jejuniis quam cibis pauperes pascit." St. Basil, to have more to give, contented himself with only one garment, one cloak, bread, salt, water, and a couch upon the ground. (Greg. Naz., *Or.* 43, c. 61.) Paula, as austere for herself as she was generous for others, gave them what she refused to herself, and thought fish, eggs, honey, and wine were too great dainties for her. (Hier., *ep.* 86, IV., part 2, p. 679.)

[1] Greg. Naz., *Orat.* 43 *in Basil.*, c. 34, 35, I. p. 797, *seq.* We possess the beautiful oration by which Bazil effected that prodigy. (*Hom. de Siccit.*, Opp., II. p. 62.

vative against monopoly, the best remedy, without contradiction, was that to which Basil had recourse. Formerly, Diocletian, in fixing the price of provisions, had only made them dearer. When Julian wished to follow his example, the high price of corn soon extended to all other provisions.[1] Law and violence against monopolizers have never produced anything but famine. Basil did better; he gained the speculators themselves, and, by their own hands, had their granaries emptied and their treasures thrown open.

Independently of these occasional largesses, promoted by the church herself, many others were spontaneously made by the faithful. It was almost a general usage for the Christians who were rich, or at their ease, to bequeath a gift more or less considerable for works of charity. The writings of the times mention a great many of these pious legacies,[2] many of which were already conceived in the form so much used in the middle ages.[3] The parents of Gregory of Nazianzen had charged their children to give to the poor all that they should leave after them. Cæsarius, the brother of Gregory, Satyrus, the brother of Ambrose, had expressed a similar wish, and their wills were religiously respected.[4]

---

[1] Amm. Marc., XXII. 14. [2] Sozom., *Hist. eccles.*, VII. 27, etc.

[3] See one of the inscriptions above related: "Eustathius, deacon of the church of St. Mary *in Cosmedin* has given for the support of the poor . . . and for *the forgiveness of his sins*, divers estates, as follows," etc. (Maio, *Coll. script. vett.*, V. p, 216.)

[4] Greg. Naz., *Orat. fun. in Cæsar.*, c. 4, I. p. 200; *Testam.*, II. p. 203; Basil., Ep. 32, *ad Sophron.*, Opp., III. p. 111; Ambr., *De excess. Satyr.*, I. 59, Vol. VIII. p. 25. The bishops and the priests

But all heirs were not equally disinterested. St. Gregory was obliged to make reclamations against two brothers who refused to pay to his church the legacy which their mother had left to it.[1] The patrimonial property left by Proba to the church of Rome was dilapidated by faithless administrators; those of Cæsarius were pillaged by pretended creditors who did not make themselves known during his lifetime.[2] Many bishops, moreover, were justly scrupulous in not accepting for their churches inheritances of which near relatives might consider themselves frustrated.[3] The most of them, finally, judged that gifts made for an epoch when the enjoyment of them would be no longer possible, manifested but little disinterestedness and spirit of sacrifice. "You will give in your will, do you say? I understand by that," says Salvianus, "that you will be generous after your death. But which are your deeds that will be recompensed?

---

who died without leaving relations, bequeathed almost always their fortune to their church and to its poor.

[1] Greg. Naz., *Ep.* 61, *ad Aer.*, *et Alyp.*, Opp., II. p. 54, *seq.*

[2] Cœlestin., Pap. I., *Ep.* 12 *ad Theod.* (Labbe, II. p. 1629); Greg. Naz., *Ep.* 32.

[3] St. Augustine was reproached for having refused some beneficial bequests to his church; he gave as the reason, that they proceeded from fathers who had unjustly disinherited their children, and declared he would ever refuse similar legacies. Aurelius, bishop of Carthage, showed the same delicacy. An inhabitant of that city, no longer hoping to have children, had given all his fortune to the church, and had reserved for himself but the use thereof. Having become a father, Aurelius sent him back his donation; valid, says Augustine, according to human law, but void according to the celestial law. (Aug., Serm. 355, c. 3, 4, XIX. p. 350–2, *De vit. et mor. cler.*)

Those done while you are living, or those which will follow your death? Besides, how do you know that you will have the time to make your will, or if it will not be broken, or your estate dissipated."[1] Really to prove love for the poor, the gifts should be made during life; that is the sacrifice truly agreeable to God, because it mortifies the flesh and exercises self-denial.

If the abundance of gifts did not equal that of the legacies, yet it was considerable.

Palladius had known at Ancyra, in Galatia, one named Severian and his wife, both animated with so great a charity for the poor, that they consumed all their revenues for them. They said to their children: "After us, all of our property will belong to you; but during our lives, let us distribute the income from it to the churches, the hospitals, the poor, and the monasteries." In a time of scarcity, their largesses were so great that they caused many heretics, who had separated from the church, to re-enter it. Pammachius gave, in his lifetime, a great part of his goods to the poor, and left the rest to them after his death.[2] Nebridius, Prefect of Constantinople, consecrated to the needy the salary of his office, and the presents made to him by the Emperor.[3] Olympias, his widow, ob-

---

[1] Salv., *De avarit.*, Opp., II. p. 160; *Cf.* Basil., *Hom. in div.*, c. 8; Opp., II. p. 60.

[2] Pallad., *Hist. lausiac.*, c. 114, 121, pp. 203, 215.

[3] Hieron., *Ep.* 85, Opp., IV. p. 2, p. 666. At an early period, the use was established at Rome that prætors and consuls recently elected, on their going to return thanks to God in the church of the apostles, should give clothes and money to the poor. This is, according to Amm. Marcell., the occasion of this custom: In the

tained this glorious testimony from Chrysostom: "From thy earliest youth thou hast not ceased to nourish Jesus Christ, to quench his thirst, to visit him in his afflictions, and, in our days, the ocean of thy charity has spread to the ends of the earth."[1] "Nonna," said St. Gregory, her son, "would have exhausted a sea by his largesses. Gorgonia, her daughter, not content with enriching the churches, received at her house all the pious, was the friend of widows, and extended to the unhappy an assisting hand. Her house was a hospital for all her neighbors in destitution, and her goods were the common patrimony of the poor."[2]

The charity of Paula and of Fabiola has been immortalized by St. Jerome, that of Mamertinus Claudian and of Eutropia by Sidonius Apollinaris.[3] But

---

year 367, Lampadius, giving, at his installation, magnificent exhibitions, "a part of the people," says Ammian, "was displeased for their being so prodigal to coachmen and actors. Then, Lampadius, *to make himself more popular*, sent for all the poor that filled up the porticos of the Vatican, and gave them abundant alms." This fact shows us that Christian ideas began to pervade the people at Rome. Thus, the example of Lampadius seems to have been followed by his successors; and 130 years later, according to Ennodius, a senatorial decree turned the custom into a law. (Amm. Marc. XXVIII. 3, *cum ann. Ennod.*)

[1] Chrys., *Ep. ad Olymp.*, c. 5, 10; Opp., III. pp. 541, 547. Chrysostom was obliged, however, to moderate the liberality, sometimes inconsiderate, of Olympias, and to exhort her to give to the poor but in proportion to their wants, that she might be able to help a greater number of them. (Sozom., *Hist. eccles.*, VIII. 9.)

[2] Greg. Naz., *Orat.* 18, *in Patr.*, c. 21; *Orat.* 8, *in Gorgon.*, c. 82, I. pp. 225, 344.

[3] Hieron., *Ep.* 84, 86; Sidon. Apoll., *Epp.* IV. 11; VI. 2.

how could we enumerate so many other examples related by contemporary authors?[1]

Provided that a priest or a bishop was reputed to be prudent and charitable, understanding the necessities of his flock, and having at heart their interests, pious offerings came in to him in abundance. St. Ambrose observed that the priests who gave the most were also those who received the most, because charitable Christians, in remitting to them their gifts, were sure of seeing them do good to the poor.[2] St. Epiphanius, Bishop of Salamis, after having given all his wealth, after having lavished that of his church, always found in the charity of the faithful wherewith to renew his liberalities. "Without ceasing," says Sozomen, "he exposed himself to the reproaches of his steward, who accused him of exhausting the treasures of the church. But he did not listen to him, and always gave and always had something to give; for those who had resolved to bestow something on the poor, did it through him, persuaded that he would fulfil their

---

[1] See, among others, those of Galla, daughter of Symmachus; St. Eupraxia and her parents, allied to Theodosius; St. Melania, widow of a Roman general; of St. Nicarete, a contemporary of Chrysostom; then those of Eleusius, Florentius, the bishop Sisinnius, the priest Constantius, etc. (Sozom., *Hist. eccl.*, IX. 3; Baillet, *Vie des Saints*, 5th Octob., p. 83; 27th Dec., p. 343; Bolland., *Acta Sanct.* ad 13 *Mart.*, p. 266–8; Pallad., *Hist. laus.*, c. 10, 117, pp. 33, 208; Hieron., *Ep.* 4, *ad Flor.*, IV. P. 2, p. 4; Socr., *Hist. eccl.*, VII. 26, 28; Chrys., *Ep.* 225 *ad Const.*, Opp., III. p. 724, etc.) Many other examples are enumerated in the work of Arnold, entitled *Erste Liebe*, a picture of Christian manners in the first centuries. lib. III.

[2] Ambr., *De off. min.*, II. 16, § 78.

intentions better than they could themselves. One day, at last, when nothing more remained to him, his steward received from a person who never wished to disclose himself nor to tell whence it came, a purse full of gold. As it cannot be supposed," adds Sozomen, "that the author of such a gift would have wished to remain unknown, this must have been a supernatural dispensation."[1] Strange caprice in the historian, to admit a miracle rather than be obliged to recognize a virtue! Were there no longer, then, in the church, souls sufficiently generous to encourage, even in secret, and solely for the love of God, the saintly prodigality of their bishop?

And, in fact, Sozomen himself, as well as his contemporaries, have transmitted to us a crowd of instances of a devotedness more complete still, as they are of Christians who made an entire abandonment of their effects to the poor. It is true that this abandonment came principally, or almost solely from those who took the vow of a monastic life.

At this epoch, when Christianity had only feebly affected general morals, as long as a Christian remained in the world, it was almost impossible for him to break a multitude of ties, to free himself from a crowd of factitious wants, of pretended duties, imposed upon him by the tyranny of opinion. Did he wish to regulate the use of his superfluities and to give a larger part to the unfortunate, a thousand obstacles withheld him: children habituated to luxury, clients to retain, friends to attend to, relatives to satisfy, an eager crowd

---

[1] Sozom., *Hist. eccles.*, VII. 27.

which, in feasts and banquets, levied tribute on the rich; finally a pack of parasites and flatterers, whom it was impossible to make understand such a sacrifice. "With your rank, your fortune, such a pitiful life, such a modest attire, so mean a service!" When Paulinus, a Roman senator and consul, wished to divest himself in favor of the poor, a frightful void was made around him; his relations, his friends, his freedmen and his slaves, even the most faithful, abandoned him; he was covered with sarcasms and ridicule, from which Sulpicius Severus, his last friend, could not succeed in defending him.[1] It must be confessed, it needed more than human courage to face such outrages; the only course that remained was to quit the world and flee to the desert. This is what Paulinus did. It is also what, about the same time, Paula, a noble Roman dame, did, when in her widowhood, she wished to consecrate herself to works of charity. "Importuned," says Jerome, "with the movements in her house, and the visits of the great of Rome, impatient to fly away, she departed with her daughter as soon as spring came, went to visit the most celebrated monasteries in the East, and founded several herself, as well as hospitals for pilgrims. She was excessive only in her liberalities; she took God to witness that she did all for His name, that she would have been willing to die a beggar and not leave a single farthing behind her, nor even a shroud for her interment. 'If I ask,' she said, 'many will be ready to give to me, but if this poor man asks something of me and does

[1] *Paulini vita in Paulin.* Opp., *præf.*, 22, *seq.*

not receive it, and he die of hunger, who must render an account for his life?' I could have wished her," adds Jerome, "more prudent in her domestic administration; but in her ardent faith, she only saw her Saviour, to whom she wished to return all his favors." At last she attained the utmost of her desires.[1] The parents of St. Melania, whom their rich friends at Rome wished to restrain from renouncing their property, saw no other means of accomplishing their project than to retire in a cloister.[2]

While these generous Christians embraced monastic life in order more freely to do good, others, animated with a different spirit, stripped themselves of their possessions in order to renounce the world more easily. St. Anthony, the father of the Anachoretes; Pachomius, the founder of cenobitic life; Hilarion, the propagator of Monachism in Syria; Basil and Gregory in Asia Minor; Epiphanius, Bishop of Salamis, in the Island of Cyprus; Porphyry of Gaza; Alexander, founder of the *Acoemetes;* Theodoret, Bishop of Cyrus; Abraham, Bishop of Carrhæ; Isidore of Pelusium; Hilary and Honorius, Bishops of Arles; St. Cloud, priest of Paris; St. Martin, Bishop of Tours; St. Gregory, Bishop of Rome; Marcellus, Archimandrite of Constantinople; Isaiah, Cledonius, and their imitators in embracing monastic life, from whence most of them were afterwards elevated to the priesthood or to the episcopate, all made a total abandonment of their for-

[1] Hieron., *Ep.* 86, *ad Eustoch.*, IV. P. 2, p. 671, *seq.*

[2] Pallad., *Hist. laus.*, c. 118, p. 212.

tunes to the poor.[1] Illustrious laymen did the same. Nepotian, the favorite of Gratian and Theodosian; Theodulus, Governor of Constantinople under Theodosius the Younger, and a certain officer who, after a conversation with Macarius, renounced all worldly hopes, distributed his goods to the poor and embraced the monastic state. And thus, too, Pelagius; Fabiola, after the death of her second husband; the virgin Demetriada, Eupraxia, and the two Melanias, Roman dames, who divided all their property among the monasteries, the churches and the hospitals, as well in the East as in the West.[2]

---

[1] Athanas., *Vita St. Ant.*, c. 2, 3, Opp., Ed. Ben. I. p. 796; Hieron., *Vit. Hilar.*, IV. P. 2; Greg. Naz., *Orat.* 43, c. 60, I. p. 815; *Carm.*, II. p. 1002; *vit. Greg. in præf.*, 55, pp. 91, 131; Thomassin, *Anc. et nouv. disc.*, I. p. 365; Bolland., *Act. Sanct.* ad 15 jan., p. 1021; 4 feb., p, 468, *seq.;* 26 jan., p. 18; 5 ma., p. 27; 16 janv., p. 223; 7 Sept., p. 101.

Some bishops made the same sacrifice without any connection with a life in the desert or in a monastery; thanks to the strong wall they had raised between themselves and the world, the episcopal palace became for them a kind of Thebaïs. St. Ambrose, on his receiving the pastoral crook, distributed all his goods to the poor, and gave all his estates to the church, reserving only the use for his sister. Gregory of Nyssa sacrificed for the relief of his flock all his patrimony. St. Spiridion, bishop of Cyprus, divided all .his into two parts, one of which was for the poor, and the other for such as might want some loan. St. Augustine, a little after his conversion, had abandoned his house and lands to the church of Tagaste, his native country, reserving for himself out of this gift but a strict subsistence for himself and his son. Having been raised up to the bishoprick of Hippone, he one day announced from the pulpit that all priests and deacons of his church had, like him, renounced voluntarily all their fortune for the benefit of pious and charitable foundations. (Aug., Serm. 355 and 356, XXI.)

[2] Baillet, *Vies des Saints*, 11th May, p. 200; Jan., p. 30; Sept.,

Finally, history relates to us still greater acts of devotion; it speaks of Christians, who, having deprived themselves of everything for the poor, took the fancy of selling themselves in order still to have something to give them. Such were Paulinus, Bishop of Nola, and Serapion, Bishop of Thmuis. In the time of Justinian, Peter, an old collector of taxes, resolved to make amends for his former harshness by his charities, and had himself sold by his own almoner, for the benefit of the indigent.[1] Let us not too lightly regard these recitals as fabulous; if such devotedness appear to exceed the measure of human power, one consideration will aid us, perhaps, in giving faith to it; namely, the instability of fortunes then, which the tottering empire continually threatened to involve in its ruin. "What do we pretend?" said two courtiers of Theodosius, belated one day in the cabin of a hermit, and struck with the reading of the life of St. Anthony: "what is it that attaches us to the court, and what can we hope there more than the friendship of the emperor? And what more fragile than such a fortune? What situation more exposed to great dangers?"

The contrast of the agitations of the court and the peace of the desert was so strongly felt by them, that from that day they renounced the world, their fortunes, and their hopes of advancement, and embraced monastic life. Such was the effect produced each day by the fall of so many illustrious parvenus, the Rufins, the Stilicos, the Eutropeouses, the Gaïnases. Added to

p. 408; Hieron., *De morte Nep.*, *de morte Fabiol.*, Pallad., *Hist. laus.*, c. 65, 118, 119, 127; Thomassin, *ubi sup.*, p. 390, etc.

[1] Bolland., *Act. Sanct.*, ad 23 Jan., p. 506, *in vit. S. Joh. Eleem.*

this, at this epoch, there was great uneasiness as to the coming of the end of the world. At the sight of the disasters of the empire, many Christians, as did their predecessors, believed every day touched the fatal moment, and exhibited, in thought of this, an indifference, that charity alone, perhaps, would not have been able to inspire.[1]

CHAPTER VI.

ADMINISTRATION OF THE FUNDS OF CHARITY.

TITHES, first-fruits, offerings on the altar, regular or occasional collections, legacies, partial or total donations, movables or immovables; such were the principal resources furnished by charity. The church, the

---

[1] The vestiges of this belief in the approaching end of the world are found everywhere in the contemporary authors. See, among others, Aug., *Ep.* 122, c. 2, XXXIX. p. 426; Serm. 105, *De Scr.*, XVIII. p. 581, etc.; Greg. Magn., *Epp.* II. 29 (*ap.* Labbe, Conc., V. p. 1114); *Dialog.* III., Opp. I. p. 1421; Chrysost., hom. 20, *in Matth.*, c. 6; hom. 35, *in Joh.*, VII. p. 267; VIII. p. 200; *De virginit.*, c. 73, I. p. 326; Greg. Naz., *Orat.* 17, c. 11, I. p. 324, etc. The conclusion of these sinister previsions is almost always with the Fathers an exhortation for doubling one's zeal and devotion in works of charity. "What do people," asks St. Augustine, "when a house is going to fall down? they take out their furniture to put it in a safe place." "The end is at hand," says St. Chrysostom; "the bridegroom is coming; let us buy a good deal of oil for our lamps, and let us transport by the hands of the poor our treasures to heaven."

depository of most of them,[1] only distributed immediately the offerings in kind, or those of less value; as to the others, especially as to lands, she put them under cultivation and employed the income, either for her own wants or for the relief of the needy. She thus found herself engaged in an administration much more complicated than in the first centuries, and which claims our attention for a short time.

It is probable, in truth, that the church had already received in gift some real estate before the days of Constantine. The edict of Milan, published in 313, mentions houses and gardens, lost to the church by confiscations, and which ought to be restored to it.[2] But, doubtless, this property was not considerable. The Roman law did not recognize in corporations the right of possessing real estate, except when expressly and by name authorized by the State, and few Christians ventured to make donations to the church, which, from one moment to another, might be annulled or seized. At most they gave, at times, under a private

[1] The very church exhorted believers to pass through her hands what they destined for the poor, in order to secure its useful application and its equitable distribution. Such was the advice given by the bishop of Cæsarea to Heraclidus, at the moment when he projected the sale of all his goods. "Instead of distributing one's self the product, it is better," says he, "to remit it to the administrator of the goods for the poor, in order that they may be given only to the truly indigent, and not thrown to the imprudent." (Basil., *Ep.* 150, c. 3, III. p. 241.) Besides, as shall be shown, this rule did not concern the occasional alms, which, on the contrary, Chrysostom loved to see remitted directly to the poor. St. Jerome praised Fabiola, who took upon herself alone the distribution of her alms. (Hieron., *Ep.* 84, *ad Ocean.*, IV. p. 662.)

[2] Euseb., *Hist. eccles.*, X. 5.

name, the houses which served as places of meeting, and the contiguous land for a cemetery. Such was that which Alexander Severus had adjudged to the Christians of Rome, in spite of a corporation which also laid claim to it.[1] Since then Diocletian had forbidden all kinds of donations in their favor. But, as soon as the church had been recognized by the State, Constantine, by a special edict, published in 321, authorized it to receive the gifts of the faithful.[2] Henceforth, dotations in its favor increased very rapidly. The revenues of the church of Cæsarea, in Cappadocia, were so considerable, that, according to St. Gregory, it was the sight of a part of its riches, transported from Tauricus to Cæsarea, that excited the envy of Anthimos, Bishop of Tyanes, against St. Basil.[3] In the time of Chrysostom, the church of Antioch had sufficient to furnish each day the support of three thousand widows or consecrated virgins, besides the strangers, the sick and the impotent whom it assisted.[4] But nothing equalled the wealth of the great metropolitan churches of Rome and of Alexandria. Besides immense sums in specie, and vases of gold and silver, the different churches of Rome possessed houses and lands, not only in Italy, Sicily, and other parts of the west, but also in Syria, in Asia Minor, and in Egypt.[5]

---

[1] Gieseler, *Lehrb. d. K. geschichte*, 1. p. 213. Such were still those the property of which had been acknowledged by Gallian, by the name of θρησκεύσιμοι τόποι. (Euseb., *Hist. eccles.*, VII. 13.

[2] Euseb., *loc. cit.*, X. 5; Cod. Theod., XVI. 2, *De episc.*, l. 4.

[3] *Vita St. Basil.*, in Basil. Opp., III., præf., p. 80.

[4] Chrys., hom. 66, *in Matth.*, VII. p. 658.

[5] Fleury, *Mœurs des chr.*, part 3, § 17; Greg. Magn., *Epp. passim.*

When St. John, the Almoner, was elevated to the Patriarchate of Alexandria, he found in the sacred treasury eight thousand pounds of gold, and received ten thousand himself. The Church of that city, it is said, possessed vessels, which she used for provisioning herself with corn. It is affirmed that on one single day it lost thirteen of them, loaded with ten thousand bushels each. This fact, if exact, will enable us to judge of the extent of its resources; and St. John, the Almoner, passes for having nourished even seven thousand five hundred poor at once.[1]

Thanks to these rich foundations, the fate of the unfortunate whom the church assisted, assuredly became less precarious. It had funds always ready to meet the caprices or necessary intermissions of private charity. But this advantage was accompanied with detriment. The church found itself engaged in details of administration, often perplexing, and which had no relation to its true, spiritual commission. It was necessary for it, whose profession was to labor only for heaven, to devote itself to cares purely worldly. To relieve them from these cares, all the bishops had not, like Ambrose, or like Mamertius, Bishop of Vienna, a brother, at the same time devoted to the church and experienced in business.[2] They were obliged, themselves, to buy, barter, and sell; they had to see that the *coloni* and the slaves worked, to keep and watch many stewards and overseers. Besides, the hands which touched the treasury of the church

---

[1] Bolland., *Acta Sanct.*, *ad* 23, Jan., pp. 518, 519, 526, 529.

[2] "Procuratorem in negotiis, villicum in prædiis." Sidon. Apoll., *De morte Claud.*, Opp. lib. IV. ep. 11.

were not all equally sure. There were superintendents of but little fidelity,[1] prodigal or interested bishops, who did not always very scrupulously distinguish the property of the church from their own, or who too liberally gave the enjoyment of them to their own families.[2] Even the firmest integrity, the most assiduous watchfulness did not prevent occasional suspicions regarding this administration.[3] The poor, whose demands were repelled or inadequately satisfied, were ready to regard the money refused to them as badly employed. The extent, even, of these funds, gave occasion to unlimited expectations, not to say exactions, and, on the other hand, furnished a thousand pretexts to the selfishness of the rich. When the church insisted upon the duty of alms-giving, its treasures, its vast domains, were objected to it, and that it was astonishing that, with its opulence, it could not suffice to the wants of all the needy.[4] Thus, in pro-

---

[1] Thus, St. Isidore charged with unfaithfulness both Maro and Martinian, managers of the church of that city. (Thomassin, I. p. 389.)

[2] An ordinance of the Apostolic Constitutions, and divers decrees of Councils, are destined to repress that misuse. Const. ap., VIII. 33; Conc. Antioch., ann. 341, can. 25; Conc. Agath., ann. 506, can. 7; Conc. 4, Aurel., ann., 541, etc. (Labbe, *Concil.*, II. p. 573; IV. p. 1383, etc.)

[3] The Fathers of the church sometimes make allusion to it; Chrysostom, for instance (hom. 21 *in Cor.*, c. 6, 7, X. p. 189; hom. 9 *in Phil.*, c. 4), and Augustine (*Ep.* 126, c. 8, XXXIX. p. 441), etc. Chrysostom was himself exposed to unjust charges of that kind. (*Vit. Chrys.*, Opp., XIII. p, 146.)

[4] "They tell us, the church is wealthy. What is that to thee? Not her gifts, nor mine, will save thee. Art thou dispensed from fasting and praying for the reason that there are priests fasting and praying? (Chrys., hom. 21 *in Cor.*, c. 6, X. p. 189.)

portion as its fixed resources augmented, it saw its eventual resources, those which came from offerings and collections, diminish; so that, if, in ordinary times, it better knew on what to rely, it had, on the other hand, heavier burdens, and, did circumstances become difficult, it had means less abundant. The spirit of benevolence, in fine, which, like all the generous sentiments, is only developed by acts, languished from day to day; the rich became habituated to send the poor for assistance to the church, reserving to themselves the privilege of indemnifying it some day by a pious legacy.

Let us not, then, be surprised if, in view of these sad effects, the most devoted bishops began to deplore the day when offerings were changed into dotations, and when the church became proprietor. Chrysostom was, in principle, much opposed to treasuring up. He said that, "That which belongs to the church perishes with time or becomes a prey to ravishers, whilst that which one gives, himself, to the poor, the devil cannot take away."[1] He recommended that the sums amassed should be promptly and largely distributed, to avoid the mishap of a steward, who, having buried the goods of the poor, had been obliged, in time of war, to deliver himself up to the enemy.[2] "It is with you all," says he, elsewhere, "that the treasure of the church should be, and it is your cruelty that causes her to be obliged to possess and to deal in houses and lands. You are barren in good works, and the ministers of God have to be occupied with a thousand objects foreign to their

[1] Chrys., *Hom. in Matth.*

[2] *Ibid.*, *De Sacerd.*, III. 16, Vol. I. p. 397.

office. In the days of the apostles, houses and lands might have been given to them; why was it preferred to sell them and to give the price? Because that was better, without doubt. Your fathers also would have preferred that the alms should have been given from your revenue, but they feared that, if left to you, your avarice would have suffered the poor to perish of hunger, hence the present order of things. Instead of praying and teaching, we must mingle with the crowd of those who sell wine and corn; suffer outrages, and receive, in place of the glorious titles fixed by the apostles, names appropriated only to those engaged in secular life. Occupied with harvests, vintages, sales and purchases, we cannot walk in the footsteps of the Lord; we do not pray as we should, and the Scriptures are neglected. Let your threshing-floor and your wine-press relieve us henceforth from these cares. Take this servitude from us, and be, yourselves, the treasure of the church. Otherwise, the poor are on your hands; we will nourish as many as we can, and we will leave the others to you, to be supported on your own responsibility. By the grace of God, I believe that the number of the Christians at Antioch may amount to one hundred thousand. If each one of them should give a loaf of bread daily to the poor, all would have an abundance; and, if each would give only one penny, we would have no more poor, and your priests might give themselves up to the discharge of their true functions."[1] St. Augustine also desired that his flock would take back all the funds and lands belonging to

[1] Chrys., hom. 85 *in Matth.*, c. 3, 4, VII. p. 808–810, *Cf.* hom. 21 *in Cor.*, c. 7.

the church, and would themselves take charge of the support of the poor and of the clergy.[1] If nothing was changed, in this respect, either at Antioch or at Hippo, let us not conclude with Thomassin, that the Christians of these two cities recognized the injustice of their suspicions and complaints;[2] let us not conclude, either, that the system of charitable foundations was, in itself, the best both for the church and for the poor, but only that it was the most appropriate for the wants of the times. To count upon individual alms, which the relaxation of zeal rendered always more rare,[3] upon private resources, which the dullness of business diminished from day to day, would have been, for the future, to be exposed to cruel disappointments. The funds given or bequeathed to the church were much more productive, much more sure in her hands than in those of their former possessors. They formed, for the poor, a safety-fund, which, at this period of disasters, nothing could well replace.

We have seen that, in the beginning, the church made three distinct parts of its revenues; one for the support of the clergy, one for the expenses of worship, and the third for the poor. When, in consequence of the extension of the Christian communities, the episcopate became more important and was subjected to

---

[1] Possid., *in vit. Aug.*, c. 23. [2] Thomassin, *ubi sup.*, I. p. 357.

[3] "Your avarice," said Chrysostom, "obliges the church to keep her possessions. . . . You heap up treasures on earth, . . . and the church must provide alone for the wants of the poor. What is to be done, pray? to put them out? to close on them all access to these harbors? Who then would remedy so many shipwrecks? You would then hear only cries and lamentations." (Hom. 21 *in Cor.*, c. 7, X. p. 190.)

greater expenses, particularly from the reception of strangers who momentarily sojourned in the capital, in order to enable the bishop to fulfil this duty of hospitality, a fourth part was constituted for him.[1] At first nothing determined the relative proportions of these four parts. The bishop, the legal depositary of the revenues of the church,[2] made, according to his disinterestedness and his charity, that of the poor more or less liberal. When Chrysostom had been elevated to the Patriarchate of Constantinople, he found in the accounts of the superintendent, relative to the person of the bishop, or to the expenses of public worship, exaggerated allowances, which he either reduced or else discontinued. Henceforth he took his repasts alone, that they might be more frugal,[3] and consecrated to the poor all that he could economise in this way.[4] He finished even, it is said, by entirely abandoning to them his part of the ecclesiastical revenues, while Olympias provided for his support.[5] Maximian, one of his successors, is praised by Pope Celestin for having been raised to the episcopacy by the suffrages of the poor, and for having aspired to this post only in order to be in a condition to do more good.[6] Honorius, Bishop of Arles, perceiving that the wealth of his church was injurious to clerical discipline, used it

---

[1] Thomassin, *ubi sup.*, I. p. 411.

[2] *Conc. Antioch.*, ann. 341, c. 25; Gelas., *ep.* 10 (Labbe, *Conc.*, II. p. 573; IV. p. 1196, etc.

[3] Socrat., *Hist. eccl.*, VI. 4.

[4] Pallad., *Dial. de vit. Chrys.*, c. 5, 12.

[5] Baillet, *Vies des Saints*, 17th dec., p. 250.

[6] Cœlest., ep. 11 (Labbe, *Conc.*, II. p. 1626.)

all in charitable distributions, only reserving for himself and his clergy what was strictly necessary for a support.[1] St. Hilary, bishop of the same city, labored with his own hands, in order that he might have the more to give. However, all the bishops did not follow such laudable examples. Theophilus, of Alexandria, too much absorbed in constructing or ornamenting churches, often neglected deeds of charity. Isidore, his manager, was obliged to remind him that the bodies of the sick are the living temples of the Lord, which, above all, are those to be repaired.[2] It was to prevent abuses of this kind that the Popes Simplicius and Gelasius, fixed regularly the division of the ecclesiastical revenues in four equal parts;[3] but, in allotting at least the fourth of these revenues to the poor, it was well understood that all of the rest, not strictly necessary for the support of the clergy, should also be given to them. This is at least the opinion of Thomassin and of Launoi, who observe, that, in general, according to the Fathers and the Latin Councils, all the real estate revenues of the church were considered as the patrimony of the poor, and that, only as such, did the clergy have any part in them.[4] In those

---

1 Bolland., *Act. Sanctor.*, *ad* 16 Jan., p. 20.

2 Sozom., *Hist. eccles.*, VIII. 12.

3 Simpl., *Ep.* 9 *ad Flor.;* Gelas., *Ep.* 9, c. 27 (Labbe, *Conc.*, IV. pp. 1069, 1195).

4 Thomassin, *ubi sup.*, I. p. 384, *seq.;* Launoi, *diss. de cur. pauper.*, Opp. fol. II. P. 2, p. 572, *seq.* In favor of that opinion they quote, among others, a passage of St. Ambrose against Symmachus, and another of St. Prosper (*De vit. contempl.* II.): "Ecclesiasticas opes egenorum patrimonia." From that principle Constantine started when decreeing, in his law of 326, afterwards abrogated, that a

cases, when the ordinary resources were insufficient for the wants of the poor, the pious bishops had the sacred vessels melted or sold. Thus, among others, did Cyril of Jerusalem, during a famine; Hilary, of Arles; Exuperus, of Toulouse; St. Ambrose and St. Augustine.[1]

According to a decree of the Council of Chalcedony, every bishop had to associate with him a superintendent (*œconomus*), whose presence, in hindering, at need, the dilapidation of property, would prevent suspicions which arose concerning its use.[2] The deacons and the sub-deacons, called "the hand, the mouth, and the soul of the bishop," were, as at the beginning, his agents for the distribution of alms. They kept, as formerly, a register of the families which they were to assist regularly.[3] Their number, which was very considerable in the principal churches,[4] proves what was

rich man could no longer be admitted into the clergy; "for," said he, "Opportet pauperes ecclesiarum divitiis sustentari." (*Cod. Theod.*, XVI. 2, l. 6.) Chrysostom likewise declared that the church owed to her ministers but what was necessary to keep them from starving of cold and hunger.

[1] Sozom., *Hist. eccles.*, IV. 24; Bolland., *Acta Sanct.*, *ad* 5 Mai., p. 28; Ambros., *De off.*, II. 6, 15, 28; Possid., *Vit. Aug.*, c. 52; Thomass., *ubi sup.*, p. 387.

[2] Conc. Chalced., c. 26 (Labb., IV. p. 768).

[3] Ἐγγεγραμμένων πενήτων; such is their designation in Chrys., hom. 21 *in Cor.*, c. 7, X. p. 190.

[4] For the cathedral of Constantinople, Justinian fixed the number of deacons at one hundred, that of sub-deacons at ninety, and that of deaconesses at forty. They were, it appears, much more numerous formerly. (Justin., *Nov.* 3, c. 1.)

The deaconesses were, as before, chosen among the assisted widows; they were to be at least sixty, or, according to the less

still the importance of their functions; though it is true that some services connected with the duties of worship had been added to them. The high-priest and the arch-deacon served as intermediate agents between them and the bishop, and assisted the latter in his ministry of charity.[1]

Let us now examine what were the different classes of persons assisted by means of these funds, and by what new institutions the church prepared to assist, out of them, the greatest possible number.

CHAPTER VII.

USE OF THE FUNDS OF CHARITY.

THE Jewish law, says one of the Fathers, recommended benevolence towards the members of one nation alone; the law of grace invites the seas and the lands to the banquet of alms. St. Paul, in recom-

---

severe ordinance of Valentinian II., fifty years old. (Cod. Just., I. 3, c. 2.) The Council of Chalcedon fixed for their admission the age of forty. (Can. 15, Labbe, IV. p. 763.) The Council of Nicea had already prohibited giving to them a sacerdotal consecration. From the fifth century their office was suppressed in the West by the authority of several Councils, and was maintained only in the East, where the separation of both sexes was more rigorous and more absolute. (Concil. Aransic., can. 26; 2 Conc Aurel., can. 18; *ap.* Labb., III. p. 1451; IV. p. 1782.)

[1] 4 Conc. Carthag., ann. 398, can. 17; 2 Conc. Bracar., ann. 563, can. 7 (Labbe, II. p. 1201; V. p. 840).

mending, above all, the servants of the faith to the Christians, prescribes to them to embrace both Jews and Gentiles in their bounties.[1] Jerome says almost the same thing;[2] and we receive with pleasure from the lips of Leo the Great, these truly evangelical words: "Though we ought to assist the faithful before all, we ought also to show compassion on the unfortunate who are disbelievers. The neighbor whom we are ordered to love, is every man, having a common nature with us; men of all ranks, just or unjust, friends or enemies, God commands us to do good to all, even as He does."[3]

Such was the impartiality with which many Christians still preached and practised the duty of giving alms. The avowal of Julian, upon this subject, is known.[4] Atticus, the Patriarch of Constantinople, learning that a famine was felt in Nicea, sent to the bishop of that city three hundred pounds of gold to be distributed, as he expressly demanded, *without distinction of faith*, among those who suffered hunger and who were ashamed to beg.[5] In the time of the younger Theodosius, the Roman army having brought into Mesopotamia seven thousand Persian prisoners, whom it refused to set free, and who, deprived of everything, were in the most deplorable condition, Acacius, the Bishop of Amida, assembled his clergy and said to them: "Our God needs neither cups nor plates, for He neither drinks nor eats. Let us sell the vessels of

---

[1] Athanas., *Comm. in Gall.*, ed. 1518, p. 122.

[2] Hieron., *Ep. ad Hedib.*, IV. p. 169.

[3] Leo Magn., 1 *Serm. de jejun. dec. mens.*, Opp., p, 7.

[4] Julian., *Ep. ad Arsac. pontif. Gal.* (*ap.* Sozom., *Hist. eccles.*, V. 16). See above, page 197, note.

[5] Socrat., *Hist. eccles.*, VII. 25.

gold and of silver, which the church possesses, and let us use them to ransom and feed these miserable captives." It was thus that he sent them to the King of Persia, after having abundantly provided for their wants.[1] Abraham, Bishop of Carrhæ, had had much to complain of some pagans in his diocese. Nevertheless, he assumed the payment of a large sum to the imperial officers for them; and, as he had not himself wherewith to do it, he was obliged to borrow it. This generous trait converted them to Christianity.[2]

It must be confessed, however, that such traits were more rare than they had been in the primitive church, and became every day more and more so as Christianity was nearer triumphing. The persecuted church had extended her charity even to her oppressors; the victorious church took from the pagans, the Jews, the heretics, oftener than she gave to them. The spirit of intolerance restricted charity,[3] and it was this that obliged the Christian sects to have each one their own treasury for the relief of the indigent. Between them and the established church, there resulted from this, an emulation which, if it did not promote union, at least favorably influenced liberality. Chrysanthus and Paul, Novatian Bishops of Constantinople, exhibited for their co-religionists an extremely active

---

[1] Socrat., *Hist. eccles.*, VII. 21.

[2] Bolland., *Act. Sanctor. ad* 14 Feb., p. 767.

[3] "Make donations to thy King," said St. Augustine, "but make them *in his church*, as the first Christians used to lay them at the feet of the apostles. Heathens, heretics, feed such as are hungry, clothe such as are naked; but, according to the expression of the Psalmist, *they have not found their nest*, for they do it all out of the church, out of which nothing subsists." August., (*in Ps.* 44, *in Ps.* 83, c. 7; VII. p. 375; X. p. 147).

charity which, while contributing to the prosperity of their sect, stimulated the charity of the orthodox bishops.[1] Sometimes hypocrisy took advantage of this emulation. Socrates, the historian, mentions a Jew, who, pretending to embrace Christianity, went about demanding baptism successively of the different communions, heretical and orthodox, and received precious gifts from them all, until Paul, the Bishop of the Novatians, discovered his fraud, it is said, by a miracle.[2] It is still to-day one of the most difficult problems, in matters of beneficence, to leave its spontaneity to private charity, and avoid useless repetitions, and to mete out a sufficiency with a distribution always equitable and judicious.

But soon, owing to the exclusive protection which the church received from the State, she was delivered from all inconvenient rivalry; the pagans and the heretics, to escape from the laws of exclusion and the penalties decreed against them, having to consent to enter into the Catholic Church, which finished, thus, by numbering almost as many members as the Empire counted subjects.

How great must have been, then, the extent of the burthens weighing upon her? If she had wished to continue, as formerly, to succor individually each one of her unfortunate children, what resources would ever have sufficed for it? At that epoch, above all, when there were far fewer hands extended to give than to receive, where could a support be found for each widow, a protector for each orphan, a paternal hearth

---

[1] Socrat., *Hist. eccles.*, VII. 12, 17.

[2] *Ibid.*, VII. 17.

for every abandoned child, a hospitable roof for every traveller, an asylum for all the poor who needed one, and nurses and physicians, for each impotent old man, for each sick person that it was desirable to have taken care of at home?

At the thought of such difficulties, Chrysostom, in one of those generous but chimerical movements, which charity suggested to him, would have been willing to transform Constantinople into a sort of vast *phalanstery*. After having described the pretended community of the first Christians, he exclaims: "What abundance among us, if we knew how to do the same! Let me enjoy it in thought, since you do not wish the reality. Let me suppose, then, that all would sell their property and put it in common. How much think you might be collected thus? Perhaps a million of pounds of gold, if not two or three millions. What resources for the daily support of our poor! Do you not think that this would be much more than sufficient for the expenses of the common table? Who does not see that the division of fortunes, by multiplying expenses to excess, is a cause of poverty? Suppose in each house ten children with the father and the mother; will they not need to spend much less when together than when dispersed, since then ten houses, ten servants, and so on, would be necessary? At present they live in monasteries as they lived formerly in the primitive church, and none died there of hunger."[1] It is true that as much could not be said of Constantinople; but Chrysostom, in his admiration of a commu-

[1] Chrys., hom. 11, *in Act. ap.*, c. 3, IX. p. 93, *seq.*

nity,[1] forgot the impossibility of reconciling it with the conditions of ordinary life. His contemporaries remembered it for him. However, repelling what was impracticable in such a system, they began to borrow from it whatever it had of economical and advantageous, the concentration of the means of succor and association, realizing the first in their hospitals, and the second in the monasteries.

ARTICLE I.

ALMSHOUSES AND HOSPITALS.

The construction of edifices specially consecrated to the amelioration of the condition of the unfortunate, forms so characteristic and so glorious a trait of Christian civilization, that it is not astonishing that the establishment of them, in the fourth century, has been considered as the effect of a redoubled charity among the faithful.

However, we have seen, that, on the contrary, the spirit of charity had rather languished in the church, since its triumph. This is the testimony of the reiterated complaints of its chiefs; and the foundation of hospitals, even, proves, in one sense, that they could

[1] Let us observe, moreover, that according to the idea of Chrysostom, such a community was to be quite voluntary; it entered not his mind that any power was to intervene to realize it; and the latter part of his speech shows that he founded his hopes upon persuasion. "Comply with my wishes," said he, at the close, "and little by little we shall ameliorate that state of things; and if God gives us life, I hope we shall soon succeed." (Chrys., hom. 11, *in Act. ap.*, c. 3, IX. p. 93, *seq*).

count less than formerly on the benevolence of individuals.[1]

But when, from this, men have proceeded to throw discredit upon this institution, when they have wished to see in the creation of hospitals only the effect of a total forgetfulness of primitive charity,[2] it was a still graver mistake. Ephraim, Basil, and Chrysostom, figure among the number of the first founders of almshouses, and assuredly no one dare reproach them with having *petrified charity* to sacrifice to a vain show, with having substituted for modest and devoted evangelical benevolence, a *pharisaic benevolence, looking to its ease* and seeking for *éclat.* Before pronouncing so severe a judgment, it was necessary to examine if individual charity in the first centuries, even supposing it as active as formerly, could have sufficed for the new wants, created either by the extension of the church, or by the increase of misery. St. John, the Almoner, who would have desired that the house of each one of the faithful should have been an infirmary for the sick, continued to have them treated in the hospitals;[3] the ideal to which he tended did not cause him to lose from view the necessities of the times. The foundation of hospitals was, before all, an economical measure, commanded by circumstances. It is probable

[1] Chrys., *in Matth.*, hom. 85, c. 4; de Recalde, *Abrégé histor. des hôpit.*, Paris, 1784, p. 7; de Gérando, *de la Bienfais. publ.*, II. p. 142; IV. p. 277; de Villeneuve, *Econ. pol. chr.*, II. p. 237; Wallon, *Hist. de l'esclav.*, III. p. 399.

[2] Moreau-Christophe, du *Probl. de la misère*, II. pp. 211, 236–239; III. p. 527.

[3] Fleury, *Hist. eccles.*, XXXVII. 11.

that before Constantine, the difficulty of separately relieving each one who, in misfortune, applied for assistance to the church, was already felt; but how then think of vast establishments, which would have attracted the attention of the authorities, and excited the ill-will or the cupidity of the enemies of Christianity? What was not possible under the pagan emperors, became so under their successors. What would have been simply advantageous when the Christians formed a feeble minority, became indispensable when the church embraced the largest number of the subjects of the empire.[1] It was above all in these times of great calamities that this necessity must have been felt. The foundation of the alms-house of Edessa, though not one of the most ancient, can here serve as an example.

About the year 375, a fearful famine appeared in that city, and, as is common, was followed by a contagious malady, which cruelly decimated the population. "Ephraim, learning that a crowd of wretched persons, without bread and without shelter, were lying

[1] In his *Histoire critique de la pauvreté*, Morin attributes the origin of hospitals to the difficulty experienced in supplying that multitude of individuals and families whom Constantine, when he relieved the church, called out of prisons and mines, almost all of them poor, sick, and suffering. (*Mém. de l'Acad. des Inscr.*, IV. p. 305.) Morin assigns a very little and a very transient cause to an institution both grand and durable. We have here to rectify the error, pretty common, of such as refer the first creation of hospitals to an ordinance of the Nicene Council. The 70th canon, generally quoted on this occasion, is obviously apocryphal, as well as all those which are interpolated in the Arabic version of the decrees of that Council.

in the public square, quit his hermitage and came to Edessa, and warmly reproached the rich, who, without pity, left their brethren to die of hunger and misery. Struck therewith, the rich replied: 'It is not the love of our property that retains us, but we do not know by whom to make the distribution; we are surrounded by greedy people, who would make of it a vile traffic.' But me, said Ephraim, what think you of me? 'That you are universally respected and worthy of all our confidence.' 'Well!' he replied, 'if it is thus, I will take charge of the affair.'" Immediately, with the sums which he received from them, he set up, in the public galleries, three hundred beds, where he himself, with others under his directions, took care not only of those of the inhabitants who suffered from the effects of the famine, but also of the inhabitants of the country and the strangers, whom the scarcity had driven into the city. As soon as the scourge had ceased, Ephraim returned into his solitude, where he died soon after.[1] It is probable, though the historian does not say so, that this alms-house survived its founder. At any rate, similar ones were established in most of the cities, not only for transient scourges, like that which had just afflicted Edessa, but for permanent scourges, and above all, for leprosy, that terrible and contagious evil, which spread such ravages in antiquity and in the middle ages.

Those lepers, "whose flesh, as if devoured by fire, seemed," says St. Gregory, "to be rather dead than alive, those unfortunates, whose names alone, but not their disfigured features, aided in recognizing them,

---

[1] Sozom., III. 15.

abandoned by their friends and relatives, attracted to the vicinity of the cities by the hunger which clung to them, and soon driven off by the horror which they inspired, warned off from the public squares and fountains, wandered everywhere, vainly essaying, with the little voice left to them, to move pity by their mournful songs."[1]

In 370, Basil first conceived the thought of opening to them a hospital at the gates of Cæsarea. "It is he," says his friend, "who has taught us not to despise those who are men as well as we are, not to outrage, in them, Jesus Christ suffering. He went to these wretched beings, embraced them as brothers, not from a vain affectation of courage, but to excite, by his devoted action, that of those whom he charged with attending to them."[2] In assembling them in the hospital prepared for them, Basil protected them from want, and at the same time preserved society from their dangerous contact.

The advantage of thus having attended, in one establishment, and with an apparatus of medical assistance, all kinds of corporeal ills, was soon understood; and hospitals for the sick, known by the name of *Nosocomia*, were multiplied throughout the empire. It is affirmed that, in the reign of Constantine, St. Zoticus, whose memory the Greek Church reveres, founded at Constantinople a *Lobotrophium*, to succor the maimed and the impotent.[3] Chrysostom, from the sums eco-

---

[1] Greg. Naz., *Orat.* 43, Opp., I. p. 818. See a similar picture in St. Gregory of Nyssa (*De am. paup., or.*, 2).

[2] Greg. Naz., *ibid.*, c. 63, p. 817.

[3] Du Cange, *Fam. Byzant., Const. Christ.* IV. p. 165.

nomized in the expenses of his bishopric, enriched or founded many of them in this same city, and had priests, superintendents, and physicians to serve in them.[1] His example was followed under Arcadius, and Theodosius, the Younger, by the Patricians Florentius and Dexicratus; under Justin, the Thracian, by Eubulus; under Marcian, by Stephen, chamberlain of the emperor. Others, again, founded there a house for the poor, afflicted with incurable diseases, which, having fallen in ruins, was re-established, later, by Justinian.[2] St. Augustine, likewise, founded a hospital for the sick at Hippo; Fabiola, a noble dame of the race of the Fabii, founded one at Rome, and united with it, in the country, under the title of *Villa languentium*, a house for the convalescent.[3] There were soon *Nosocomia* established in all the principal cities; yea, in cities of the second order, and sometimes, even, in the country places. The establishment of these hospitals enabled many necessitous to be cared for, who formerly were treated as criminals. Thus they ceased from shutting up the insane, as before this the custom had been, in perpetual confinement in the public prisons.[4]

The services in these hospitals were performed by nurses, known by the name of *Parabolani*, from the devotion which they showed, and the real dangers

---

[1] Pallad., *Chrys. vita*, Chrys. Opp. XIII. p. 19.

[2] Du Cange, *ubi sup.*; Procop., *De ædif. Just.* 1, 2.

[3] Hieron., *ap.* 84, *ad Ocean.*, IV. P. 2, pp. 660, 662.

[4] Moreau-Christ., *Du Problême de la mis.*, I. p. 123, note; Villeneuve, *Econ. pol. chr.*, II. p. 273.

which they incurred in times of contagious diseases.[1] They were associated with the clergy, of whom they formed one of the minor orders, and the immense number of them to be found in many cities, at Alexandria, for example, proves the rapid extension of the establishments to which they were attached.[2] The widows assisted by the church were charged with the same cares.[3] In fine, to these retained servants many volunteers were joined. Christianity, which teaches to overcome evil with goodness, to divert the mind from our own sufferings by relieving the sufferings of others, led into the hospitals, placed by the pillow of the sick, some, suffering with misfortune, who had come there for a different kind of cure. This is the remedy advised by St. Anthony to one of his brothers, afflicted with melancholy.[4] Palladius speaks of a young virgin, who, having yielded to the artifices of a seducer, expiated her fault by consecrating herself during thirty years to the relief of the sick and helpless.[5] The illustrious widow, Fabiola, when founding a hospital at Rome, had, the first, solicited the honor of nursing the unfortunate inmates. "How often," says St. Jerome, "she carried them upon her

---

[1] Gothofr., *in Cod. Theod.*, XVI. 2, l. 42, p. 83.

[2] The turbulence of *the parobolani* of Alexandria, during the Eutychian controversies, the support they had given to the fanaticism of some bishops, had determined, in 416, Theodosius the Younger, to reduce their number to five hundred; two years after, it was necessary to increase it again by one hundred. (Cod. Theod., XVI. 2, *De parab.*, l. 42, 43.)

[3] Chrys., hom. 14 *in* 1 *Tim.*, c. 1, XI. p. 626.

[4] Socrat., *Hist. eccles.*, IV. 23.

[5] Pallad., *Hist. laus.*, c. 140, p. 222.

shoulders, and washed wounds which others could not have looked upon. Not less generous of herself than of her purse, she braved what would have caused others to pause with disgust; and believed that in the wounds of the poor she dressed those of her Saviour.[1] Theodoret praises the same devotedness in the Empress Flaccilla. "She went, herself, to the hospitals, took care of the sick, prepared their meats, tasted their broths, and waited upon them in all the duties of a servant; and, when others sought to turn her from such cares, she said, 'Let the Emperor distribute gold; I wish to do all this for Him from whom he holds the Empire.'"[2]

Next to the care of the sick, that which, by its extent and complication, the most required a common administration, was the care of children deprived of their parents. For them were established at first the *Orphanotrophia*, and then the *Brephotrophia* for orphans still at the breast. As for exposed or abandoned children, it does not appear that there were establishments founded specially for them, at this epoch, unless the Brephotrophia may be so regarded, and upon the destination of these, moreover, the learned are not of the same opinion.[3] The foundation of St. Galla, the daughter of Symmachus, who assembled at her house the poor little children whom she had found out, appears to have been a work of charity wholly individual.[4] A passage of St. Au-

---

[1] Hieron., *Ep.* 84, IV. p. 660.

[2] Theodoret., *Hist. eccles.*, V. 19.

[3] Naudet in them sees hospitals of maternity; Rheinwald, hospitals of foundlings; Fleury, hospitals for babes, exposed or not.

[4] Thomassin., *ubi sup.*, I. 283.

gustine indicates that often abandoned children were received by the consecrated virgins, who, in presenting them for baptism, exerted themselves to find some charitable person who would charge himself with raising them.[1] In the fifth century the usage was introduced at Arles, at Treves, at Macon, at Rouen, and in other cities of Gaul, of receiving them in a scollop of marble, placed at the entrance of the church. The sacristan (*matricularius*) received them; the priest inscribed them on a register, and sought some one who would be willing to take charge of them. If no one offered, the church itself took care of them, and had them brought up at its expense in the hospitals of the orphans.[2] In all cases, the monasteries were open to them, almost without distinction, as soon as they had arrived at a certain age.[3] The first refuges of foundlings, of which history presents any traces, are that of Treves, obscurely mentioned in a legend of the times of Childebert; that of Angers, in the life of St. Maimbœuf, and that which the high-priest Datheus founded, in 787, at Milan.[4]

The same economical considerations which led to the foundation of the *Nosocomia* and the *Orphanotrophia*, also caused the *Parthenones* or *Parthenocomia*,[5] and the *Cherotrophia*, for the virgins and the widows

---

[1] August., *Ep.* 23, *ad Bonif.*

[2] Terme et Montf., *Hist. des enf. tr.*, Paris, 1837, p. 82, *seq.*; de Gérando, *Bienf. publ.*, II. p. 142, *seq.*: Villeneuve, *ubi sup.*, II. p. 265.

[3] Such was the prescription of St. Basil's rule.

[4] De Gérando, *Bienf. publ.*, Terme, p. 85, *seq.*

[5] Greg. Naz., *Orat.* 43, c. 34.

whom the church supported, the *Ptôchotrophia* or *Ptôcheia*,[1] for the poor whom it lodged and assisted, the *Gerotrophia* or *Gerontocomia* for the infirm old men, whom it took under its care.[2]

In short, the bishops, whom we have seen from the beginning always ready to give hospitality to strangers, travellers, and pilgrims, recommended by other churches, thought, also, of simplifying this charge, and of rendering it less onerous and more easy through the instrumentality of special establishments.[3] Hence the foundation of the *Xenones* or *Xenodochia*, so common since the fourth century in all parts of the empire, especially in Constantinople.[4] St. Jerome had laid the foundation of a similar hospital for pilgrims, at Bethlehem; to finish it, he charged his brother Paulinian to sell the rest of their common patrimony. He himself felicitates Pammachius, who had just endowed Ostia with a house of hospitality. Pammachius, after the death of his wife

---

[1] Or still, *πτωχῶν καταγώγια*. (Greg. Naz., *Orat.* 43, c. 34; Chrys., I. p. 222, *seq.*)

[2] These various establishments are mentioned especially in Justinian's code, 1, 2, l. 19, 23, 24, etc. If, like those preceding, they are not yet to be found in the Cod. Theod., the reason is that Justinian's predecessors were much less than he engaged with the details touching the ecclesiastical administration.

The *Parthenones* and the *Cherotrophia* were at an early period confounded with the monasteries; hence they are not so frequently mentioned as the other hospitals. Nicephorus speaks, however, of those which Eleusius, bishop of Cyzicus, founded under Julian's reign. (Niceph., *Hist. eccles.*, X. 20.)

[3] Thomassin., *ubi sup.*, p. 173.

[4] They were the substitutes for the old *diversorium episcopale*, *ἐπισκοπικὸν καταγώγιον*. (Sozom., VI. 31.)

Pauline, only found consolation in works of charity, of which she herself had given him an example. Not content with expending on the poor of Rome the immense treasures which she had left to him,[1] this noble descendant of Camillus, after having exchanged the senatorial purple for the coarse, black robe of the monks, had created an establishment like that of Fabiola, but specially destined for travellers. "I learn," said St. Jerome to him, "that you have founded a *Xenodochium* at the Roman harbor, and planted an offshoot of the hospitable oak of Abraham upon the shores of Ausonia. Like Æneas, you encamp on the banks of the Tiber, and build a Bethlehem (a house for food) upon those shores long since made desolate by famine."[2] Pæsius, from the rich inheritance which he had received from his parents, constructed a house, where he received and took care

[1] "Paulina," says St. Jerome, "has given us, by her death, the children whom in her life-time she had so ardently wished for. Rejoice, O Pauline! leap for joy, O sterile one! since thou hast brought forth as many children as there are poor at Rome! . . . All that was used for delights and luxury of life is used now for virtue. That blind man who stretches out his hand, and so often cries in the desert, has become the heir to Pauline, the joint heir to Pammachius! . . . That door, out of which went so many flattering clients, is now besieged by a crowd of unfortunates. Thou relievest Christ in all of them. . . . Others spread out flowers on the tomb of their spouses, thus seeking a balm for their grief. Thou, thou spreadst upon the ashes of thy own the precious balm of alms which extinguishes sin. . . . She has no longer regret for having left here below riches that thou art spreading, according to her desires; she rejoices, on the contrary, seeing the accomplishment of her most ardent wishes." (Hieron., *Ep.* 54; IV. p. 583, *seq.*)

[2] Hieron., *ibid.*, p. 586.

of strangers. On Saturdays and Sundays he had tables set there, to which he admitted all the poor.[1] The same is told of Alethius, of Eucharistus, and of Spiridion.[2]

The different hospitals, which we have just passed in review, were sometimes distinct, especially in the capitals; more often they were united in one common establishment consecrated to these different usages, and to which the generic name of *Xenon* or *Xenodochium* was given.[3]

That which St. Basil had founded, near to Cæsarea, and which Gregory of Nazianzen celebrates in the funeral oration of his friend, under the name of *Basilias*, was probably of this kind, though originally it was destined for lepers. "Take," says Gregory, "some steps out of the city and see that new city, that sanctuary of charity, that treasure, where, at his call, came the superfluity of the rich, and what was necessary to the poor, to be deposited where thieves and moths and envy come not. Shall I compare with this edifice, Thebes, with its hundred gates, or the walls of Babylon, or the Mausoleum, or the Pyra-

---

[1] Pallad., *Hist. laus.*, c. 15, 16, p. 39.

[2] Arnold, *Erste Liebe*, p. 486, *et seq.*

[3] A passage in Chrysostom shows, indeed, that the *Xenones* also contained the sick (Chrys., *ad Stagyr.*, III. 13, I. p. 222). The choice of this word to designate charitable institutions in general, shows the importance of such as were destined for foreigners and travellers. Thus it is rightly that De Melun has said in his return on the project of a law recently adopted for hospitals in France: "The most ancient foundations, and often the riches, were destined for travellers and pilgrims," etc. (*Ann. de la char.*, 31, August, 1851.)

mids, or the Coliseum, or those magnificent temples, constructed with so much art, and to-day in ruins, and all those monuments which have secured to their founders only a barren glory? And it is not this city alone that he has thus endowed. All around, elsewhere, the *chorepiscopi*, and the governors, animated by his example, vie with each other in their bounties to the poor;" so that *Xenodochia* were to be seen in all his diocese, and even in the country places and hamlets of Cappadocia. "For others," continues St. Gregory, "let them have skilful cooks, tables well served, rich equipages, and sumptuous garments, but as for Basil, let him have the care of the unfortunate and infirm; to him, as to Jesus, is the gift of healing the lepers, by his hands, at least, if not by his word."[1] It is the destiny of the best institutions to find adversaries and detractors at their origin. This one had been decried to the Governor of Cappadocia, and Basil had humbly to explain to this magistrate that "to found a hospital for the poor who are sick, to receive travellers, to assemble there, for this object, nurses and physicians, to establish workshops in it, in a word, to have there all that is necessary for the support of its guests, was not to injure public interests, but, rather, was to contribute to the embellishment and the honor of the province."[2]

St. Basil's example found imitators, not only in Cappadocia but in all the empire. Marcian, grand superintendent of Constantinople, consecrated all his

---

[1] Greg. Naz., *Orat. fun. in Basil.*, c. 63; *Vita S. Basil.*, c. 241 (*in Basi.*, *Opp.*, III. *præf.*, p. 115); Basil., *ep.* 143, *ibid.*, p. 235.

[2] Basil., *ep.* 94, *ad El.*, III. p. 188.

property to the founding of a *Xenodochium* for his church; Saint John, the Almoner, did as much for Alexandria and for Cyprus, of which he was a native;[1] St. Marcellus, the same in Mesopotamia; the Pope Symmachus at Rome; Pope Gregory the Great in the islands of Sicily and Sardinia, and in the other suburbicarian provinces.[2] Several hospitals had laymen for founders; besides the examples above cited, Gallicanus, patrician and consul, established one at Ostia; Sampson another at Constantinople;[3] Belisarius two at Rome, one upon the Via Lata, the other upon the Flaminian Way; Childebert, that of Lyons, regarded as the first one founded in France, the utility of which was celebrated in the Council of Orleans.[4]

The most of these establishments were placed under the inspection of the bishops, whether they had been founded by them or not. It was the bishop of the place who named the *Magistri hospitalium*, the *Xenodochi*, the *Paramonarii*,[5] the *Orphanotrophi*, the *Brephotrophi*, *the Ptôchotrophi*, in a word, the immediate

[1] Besides seven lying-in hospitals for poor women, he founded several *ptôchotrophia* and *xenodochia*, to which he gave daily distributions of wheat. (Boll., *Act. Sanct.*, *ad* 23, jan., p. 518).

[2] Baillet, *Vie des Saints*, 10 jan., p. 118; Gregor. Magn., *Epp.* III. 24, X. II (*ap.* Labb., *Conc.*, V. pp. 1151,1488: August., Serm. 356, *De Scr.*, c. 10. Thomassin quotes numerous examples of it. See also De Gérando, *ubi sup.*, IV. p. 283, etc.

[3] Ducange, *ubi sup.*, IV. 9.

[4] Fleury, *Mœurs des Chr.*, p. 3, § 18; De Gérando, *ubi sup.*; De Recalde, *Abr. hist. des hôp.*, p. 47, etc.

[5] *Paramonarii*, managers of *hospices* wherein travellers were received.

superiors of these institutions; the nurses themselves and the subaltern officers, held their tenure mediately or immediately of him.[1] He had, in like manner, conjointly with his superintendents, the management of affairs for the support of the hospitals, at least when the donors had not made another disposition of them, or when he had not rendered himself unworthy of their confidence.[2] In a word, the administration of the hospitals was considered as an affair essentially ecclesiastical.[3] It was, in the first place, an homage rendered to religion, which gave the impulse to all the works of charity; then, it was a guaranty of good administration and discipline. The church, then the sole guardian of spiritual and moral interests, disposed, moreover, of the means of repression, which rendered its intervention so much the more desirable. St. Basil refused admission to the poor, whose lives were scandalous, into the monasteries and hospitals, saying that the image of Jesus Christ could no longer

---

[1] Conc. Chalced., can. 8. "The clerks of the *ptôcheia*, as well as those of the monasteries, must remain submitted to the bishop of the place. Labbe, IV. p. 759; Greg. Magn., *Epp.* III. 24 (Labb., V. p. 1152); Epiph., *De hær.*, 75, *init.* Theodosius the Younger, by his law of 416, had remitted the election of the *parabolani* of Alexandria to the augustal prefect and the principals of the city; two years afterwards, he restored it to the bishop. (Cod. Theod., XVI. 2, l. 42, 43.)

[2] The acts of the Council of Chalcedon relate that Dioscorus, bishop of Alexandria, irritated with not having had the management of the fortune left by Peristeria to various pious institutions, seized upon them violently and made of them a distribution both profane and sacrilegious.

[3] Thomassin, *Anc. et nouv. discipl.*, I. p. 174.

be recognized in them.[1] This moral supervision itself turned to the advantage of charity. Establishments for the poor who were truly commendable, were more willingly sustained; funds for relief, the good use of which appeared assured, were accorded more generously.

Those who created hospitals, commonly assigned a certain fund in money or real estate for their current expenses. When these funds were found to be insufficient, the deficiency was supplied either by the ordinary revenues of the church,[2] or by gifts and legacies, often very abundant, obtained in their favor.[3]

We repeat it, however, neither the number nor the riches of these establishments, seems to us to indicate in Christian charity a progress proportioned to the extension of the church itself. The manifestation of benevolence had rather changed its form and nature. From individual, as it was, it had become collective.

---

[1] Basil., *Reg. fus. int.* 10; *Reg. Brev.*, c. 155 (II. p. 352, 467).

[2] At Antioch, for instance, the church contributed to the relief of the sick at the hospital. (Chrys., hom. 66, *in Matth.*, c. 3, VII. p. 658.)

[3] Vid. *Cod. Just.*, lib. I. Palladius relates that St. Macarius, overseer of the hospital at Alexandria, having never been able to obtain anything from a rich and avaricious lady, told her once that he knew of a set of precious stones for sale at 500 pieces of silver. As soon as that sum was handed to him, he used it for the benefit of his hospital; then he took thither the donor, and showing to her the sick whom he had relieved in this manner, "Here are," said he, "your jewels; if you are not pleased with them, I am ready to give them back to you." Confounded by the artifice to which he had resorted, the lady addressed her thanks to St. Macarius, and promised him to show more liberality in the future. (Pallad., *hist. laus.*, c. 6.)

If there were no hospitals before Constantine, it was, above all, because in those times of fervor, private charity was sufficient for the necessities, then, too, still limited; because Christians then did good during their lives, not after death; because the house of each brother was, in turn, an asylum for strangers, an infirmary for the sick,[1] and a refuge for the orphan. Charity was everywhere, though its advertisement was nowhere, like those hidden springs, only detected by the freshness and fertility which they impart to the soil.

But we do not the less persist in believing that, since the fourth century, the creation of hospitals was an indispensable necessity. Only establishments founded upon a large scale could provide for such multiplied wants, such pervading and profound misery. We comprehend, then, that in view of these monuments of charity, unknown to pagan antiquity,[2] the hearts of the Christians swelled with a just pride. We comprehend, too, that Julian, the Apostate, envied them this glory, and sought to transport into his *Pagan Church* an institution so admired. His error was in believing that an imperial order was sufficient to found it.[3]

---

[1] St. Paul, 1 *Tim.*, V. 10; Tertull., *ad Uxor.*, II. 4.

[2] For the evidence of this fact, which has been often contested, but which touches our subject only indirectly, we refer to the works of Ryan, *Bienf. de la rel. chr.*, transl., p. 194–198; of de Gérando, *Bienf. publ.*, IV. p. 271; de Villeneuve, *ub. sup.*, II. p. 233, as well as to the special treatises of Percy, Villaume and Mongez, etc. St. Jerome speaks of the astonishment which heathens were filled with at the first foundation of hospitals, (ep. 26).

[3] Julian wrote to Arsacius, pontiff of Galatia: "Built *Xenodo-*

ARTICLE II.

MONASTERIES.

MONASTIC life, the origin of which nearly coincides with the foundation of hospitals, had not, like them, the practice of beneficence for its direct object. It was simply a new form, a new organization given to the Christian asceticism of the first centuries. Those who formerly had given themselves up to a life of renunciation and of mortification in their own homes, now, that the world had invaded the church, felt themselves too feeble to struggle alone against the torrent, and to follow an isolated career of painful abstinence, united to undertake it together, protected from the examples and temptations of the world, and under a common discipline which would keep them from backsliding. "They wished," Fleury says, "to keep the exact observance of the Gospel, which they saw relaxed from day to day!"[1] St. Chrysostom said,

chia in all cities, not only for the use of strangers to our religion, but of all poor travellers. For that purpose I have ordered the delivery of 30,000 bushels of wheat, and 60,000 setiers of wine for the whole province. Use the fifth part for the poor who are in the service of the priests; the remnant shall be distributed to travellers and beggars. . . . Exhort our co-religionists to contribute for this object; accustom them to offer to our gods the first fruits of their fields for deeds of benevolence; and, whilst Homer boasts of the hospitality of Eumeus, let us not permit any others to ravish from us a glory that belongs to us." (Sozom., V. 16, *Cf.* Greg. Naz., *Orat.* 4, in Jul., c. 111, I. p. 139).

[1] Fleury, *Moeurs des Chr.*, part 3, § 19.

"If we call the Christians to the desert, it is to withdraw them from the pernicious examples of our cities; it is, in fine, that they may avoid vice, and practise virtue."[1]

But, if monastic life was not directly inspired by a principle of charity, it was still a useful auxiliary to this virtue; and, in more than one way, it efficaciously contributed to the relief of misery.

Not only, as we have already seen, it enabled the rich who wished to divest themselves of their property in favor of the poor, to break the ties which would have been a hindrance to it; not only did the attraction presented by these pious retreats engage many of the rich to renounce their wealth in order to enter therein, but also, even the constitution of monastic communities, and the resources at their disposal, placed them in a condition to grant many favors, both within their own organization and without.

All who entered a monastery had to give to it, for the benefit of the community, the goods they were actually in possession of.[2] They were pledged to make the same disposition of all they might subsequently obtain, whether by gift or by inheritance.[3]

---

[1] Chrys., *Adv. opp. vit. mon.* I. 8; Hom. 55, 69, 70, *in Matth.*

[2] Basil., *Const. mon.*, c. 34, II. p. 580.

[3] Some parents, to maintain after their death the integrity of their domains, contented themselves with securing such of their children as entered the monasteries, a sum equivalent to the expense of their support, and under pretext that, devoted to God, they would not want terrestrial goods, they disinherited them from the rest of their fortune, or left them but the use of the part of the inheritance which would have fallen upon them. St. Basil and Salvian especially bitterly resist such reserves, and blame likewise

Besides, the monastic communities were enriched by the offerings of pious persons, who, not being able or willing to embrace the life of a monk, sought at least, by their liberalities to those who had entered into orders, to ensure for themselves a portion of their merits.

To the resources derived from these gifts, the majority of the convents joined that of labor. St. Anthony set the first examples of this. "He worked with his hands, says Athanasius, and thus procured not only a support, but also something to give to the needy. The monasteries which he founded were filled with monks, who, to reading, singing and prayer, united labor, so that they might be in a condition to give.[1]" The principal promoters of monastic life, St. Pachomius, St. Basil, and St. Epiphanes, subjected their disciples to the same obligation; they taught them to disdain no trade, and principally recommended to them the occupations of agriculture.[2] Those of Antioch ploughed, planted, and made sacks;[3] those of Egypt, to the number, it is said, of sixty thousand, were engaged in almost all the avocations necessary to life. Palladius, visiting those of Panopolis, found a great many of them occupied in divers trades. Theodosius

---

the monks, who, at their death, bequeathed to their relatives rather than to monasteries, (Basil., *Reg. Brev. int.* 187, II. p. 478; Salvian, *De avar.*, lib. III, IV.) Hence we see that custom still granted a certain latitude in this respect. Nevertheless, in most cases, the monasteries inherited from such members of the community as left no near relatives.

[1] Athanas., *Vit. Ant.*, c. 3, 44, Opp., ed. Ben., I. p. 797, 829.

[2] Pallad., *Hist. laus.*, c. 39, p. 98; Basil., *Reg. fus. tract. int.* 38, II. p. 385.

[3] Chrys., hom. 72 *in Matth.*, c. 4.

of Rhosus, in Cilicia, worked constantly with his own hands at tissues of rushes, or in the cultivation of the fields, and exacted the same labor of those who collected about him.[1] Epiphanes condemns the Massalians or Euchites who professed to live on alms and to replace work by prayer.[2] St. Augustine censures, still more rudely, certain idle monks, who wandered about in Africa, and when they complacently cited these words of our Saviour, "the birds of the air sow not, neither do they reap; the lilies of the fields toil not, neither do they spin," he answered with St. Paul, he who is not willing to work ought not to eat.[3] But it was St. Benedict, of Nursia, who made the cause of labor prevail in the monasteries. Whilst the monks in the East, in spite of the positive prescriptions of St. Basil, gave themselves up more and more to a life of idleness and contemplation, St. Benedict, reforming those in the West, placed labor among the number of the fundamental duties of their order. "Idleness," says he, "is the enemy of the soul. Consequently the brethern ought, at certain fixed hours, to occupy themselves with manual labor, after having consecrated the others to religious reading." Seven hours of the day were set apart for labor, the products of which were sold without for the benefit of the community. The Superior prescribed to each one his special occupation,[4] and the spirit of obedience, the invariable discipline of the monastery, the persuasion,

---

[1] Theodor., *Rel. hist.*, c. 10, Opp., III. p. 827.

[2] Epiph., *Hær.* 80.

[3] Aug., *De op., monach.*, I. 33-36, XXVI. p. 519-563.

[4] Fleury, *Hist. eccles.*, XXXII. 15.

above all, that labor was one of the conditions of salvation, stimulated this indispensable element of prosperity in the convents, which, in civil society, we have seen languishing and almost dead. Free labor, discredited by Roman prejudice, continued to be honored, having been ennobled by Christianity.

Finally, to the profits derived by the monasteries from these different sources, add the economy resulting from a life in common, and the still greater economy from the severe regimen observed in the cloisters,[1] and the services which these communities might render to the cause of beneficence will be understood.[2] Among those whom they admitted into their bosom, and whom they supported from the common funds, were a crowd of poor, who would have found elsewhere no means of subsistence;[3] many slaves set free, for whom liberty, without this resource, would have been but misery; children abandoned by their parents; the distressed fleeing from public disasters. All, according to Basil, found there together with what was necessary, though frugal, truly, those mutual cares and services which brethren well united together can render to each other. "The sick, he said, receives there the assistance and the consolations of his brothers. They are all at the same time masters and servants; all free, and, nevertheless, subjected to each other by the sacred bondage of charity.[4] You see at their table, adds Chrysostom,

---

[1] Sozom., *Hist. eccles.*, I. 12; Evagr., *id.*, I. 21.

[2] Martin-Doisy, *Hist. de la charité*, p. 325, *seq.*

[3] August., *Reg. ad serv. Dei*, c. 1, XXVI. p. 573.

[4] Basil., *Const. monast.*, § 2, II. p. 561.

the maimed, and beggars; you see one attend the wounds of the sick, another conduct the blind, a third carry the lame."[1]

Monastic charity, so attentive within, was not less liberal without. With the surplus of their revenues, the religious communities exercised around them a hospitality often very generous.

During a famine which desolated Egypt, St. Pachomius distributed, without thought for the morrow, all the provisions of his monastery. While the same scourge raged in Pontus and Cappadocia, Peter of Sebaste, brother of St. Basil, extended his charity over the whole sphere of his observations; and, the wretched sufferers, fleeing to him from all parts, his desert presented rather the aspect of a city.[2] St. Apollo did as much in the Thebais, and was believed by the inhabitants to possess, like our Saviour, the power of multiplying loaves. The monks of Arsinoë, united around Serapion, to the number of ten thousand, carried

---

[1] Chrys., hom. 72 *in Matth.*, c. 4; Aug., *De moz. eccl. cath.*, I. 67–70, XXVII. p. 535, *seq.* Indeed, those were the most flourishing times of monastic life, still embellished perhaps by the imagination of these two writers. Others have added several shades to this picture. According to Julian Pomère, there were men who seemed to have entered the monastery to escape spending their patrimony by assisting the poor, or in receiving foreigners; others who inflated themselves with pride for their paying a pension proportioned to their expense, whilst the community supported monks who had brought no money. St. Augustine, himself, points out some lazy persons who entered orders only to live at the expense of others. It is true enough, that even in the most favorable conditions, the system of community is exposed to great misuses.

[2] Bolland., *Act. Sanct.*, *ad* 9 jan., p. 587. The same is related of St. John of Réome, (*Ibid.*, *ad* 28 jan., p, 561).

each of them, to this abbot, their crop of wheat, which he distributed to the peasants around him; sometimes he sent even to Alexandria, vessels loaded with corn and clothes for the needy. Maysimas of Cyrrhus, in Mesopotamia, was so devoted to strangers and the poor, that his door was, so to say, open to every comer; he had two kinds of provisions for alms-giving, oil and wheat, which were believed to be inexhaustible with him from his liberality.[1] The monks of Nitria to their convent had joined a hospital, where every traveller was lodged gratuitously for eight days; but, if he wished to sojourn longer, he had to work like the brothers, for the profit of the community. Their guests found with them also medical aid; Apollonius, a rich merchant, established himself there for twenty months with a supply of medicines purchased at his own expense, and passed whole days in taking care of the sick.[2] A great number of other convents had like hospitals, which fulfilled in the country and desert places, the part of those in the cities. Between the monasteries in the neighborhood of Oxyrinchus, in Egypt, reigned an emulation of hospitality truly admirable; and it is assured that travellers arriving in the Thebais, sometimes had their garments torn by the monks in disputing the honor of receiving them.[3]

The monasteries were also places of refuge and of education for children; St. Chrysostom extols the

---

[1] Theodoret., *Rel. hist.*, c. 14, Opp., III. p. 842. See, besides, the example of the monk Abraamès, c. 17, p. 849.

[2] Pallad., *Hist. laus.*, c. 14, 52, 76.

[3] Theodoret., *Rel. hist.* c. 30, p. 895.

services which they rendered in this respect.[1] Basil, in his great Rules, strongly recommends functions so honorable, and prescribed by the Saviour himself to the monks. He advises that children of every age should be received, particularly those who have lost their parents, and that they should be brought up in all charity, as if they were the children of the community; that those of each sex should be formed to an appropriate kind of life, prepared for piety by prayer; that the histories and the maxims of the Scriptures should be taught to them; that a director, at once mild and prudent, should watch over their habits and practise them in virtue; lastly, that they should frequent the shops of workmen, skilful in those arts and professions for which they seemed apt, while still remaining under the assiduous supervision of their protectors.[2] Theodoret relates the cares taken of his infancy by a monk to whom his mother had confided him, and the good which two monks from Edessa, had done in Egypt, by the schools which they had founded there.[3] The Benedictines of Mount Cassino rendered the same service to the people of Italy.[4]

Thus it was that the monastic communities preluded in the mission of charity and of civilization, which they were to perform during a part of the Middle Ages. This mission explains, and justifies at the same time, the liberalities of which they were

---

[1] Chrys., *Adv. opp. vit mon.*, III. 12, 17.
[2] Basil., *Reg. fus.*, *int.* 15, II. p. 355, *seq.*
[3] Theod., *Hist. rel.*, III.
[4] Greg. Magn., *Dial.*, II. 3, Opp. I. p. 1356.

already the object. To give or bequeath to monasteries, was for the future, it is true, to sow the seeds of a degeneration, which, among many of them, was to be but too precocious; but, for the present, it was to commit into industrious and charitable hands the riches, which, otherwise, would have remained barren for the material and moral good of the people.

CHAPTER VIII.

CONTINUATION.—WORKS OF CHARITY INDEPENDENT OF MONASTERIES AND HOSPITALS.

THE collective action of hospitals and of monasteries by no means exhausts the catalogue of the works of beneficence during this period. Individual charity, though more limited, had not entirely lost its former activity. Many unfortunates were relieved; many strangers received, and widows and orphans succored; even many sick were nursed out of the hospitals which were appointed for them. Many alms were given at the door of the churches, by the faithful and the deacons, to the mendicants who had a permission to remain under the sacred porticoes. Poor persons, ashamed to beg, according to the charitable invitation of Leo the Great, were discreetly assisted in their own abodes.[1]

[1] Leo Magn., Serm. 4, *De collect.*, Opp., p. 6: Fleury, *Mœurs des chr.*, part 3, § 18.

Christian women, in-doors, imitated that Peristeria, whose prodigality towards the poor is praised by St. Nilus, in her maternal cares for travellers, for the sick, and for all who were victims of any suffering.[1] Ephraim, the Syrian, Gallicanus, of consular dignity, and Victor, a military count, are celebrated by the authors of their times for the devotion they manifested at the bed of the infirm and expiring.[2] Aetius, chief of the Eunomians, availed himself of his knowledge of medicine to attend the sick gratuitously.[3] Paulinus says of Sulpicius Severus, that, to afford an asylum to his guests, he was like a guest in his own house, and that he hardly found a place there for himself, so full was it of strangers and of the necessitous.[4] A *protocomes*, whose life Palladius recounts, congratulates himself for having always shown a generous hospitality, for having never sent away the poor without relief, and for having never suffered a stranger to depart from his house with empty hands.[5]

The bishops, above all, distinguished themselves by the profusion of their alms. After the ravages of the Visigoths in Gaul, and a war during which all the crops had been burned, St. Patientius, bishop of Lyons, imported, at his own expense, an immense supply of corn, filled with it two store-houses on the banks of the Rhone, and of the Saone, and caused it to be gratuitously distributed to the famished popula-

---

[1] Nili *Perister.*, sect. 1, c. 3. (*Bibl. Patr.*, XXVII. p. 183).
[2] Sidon. Apoll., *Epp.* VII. 12; Arnold, *Erste Liebe*, p. 478.
[3] Philostorg., *Hist. eccles.*, ed. Gothofr., p. 52.
[4] Paulin., *Ep. ad Sever.*, 24, c. 3. Opp., p. 150.
[5] Pallad.. *Hist. laus.*, c. 64, p. 158.

tion of Arles, Avignon, Orange, Alby, Valence, and Clermont. "We have seen," says St. Sidonius, who is rendering thanks to him in the name of this last city, "the routes too narrow for the convoys of grain which thou didst cause to pass, more admirable still than Joseph, since thou hast remedied a famine which thou hadst not foreseen."[1] Saint Sidonius himself, having sold his plate and sacrificed all his revenues, nourished, it is said, four thousand poor with the aid of his brother-in-law, Ecdicius.[2] Pope Saint Gregory, on the first of every month, caused different kinds of provisions, according to the season, to be given to the poor. Every day he had distributed, at his home, succor for the sick and infirm, and sent from his own table, portions to those who were ashamed to confess themselves necessitous. John, the Deacon, found in the palace of the Lateran, a voluminous register, containing the name and designation of the unfortunate whom he habitually assisted. As soon as he learned that any member of his flock was in embarrassment, he caused him to be assisted by the church, in each particular case fixing the value and duration of the aid. More than once, Rome was indebted to his care for escaping the horrors of famine. He received and assisted, by crowds, the unfortunate who fled before the Lombards.[3]

---

[1] Sidon. Apoll., *Epp.* VI. 12, Opp., p. 134, *seq.*

[2] Baillet, *Vie des Saints*, 23d August.

[3] Greg. Magn. *Epp. passim.;* Fleury, *Hist. eccl.*, XXXV. 16; *Law*, Greg. Magn., p. 135, 302, *seq.* St. German of Auxerre, St. German of Paris, Exuperus of Toulouse, Gregory of Antiochia, Domitianus of Melitene, and many others, were also renowned for their benevolence. (*Act. sanct.*, *ad* 10 jan., p. 618; *ad* 31 July, etc., Evagr., *Hist. eccl.*, V. 6.)

Besides, there were many charitable deeds that could not be accomplished either in the hospitals or in the monasteries.

I might here again mention the love-feasts which were still maintained with the charitable destination which the first Christians had given to them.[1] The love-feasts of dedications, of funerals, and those which accompanied the festivals of the martyrs, were still in the days of Chrysostom and of St. Augustine, considered as a means of relief to the poor.[2] It was on this account, principally, that the Council of Gangres supported them against the excessive asceticism of the disciples of Eustathius;[3] and for the same reason that Julian recommended the imitation of them to the ministers of the religion he had undertaken to restore.[4] But it was not long, even in the church, before the disadvantages of these festivals were recognized. They had come to be, for most of the rich who celebrated them, but a charity of ostentation. Then, as true charity disappeared, sensuality took its place at these feasts.[5] Heathen dissoluteness, which got into them,

---

[1] Drescher, *De agapis*, p, 37–38.

[2] Chrys., *Hom. in dict. Paul.*, c. 3; August, *adv. Faust.*, XX. 20. "Agapes nostræ pauperes pascunt." Serm. 178, *De scr.*, c. 4. "I am not, sayest thou, like the bad rich; I celebrate agapæ; I support the poor." . . . Drescher, *ub. sup.*, p. 130–136. Pammachius, in the funeral agapæ he gave in honor of Pauline, entertained in a church all the poor of Rome. (Paulin., *Ep.* 13, § 11.) See, moreover, Gieseler. *Lehrb. der K. Gesch.*, 4th ed., I. P. 2, p. 299.

[3] Conc. Gangr., can. 11. (Labbe., *Conc.*, II. p. 419.)

[4] Julian., *Fragm.*, Opp., I. p. 305.

[5] Drescher, *De agap.*, p. 39, 40; Augusti, *Denkm. d. christl. Archæol.*, II. p. 221.

gave occasion for the attacks of the heretics.[1] As early as in the fourth century it was necessary to prohibit them in the churches and chapels, as St. Ambrose did at Milan, Aurelius and St. Augustine at Carthage, and several councils in the East and West.[2] Since then, they ceased to form an integral part of divine service. Soon the private celebration of them was abstained from. The usage may be regarded as having entirely ceased in the fifth century, and if it was still maintained or revived in any place, as, for example, we see under Gregory the Great, it was as a transitory compensation for the converted pagans, who complained of the abolition of their sacred repasts.[3] In most of the churches there remained of these love-feasts only the custom, still in vigor in our times, especially in Italy, of making distributions of provisions to the poor at funerals.[4]

The redeeming of captives was at this fatal epoch, a work of charity of much greater importance. "What is more honorable, said St. Ambrose, than to rescue men from death, and women from dishonor; to restore children to their parents, and citizens to their native country!"[5] Whilst Nebridius was at the Court of Constantinople, he never solicited for any

---

[1] See, above, the reproaches of the Eustathians; those of the Manichæans are mentioned in St. Augustine's work against Faustus. XX. 24.

[2] Conc. Laod., can. 28. (Labbe, I. p. 1501); Aug., *Ep.* 22, 64. *ad Aurel.;* Concil. Aurel. 2, can. 12; conc. Trull., can. 74. (Labbe, IV. p. 1781; V. p. 1175.)

[3] Greg. Magn. *Epp.* XI. 76, *ad Mellit.* (Opp., II. p. 1176.)

[4] Raoul-Rochette, *ub. sup.*, p. 137.

[5] Ambros., *De off.*, II. 15, VII. p. 301.

object but this. Chrysostom, even in his exile, consecrated to it a part of the alms which he received from Constantinople. It was, also, one of the acts of beneficence to which Mamertius Claudian, brother and coadjutor of the Archbishop of Vienna, gave himself up with the most ardor.[1] When Pavia was taken and pillaged by the troops of Odoacer, St. Epiphanes, its bishop, ransomed the most of the inhabitants which they had taken.[2] For the same object, St. Ambrose,[3] St. Hilary of Arles,[4] Acacius of Amida, and Pope St. Gregory sold, as we have said above, the precious vessels of their churches.[5] When the Vandals, after the sack of Rome, made many thousands captives, St. Paulinus of Nola, at once redeemed the most of them. Among those who remained in captivity was the son of a poor widow. Paulinus, having nothing to secure his freedom with, gave himself up in his place. But the barbarians, seized with admiration, freed them both, and were, after that, much more easy in regard to the ransom of the other prisoners.[6] As to those whom the Vandals carried into Africa, they found still more sympathy, if it is

---

[1] Hieron., *Ep.* 85, IV. p. 666; Sozom., *Hist. eccles.*, VIII. 27; Sidon. Apoll., *Epp.* IV. 11.

[2] Baillet, *Vie des Saints*, 21 jan., p. 270.

[3] Ambros., *De off.*, II. 28, § 136.

[4] *Bolland.*, *Act. SS. ad* 5 maj., p. 28.

[5] Greg. Magn., *Epp.* VI. 13, 35. (Labbe, V. p. 1258, 1280.) St. Gregory had received from two rich laymen the sum of 30 pounds of gold for the redemption of the prisoners taken by the Lombards; but that sum was found insufficient because of the exigencies of the conquerors. (*Ibid.*, *ep.* 23, p. 1260.)

[6] Greg. Magn., *Dialog.* III. Opp., I. p. 1380.

possible, in Deogratias, Bishop of Carthage. Seeing that the conquerors, in dividing these poor slaves, separated, without scruple, husbands from wives, and mothers from children, the charitable Pontiff sold, to redeem them all, the gold and silver vases of the sacred treasure; then he caused two large churches to be opened, where he received them, providing for their subsistence, and taking care of them himself day and night.[1] After the taking of Jerusalem by the Persians in 614, St. John, the Almoner, not content with receiving with the greatest hospitality the fugitives who retired to Alexandria, sent several ecclesiastics into Palestine, charged with large sums to assist the unfortunate, and to redeem the captives.[2] The mind recalls the example of the young Angles, in the market-place of Rome, delivered by Gregory the Great.

Such is what Christian charity did, *by itself*, of most importance for the mitigation of the evils that weighed upon the Roman world.[3] In order to show of what it was capable in this respect, we had to show it at first, alone at the work, left to its own resources, acting by its own proper means, and without the help of any other power. But our talk would be incomplete if

---

[1] Victor. Vitens., *De persec. Vand.*, I. 8. (*Autor. Hist. eccles.*, ed. 1544, p. 621.)

[2] *Bolland.*, *Act. SS.*, *ad* 23 jan., p. 521.

[3] We might still speak of the acts of charity for the sepulture of the dead. We might relate yet what several bishops did for the material welfare of their dioceses, by consecrating, as Theodoretus of Cyrus, the surplus of the income of the church to the construction of bridges, baths, and other objects of public utility and salubrity. (Theodor., *ep.* 79, 115, III. p. 950, 968.)

we did not also take into account, as we have done for the three first centuries, and for a still stronger reason, the aid it received from the State; if we did not retrace what the civil power, inspired or solicited by it, has done since the fourth century to fructify its beneficent action. Grave questions touching public charity may receive some light from the facts which remain for us to relate.

CHAPTER IX.

CO-OPERATION OF CIVIL POWER IN THE WORK OF CHARITY.

As long as the church had been separate from the State, it was only in an indirect way that the principles of charity were introduced into the Roman legislation and administration. In ameliorating the condition of slaves, of children, of debtors, and of the poor, the first Emperors believed that they were only the organs of the enlightened opinion of some philosophers, when in fact they were, without suspecting it, the organs of a despised and persecuted religion.

Now that the church had not only acquired the right of existing, but, besides, had caused itself to be recognized and adopted by the State, it was no longer unconsciously, but with deliberate purpose, that the emperors opened a place to charity in the civil administration, no longer conducted by philosophy, but by the direct action of Christianity, to adopt measures conformable to its spirit. Since the epoch of Constantine, this new element, hardly seen till then, is observable in the Roman law, in which is perceivable less than before, the severe harshness and inflexible rigidity of rights; but, on the contrary, more of the character of a charitable sympathy; under the toga of the legislator we begin to perceive the movements of a Christian heart; it seems as though Constantine may be seen at the close of a moving sermon, of an evangelical conversation, or at the reception of those short but solemn lines, in which the hero of the desert, the prince of Anachorets, exhorted the Master of the world to the love of the poor, to justice and to charity.[1]

Henceforth, then, the Emperors, as a matter of duty, introduced into the administration of the Empire all they could of Christian principles; they attempted to put their government in harmony with the maxims of charity and evangelical purity.[2] Often, without doubt, they saw themselves arrested in their efforts; Roman society, originally cast in a pagan mould, resisted the action which its Christian masters wished to exercise upon it, and grew rigid against the transformations which they wished to effect in it; and the Empire will have succumbed ere the metamorphosis be accomplished.[3] No matter; though slow and diffi-

---

[1] Athanas., *Vit. Anton.*, c. 81, Opp., I. p. 856.

[2] De Roehr, *De effect. rel. christ. in jurisp. rom.*, diss. 4, § 3, 10 et passim.; Troplong, *De l'influence du chr. sur le droit civil des Rom.*, p. 115.

[3] Troplong, *ibid.*, p. 128; *Giraud, Elem. du droit rom.*, introd., I. p. 338, *seq.*

cult, the work advances; each emperor deems it a glory to have surpassed his predecessors in this career. The Theodosian code already bears the evident marks of an infusion of Christian maxims; the Justinian code bears the impress still more deep. Many acts, not of the legislative department, but which have been transmitted to us by history, equally attest the efforts of the emperors to second the work of evangelical charity. In this and the following chapter, it is proposed to describe the measures they have taken in this regard, beginning with those which relate the least directly to the exercise of charity properly so called.

We have seen the church, primarily, undertake a charitable intervention in favor of the feeble or oppressed classes; the Christian emperors not only tolerated, but authorized and encouraged this intervention, in many cases.

Struck with the evils which had followed, since Theodosius I. and Arcadius, the momentary suppression of the right of asylum in the churches,[1] and with the abuses, not less injurious, brought on by the illegal exercise of that right, Theodosius, the Young, thought it a duty to re-establish it, and, moreover, not to prejudice the exercise of worship and the majesty of the sanctuary, he extended it to the whole enclosure of the edifices and of the consecrated places; at the same time he forbade that any should be admitted

---

[1] See the edicts of those two emperors in the Cod. Theod. IX. 45, *de his qui ad eccles.*, l. 1, 3, ann. 392, 398, and the comment. of Gothofr.

there who should come armed.[1] Justinian, besides, excepted those who should be pursued for the crime of homicide, or of adultery, or rape.[2] As for slaves who sought a refuge in the sanctuary, Theodosius, the Young, ordained that the master should be immediately informed of their flight and summoned to take them home, after having pardoned them.[3]

It was thus, in part, to mitigate, by a just and equitable intervention, the rigor of strict law, that the emperors authorized the arbitrations of the bishops in civil matters, and obliged the parties who had once accepted it, to abide by the decisions of this spiritual tribunal,[4] "more human, even from that, observes M. Troplong, more removed from the spirit of contention than the official justice of the prefect of the prætorium, and whose awards, disengaged from the apparatus of judiciary forms, brought back law to reason and justice."[5]

The emperors did not pause with authorizing the charitable intervention of the church. On more than one occasion they solicited and required it themselves, for example, in charging the bishops to provide in concert with the magistrates, by regular visits and inquests, that no prisoner should be unjustly detained or submitted to inhuman treatment,[6] to cause to be

---

[1] Cod. Theod., IX. 45, l. 4, ann. 431. Socrates relates on what occasion this decree was published. (*Hist. eccles.*, VII. 33.)

[2] Justin., Nov. 17, c. 7.

[3] Cod. Theod., *ub. sup.*, l. 5, ann. 432.

[4] Cod. Just., 1, 4, *De episc. aud.*, l. 8, ann. 408, Nov. 86; *Cf.* Const. apost., II. 45–47; Gieseler, *K. Geschichte* I. p. 470.

[5] Troplong, *ub. sup.*, p. 117, *seq.*

[6] Cod. Theod., IX. 3, *De custod. reor.*, l. 7, ann. 409; Cod. Just. I. 4, l. 22, ann. 529.

released those who, despite the laws, had been shut up in the private prisons,[1] to protect against every attempt at spoliation those Romans who returned from captivity,[2] to denounce the extortions of the governors of provinces,[3] to defend free women or slaves from the infamous speculators, who would constrain them to prostitute themselves or to go upon the stage,[4] to watch over the lot of exposed children, the rights of persons under guardianship, of minors,[5] and in general of those most exposed by their feebleness to acts of injustice or of tyranny. Justinian, above all, counted much in this respect, upon the active and charitable supervision of the bishops.

But it was futile to depend upon the church to prevent by its moral influence some particular acts of oppression, if the law continued to favor them by its complicity, or at least by its tolerance. The Christian emperors comprehended the necessity of modifying legislation upon this point; they applied themselves little by little to remove from it all that could too openly shock the principles of charity, and to introduce into it, as much at least as the state of morals would permit, the spirit of the new religion.

The Romans, carried into captivity by the Barbarians, often found on their return to their homes,

---

[1] Cod. Just., I. 4, l. 23, Cod. ann.

[2] Cod. Theod. V. 5, *De postlim.*, l. 2, ann. 409.

[3] Justin., Nov. 8, c. 8, ann. 535.

[4] Cod. Theod., XV. 8, *De lenon.*, l. 1, 2, ann. 343, et 428; Cod. Just., I. 4, *De episc. aud.*, l. 12, 14, 33, ann. 534.

[5] Cod. Theod., V. 7, *De expos.*, l. 2, ann. 412; Just. Nov., 153; Cod. Just., I. 4, *De episc., aud.*, l. 27, ann. 530, l. 30, etc.

their property seized by the fisc, or passed into the hands of third persons by the gift of the Prince; sometimes, also sold by the Barbarians to other Romans, they were retained in perpetual slavery by these latter in consideration of their purchase and support. Valentinian, the First, hastened to reinstate them in their possessions, and Honorius assured liberty to them in consideration of the reimbursement of the price paid for them, or of a service of five years longer, if they could not effect this reimbursement.[1] The church did more in such a case; it redeemed the captive from the hands of his new master, or obtained from him his voluntary and gratuitous enfranchisement; but the law was obliged to respect acquired rights by offering in return an equitable compensation.

Despite the gradual ameliorations, which, from Nero to Diocletian, had taken place in the condition of slaves, this condition was far from being happy. The Christian emperors, without attempting, as in the fourth century the usurper John had done,[2] the essay, then chimerical, of abolishing servitude, and, even leaving to the masters the means of repression which were necessary to ensure their authority,[3] tried to render the condition of slaves more tolerable.[4] Constantine condemned as guilty of homicide every master who inflicted upon them any chastisement, or any tor-

---

[1] Cod. Theod., V. 5, *De postlim.*, l. 1, 2, ann. 366, 409; Peyron, *Fragm. Cod. Theod.*, p. 119, *seq.*

[2] Troplong, *ub. sup.*, p. 111.

[3] Cod. Theod., IX. 12, *De amend. serv.*, l. 1, 2, ann. 319, 326.

[4] Wallon, *Hist. de l'esclavage*, III. last chapter.

ture, with the intention of bringing them to death.[1] From the epoch of the Council of Nicea, and probably at the solicitation of the bishops who were assembled there, it prohibited gladiatorial combats which annually cost the lives of a great number of slaves.[2] In regard to this, Roman manners were particularly alien to the acts of the Christian legislator. These fatal combats, in effect, continued to the time of Honorius; nothing less effected their abolishment under that prince than the devotion of a martyr.[3]

The religious law of the sabbath, transported by the Christians to the first day of the week, served among them, as among the Jews, to temper the fatigues of the servile class. Constantine made of it a civil law, applicable to the whole empire. He ordered for Sunday and festivals the suspension of all labor in the city and in the country, except where it would be necessary for the preservation of the crops.[4] On the contrary, he permitted on these same days the vacations of the courts to be interrupted for deeds of charity, in particular for the emancipation of slaves.[5] The same year he authorized enfranchisements in the churches, on condition that they should take place in the presence of some member of the clergy.[6] Justinian abolished servitude inflicted as a punishment.[7]

---

[1] Cod. Theod., IX. 12, *ub. sup.*

[2] Cod. Theod., XV. 12, *De gladiat.*, l. 1, ann. 325; Euseb., *De vit. Const.*, IV. 25.

[3] See above, p. 146.

[4] Cod. Just., III. 12, *De fer.*, l. 3, ann. 321.

[5] Cod. Theod., II. 8, *De fer.*, l. 1, ann. 321.

[6] *Ibid.*, De *manum.*, *in eccl.*, IV. 7, ann. 321.

[7] Just., Nov., 22, c. 8, *De pœn. servit.*, ann. 336.

Already his predecessors had pronounced free, those who by any title had enjoyed liberty for sixteen years [1] He extended this privilege to every slave who should have been mutilated by his master; declared free him who, by the consent, even tacit, of this latter, should have taken orders, or have entered into a monastery;[2] he referred to the superior tribunals every decision touching the state of persons; accorded legal guarantees to those whose liberty was contested;[3] abolished the restrictions which the ancient law had placed on testamentary manumissions;[4] and closed several sources which it had left open to slavery.[5] He also effaced the distinctions it established between the different classes of the enfranchised, and assimilated them all to free persons, maintaining, however, over them the rights which the preceding emperors had reserved to the patron and his heirs.[6] The work of the abolition of slavery thus made incontestable progress without being precipitated in an imprudent manner.

The same spirit of humanity manifested itself in regard to the *Coloni*. While obliging them to fidelity, while punishing their flight by slavery, the law pro-

---

[1] Cod. Theod., IV. 8, *De liber. caus.*, l. 3.

[2] Just. Nov., 123, c. 17.

[3] Cod. Just., III. 22, *ubi caus. stat.*, l. 6, VII. 17, *De assert. toll.*

[4] Just. Instit., I. 7, *De leg. Fus. can. tollend.;* Troplong, *ub. sub.*, p. 161; Wallon, *ub. sup.*, p. 446.

[5] Cod. Just., VII. 24, *De Sen. Cons. Claud. toll.*, etc.; Wallon, *ub. sup.*, p. 441, *seq.*

[6] Cod. Just., VII. 5, 6, *De libert. dedit. et lat. tollend.*, Justin. Nov., 78, *præf.*, c. 1, 2, ann. 539; *Cf.* Cod. Theod., IV. 11, l. 1–3; Hugo, *Hist. du droit rom.*, II. p. 282.

hibits the proprietors, by sale, or by testament, from tearing them from the estates which they cultivated, as well as from assigning, in the partition of an estate, to different proprietors, Coloni, who are members of one same family; for, says Constantine, the author of this law, with an accent full of humanity, "who could endure to see children separated from their parents, sisters from their brothers, wives from their husbands?"[1] Honorius protected the prisoners taken from the barbarous nation of the Scyres, against those who wished to make slaves of them, whilst, according to the treaty, they were to be mere *Coloni*.[2]

As to the slaves and *Coloni*, who, to escape the abuse of their masters, came into the large cities to swell the crowd of mendicants,[3] the emperors, renouncing the rude decrees of expulsion with which these unfortunate creatures had been overwhelmed in former times, thought, however, that they must take measures for the public safety against them. It was to repress their roving and their mendicity, that Valentinian II. published, in 382, the following ordinance: "let all beggars who live on the city of Rome, be carefully examined and interrogated; and let those who shall be found of an age, and in a state to work, if they are of a servile condition, be adjudged as slaves; and if they are of free condition, let them be

---

[1] Cod. Theod., II. 25, *De comm. divid.;* Cod. Just., III. 38, l. 11, ann. 334. See the remarks of Baudoin, (Bald., *Const. Magn.*, Basil, 1556, p. 220.)

[2] Peyron, *Cod. Th. fragm.*, p. 120–123.

[3] Gothofr., *in Cod. Theod.*, V. p. 257; Moreau, *du Probl. de la mis.*, I. p. 152, *seq.*

adjudged as *Coloni*, to those who arrest them. We reserve, however, the judicial rights of masters against those who may have favored the escape of their *Coloni*, or of their slaves."[1] Justinian, after having at first purely and simply reproduced this ordinance,[2] modified it afterwards in what concerned Constantinople. Distinguishing between beggars of free condition, those who were strangers in the city, and those who were born there, he ordered the latter to be subjected to public works, and the others to be sent into their provinces. As for slaves, he ordered them to be remitted, as far as possible, to the hands of their respective masters.[3] The law of Justinian is obviously more humane and more wise than that of his predecessors. It was, however, always the same remedy for beggary; for let us not forget that under the emperors, the public works were but another sort of slavery.[4] At any rate, these two laws, the only ones to be found in the Roman code on the subject of beggars,[5] ameliorated, in no respect, the situation of the indigent class. Mendicity is but one of the exterior forms under which poverty manifests itself. The State can, according to circumstances, have good reasons for suppressing it. It ought to do so, even, when it becomes threatening to the public safety.

[1] Cod. Theod., XIV. 18, *De mendic., non valid.*, ann. 382.

[2] Cod. Justin., XI. 25.

[3] Just. Nov., 80, *De quæst.*, c. 4, 5, ann. 539.

[4] Wallon. *Hist. de l'escl.*, III. P. 3, 4, 5.

[5] De Gérando, *Bienf. publ.* IV. p. 476; Moreau, *du Probl.*, I. p. 419, 423.

But in doing so, it no more remedies pauperism itself, than an ulcer is cured by being struck in.

It is known that Roman legislation, like that of almost all pagan people, authorized the sale, or the exposure of new-born children whom their parents could not, or would not support;[1] those who took them up, or bought them, could, at pleasure, make of them their slaves, and sometimes based horrible speculations upon them; some prostituted them for money, others maimed them, or mutilated them to make beggars of them, for their own profit; every one could abuse these poor forsaken creatures with impunity.[2] Diocletian had tried to put an end to this abuse, by declaring every exposed child free;[3] but he had not seen that this was, in some sort, to condemn it to death, by suppressing the sole interest which could induce men, mostly without compassion, to preserve and support it. Constantine, struck with this danger, returned to the edict of his predecessor. He decreed that he who should receive and nourish an exposed child, might, as he judged fit, treat it as his son or his slave, without the parents, who had abjured in regard to it, the sentiments of nature, ever having the right to reclaim it.[4] The same emperor con-

---

[1] Dureau de la Malle, *Econ. pol. des Rom.*, I. p. 413–417.

[2] Naudet, *Sec. publ.*, *ub. sup.*, p. 73, etc.

[3] Cod. Just., IV. 43, l. 1.

[4] Cod. Theod., V. 7, *De expos.*, l. 1, ann. 331. If, however, a new-born child had been sold or given by necessity to one who took the charge of feeding him, he could afterwards be bought back by his father or any person, by paying an equitable sum, or by substituting another slave. (Cod. Theod., V. 8, *De his qui sanguinol.*, etc., ann. 329.)

demned to the punishment of parricides the father who put his child to death;[1] but exposure was not then, in the eyes of the law, considered as a murder. Valentinian I. ventured first to introduce the Christian spirit, in this regard, into legislation, and to condemn the father who was guilty of this crime.[2] As for the lot of the child himself, after many fluctuations, caused by the difficulty of reconciling the interests of humanity with those of justice,[3] under Justinian, a final return was made to the law of Diocletian, and all exposed children without exception were declared free, with a prohibition even to those who should nourish them, to hold them as *Coloni* or slaves.[4] It is true, that at this epoch the sentiments of Christian charity were already more prevalent, and that the *brephotrophia*, established in the most of the cities, offered a means of preserving the life of those unhappy beings, otherwise than by reducing them to servitude.

Kidnapping, or the theft of free children and men, so frequent among the Romans,[5] was forbidden under pain of death by Constantine,[6] who published many

---

[1] Cod. Theod., IX. 15, *De parricid.*, l. 1, ann. 319.

[2] Cod. Just., VIII. 52, *De infant. expos.*, l. 2, ann. 374. "Unusquisque sobolem suam nutriat. Quod si exponendam putaverit, animadversioni constitutæ subjacebit."

[3] See for particulars in de Gérando, *ub. sup.*, II. p. 139, *seq.*; Wallon, *ub. sup.*, II. p. 435, *seq.*; Troplong, p. 277–280; Naudet, *ub. sup.*, p. 79–81, etc.

[4] Cod. Justin., IV. 43, l. 1, VIII. 52, l. 3, ann. 529; Just. Nov., 153, *De infant. exp.*, c. 1.

[5] Mor. Christ., I. p. 68.

[6] Cod. Theod., IX. 18, *ad leg. Fab.*, l. 1, ann. 315.

other laws against those who, in any manner should tamper with the liberty of the subjects of the Empire.[1]

The same Prince declared himself the patron of orphans, so imperfectly protected by the ancient Roman law. Not content with assuring the maintenance of their rights against the malversations of their tutors,[2] he freed them from the obligation of appearing in court out of their provinces, permitted them to appeal, in case of need, to the tribunal of the emperor,[3] and accorded to them some precious exemptions.[4] Finally a great number of decrees were published with the intention of assuring to them a paternal and protecting tutelage.[5]

Almost the same privileges were accorded to widows.[6]

Debtors, who, under the republic, and in the three first centuries of the empire, had been, according to the vicissitudes of politics and the alternate rule of

---

[1] Cod. Theod., IV. 8, *De lib caus.*, l. 1, 2; V. 6, *De ingen. qui, etc.*, l. 1, etc.

[2] Cod. Theod., II. 16, l. 1, 2; III. 17, l. 1, tit. 19, *De adm. et peric. tut.*, l. 1–3, etc., Peyron, *Cod. Th. fr.*, p. 80.

[3] Cod. Theod., I. 10, *De off. judic.*, l. 1, 2; Cod. Just., III. 114, *quando imper., etc.*, ann. 334.

[4] Cod. Justin., IX. 24.

[5] Peyron, *Cod. Theod., fragm.*, p. 14, 82; Cod. Just., I. 4, l. 30; V. 28, *seq.*, Nov., 72, etc.

As for illegitimate children, if the laws of Christian princes were rather adverse to them; if Constantine, in particular, displayed enough of rigor against them, it was the result of the efforts of those princes to draw closer, and to strengthen the conjugal bond and repress debauchery. (De Roehr, *De effect. rel. chr.* diss. 4, § 16–20.)

[6] Cod. Th., I. 10; Cod. Just., III. 14, IX. 24.

parties, at one time pitilessly given up to the scourge of usury and the harshness of their creditors;[1] at another time, freed from their obligations by other laws not less tyrannical, saw, under the Christian emperors, their lot adjusted, not, surely, in the most satisfactory manner, but, at least, in a way more equitable for the two parties. The interest of money, which, until then, in spite of the laws of Augustus, had always depended more or less upon the caprice or the avidity of the lender, was fixed by Constantine and Theodosius, at a high rate, it is true, but which could not be exceeded under penalty of the loss of quadruple.[2] It was afterwards lowered by Justinian to four per cent. for the loans made by the nobility; to eight, for those of the merchants; to six, for those of other private persons. Only five per cent. could be exacted of the peasants.[3] We are far from ap-

[1] As to the rights of creditors according to the ancient Roman law, and particularly, as to the barbarous right pretended to have been theirs, to put to death their insolvent debtor, and to partake of their body, see the discussion in the Acad. of the moral and political sciences, between Troplong and Berriat-St.-Prix. (Sessions of the Acad., ann. 1847, vol. I. 2d series.) At any rate, the privileges of Roman creditors were exorbitant. (*Ibib.*, V; Mémoires de Giraud et Berriat-St.-Prix; Naudet, *Mém.*, *sur le prêt à intérêt chez les Romains*, Acad. des inscript., public session of 1849, p. 75, *seq.*; *Des secours publ.* Mém. of that Acad., XIII. p. 29–31; Dureau de la Malle, *ub. sup.*, II. p. 201; Gothofr., *ad Cod. Theod.*, I. p. 231.)

[2] Cod. Theod., II. 33; *De usur.*, l. 1, 2, ann. 325, 386. It was the former rate, or the *centesimus* by month, or the 12 per cent.; but previously that rate had risen sometimes as high as 36 per cent. more; for the loan in kind on the country, the rate was 50 per cent.

[3] Cod. Just., IV. 32, *De usur.*, *Naudet ub. sup.*, p. 83, *seq.*

proving unreservedly this intervention of the law in the domain of private contracts; still less do we guarantee that it was more happy or more efficacious than it had been in other times.

Justinian was better inspired, it seems, when he condemned to restitution those, who, taking advantage of the misery of the agriculturist, took a mortgage of his land, his cattle, his sheep, and his slaves, for the goods which they had furnished him in a time of pressing want;[1] and is very severe against creditors who invaded with violence the domicil of the dying, or troubled the sepulture of the dead.[2] He, as well as his predecessors, opened the asylum of the sanctuary to debtors too rigorously prosecuted; but, in protecting their persons, he did not free them from their obligations; and, in case of a refusal of payment, he ordered that their goods should be sold to the amount of their debt.[3] The asylum of the churches was thus, and under the same condition, open to the debtors of the fisc.[4] Already, besides, before Justinian, many charitable regulations had been published in their favor. Except in case of contumacy, it was no longer permitted, as formerly, for every delay of payment to seize immediately the pro-

---

[1] Let this law, adds Justinian, dictated by principles of piety and humanity, serve as a safeguard for the indigent against an odious and barbarous process. (Justin., Nov., 32; *Ne quis mutuum, etc.*, Nov. 34.)

[2] Just., Nov. 60, *Ut defuncti*, etc., c. 1, ann. 534.

[3] Cod. Just., I, 12, *De his qui ad eccles.*, l. 6. It is the reproduction of a law of Leo the 1st, decreed in 466.

[4] Cod. Just., 1, 12.

perty of the debtor.[1] According to an edict of Constantine, it was not permitted to take in pledge for taxes either the slaves or cattle of the farmer, or any thing useful to him for working the land.[2] In case the pledges seized were not sufficient, instead of a criminal prison decreed by the ancient law, instead of a whip armed with lead, and other kinds of torture, to which the exactors usually had recourse, Constantine and his successors only permitted the use of the *custodia libera*.[3] They prohibited all abuse in the levy of imposts, and accorded to whom so ever believed himself injured in their assessment, a full right of recourse against the collectors.[4] Finally, edicts for the alleviation, or the momentary relief from tributes of the provinces or the cities over-taxed, abound in the codes and annals of the Christian emperors.[5]

Other abuses of power were equally repressed. Different laws, insufficient, without doubt, but dictated by undoubted motives of charity, protected the subjects from the extortions of advocates and the officers of justice, from the iniquity and venality of judges, and from the rapacity of provincial governors, the exactions of tax-gatherers, soldiers and military

---

[1] Cod. Just., X. 21, *De capiendis, etc.*, l. 1, 2, ann. 327, 354.

[2] Cod. Th., II. 30, *De pignor.*, l. 1, ann. 315.

[3] Men put in the house of a debtor in arrears.

[4] Cod. Th. XI. tit. 7, *De exact.*, l. 1, 3, 7; Cod. Just., X. 19, l. 2, etc. ann. 315, 320, 346.

[5] Euseb., *De vit. Const.*, IV. 2; Evagr., *Hist. eccles.*, Ed. Vales., III. 39; V. 13; Cod. Theod. et Justin., *passim, tit. de indulg. relig.*, *de indulg. debit.* Honorius, among others, published ten laws for the abatement of imposts, and Theod. the Younger, six. (Gothofr., IV. p. 192.)

tribunes.[1] The property of the wives and the children of the proscribed, instead of being seized at the same time with those of the guilty man, were distinguished and returned to their possessors.[2] It was forbidden to the magistrates to shut up any one any where except in the public prisons.[3] Such as appealed, in civil matters, were to be exempt from imprisonment and corporal penalties.[4] In fine, we have seen that, at the request of St. Ambrose, Theodosius, to prevent the effects of rash judgments, prescribed a delay of 30 days before every criminal execution.

It is thus, that the Christian emperors attempted to introduce into the law principles of charity, which, till then, had only penetrated these indirectly, and almost furtively. Through the texts we observe this marked tendency of civil morals to approximate Christian morals; a tendency so much the more praise-worthy, as, in general, it was in harmony with the respect due to acquired rights. The Christian emperors did not suppress the imposts, did not arrest the course of justice, but they tempered the rudeness, re-

---

[1] Cod. Theod., VIII. 10, l. 12, etc.; II. 10, *De postul.*, l. 1; *ibid.*, I. 7, 1, ann. 331, etc.; Evagr., *Hist. eccles.*, V. 13, *ad fin.;* Cod. Just., II. 20, l. 11, 12. XII. 42; IV. 61, l. 5. Peyron, Cod. Th., fr., p. 110, *seq.*, etc.

[2] Cod. Th., IX. 42, *De bono proscr.*, l. 1, ann. 321.

[3] *Ibid.*, tit. 11, *De priv. carc.*, ann. 388.

[4] *Ibid.*, XI. 30, *De appell.*, l. 2, ann. 314. Valentinian and Gratian had ordered that any confinement for a cause of importance, should cease from Easter. This regulation, dictated less by a feeling of humanity than by a principle of ill understood devotion, was not admitted in the Code Justinian. Only all prosecutions and criminal executions were prohibited during the whole of Lent.

pressed the violence of their agents; they neither abolished debts nor servitude; they did not force the master to enfranchise his *Colonus* or his slave, nor the creditor to discharge his debtor; they simply hindered them from an abuse of their rights; they prevented, on their part, as they denied to themselves, all gratuitous cruelty, all useless rigor, all that exceeded the measure of severity necessary to ensure the execution of the law; they introduced the unction of evangelical sweetness into the hard machinery of the civil administration; they covered feebleness and suffering with the shield of charity.[1]

But it is time to examine more especially what they did in behalf of the indigent.

CHAPTER X.

CONTINUATION. — SPECIAL MEASURES OF CIVIL POWER IN FAVOR OF THE INDIGENT.

As soon as Constantine was converted to Christianity, he authorized gifts and legacies in favor of the church, and thus secured for charitable foundations

[1] The heathen Libanius acknowledges, that under Constantine and his sons, legislation had become singularly tempered in behalf of the low classes, and that the unfortunate had been sheltered from fraud and violence. But he does honor for those measures only to the personal clemency of the emperors, and does not recognize the Christian principle, which had dictated them. (Libanius., *Basilic.*, II. p. 146, *seq.*)

the protection of the established laws which guarantied property. However, these foundations, so rapidly multiplied, were sometimes a temptation to cupidity, dilapidated by faithless administrators, turned aside from their destination by prodigal bishops, or, under pretext of nullity, confiscated by rapacious proconsuls. The Christian emperors, then, judging that the ordinary laws were insufficient, believed that they ought to take these foundations under their protection, and provide, by special measures, that the wish of the donors should be faithfully observed.

Whilst ordinary gifts were liable to be declared invalid when they had not a regular and determined destination, Valentinian III. and Marcian declared that legacies in favor of the poor should be maintained, even if the legatees were not designated.[1] Leo and Anthemius equally decreed that, notwithstanding the uncertainty of persons, every legacy or *fideicommissum*, made for the redemption of captives, should be in the course of the year, consecrated to that by the bishop of the place, unquestioned by any authority.[2] Justinian, whilst confirming these regulations, determined still more precisely to whom such donations were to be attributed. Some individuals, in their wills, designated Jesus Christ as the heir of all or part of their possessions, without indicating the church or chapel which was to profit by the legacy. Justinian, to prevent the breaking or contesting of wills, which might arise from this vague designation, decided that the legacy should be attributed to the church of the place

---

[1] Cod. Just., I. 3. *De episc et cler.*, l. 24, ann. 452.
[2] *Ibid.*, l. 28.

where the will was made, and should be employed by the steward of that church for the benefit of the poor.[1]

The private property of the bishops was to be carefully distinguished from that of the churches which they directed, in order that the latter might remain entirely appropriated, particularly to the relief of poverty.[2] The stewards were obliged, every year, to render an account of their administration to the bishops, and to restore to the ecclesiastical domain all that they had appropriated to themselves, in any manner, from it. The same rule was applied to the directors of the hospitals and houses for orphans, and it was provided, by severe rules, that they could not turn to their own profit, funds appointed for the poor.[3]

If any one had made a gift for the construction of a hospital, it having been commenced, was to be finished, even after the death of the donor, by the diligence of the steward and of the bishop of the place. The bishop, likewise, was to recover from heirs every pious or charitable legacy, and to transmit immediately the administration of it to the director most specially interested.[4]

It was forbidden to the bishop and every other person, to convert annuities constituted in favor of

---

[1] Cod. Just., I. 2, *De sacros. eccles.*, l. 27, ann. 530. Justinian settled also the case when a donation should be made in favor of a saint, an angel, or an archangel.

[2] Cod. Just., I. 3, l. 42, ann. 528.

[3] *Ibid.*, § 5, *et non. passim in Cod. Just.*, I.

[4] *Ibid.*, I. 2, l. 15 ; tit. 3, l. 46, ann. 530.

churches, and which were secured by mortgage on the property of the testator.[1] It was equally forbidden to alienate or exchange property given to hospitals, and, in general, to pious establishments, which "were to exist as long as the Christian name, that is, till the consummation of the ages. To these guarantees, and others like them, destined to secure the maintenance and integrity of establishments for benevolent purposes, the Christian emperors joined various privileges destined to favor their growth.

Justinian exempted from the obligation of being recorded (*intimatio in actis*) all donations made to the church, to hospitals or to the poor, which did not exceed the value of five hundred *solidi*, as well as those of any value which came from imperial largesses. He likewise freed from the duty of inscription (*lucrativorum inscriptionibus*) pious donations in general;[2] "for why, says he, should we not make a difference in human possessions and those of God?" The same motive caused Anastasius and Justinian to extend prescription in favor of the property of the churches and hospitals to forty years.[3]

---

[1] Cod. Just., tit. 3, l. 57, ann. 534; tit. 2, l. 14, 17, 22; laws of Leo the 1st, Anastasius and Justinian; Just., Nov. 7, *De non alienandis*, etc.

[2] *Ibid.*, I. 2, l. 19, 23, ann. 528, etc.

[3] Justinian extended it to 100 years, (Cod. Just., I. 2, l. 24, ann. 528;) so that the church had for one century an open recourse for the goods she thought to be hers. But, in 541, he deemed it proper to come back to the decree of Anastasius. (Nov. 131, c. 6.) The church of Rome alone preserved the privilege of the centennary prescription. (Nov. 9.)

Upon the reiterated solicitations[1] of the heads of the church, its possessions were freed from *corvées* and imposts, principally the extraordinary imposts, which were levied upon all other property.[2] Those who managed them, particularly the directors of the establishments for orphans, were assimilated to tutors, protected from all vexation, and freed from all expense for judiciary formalities.[3] Constance exempted from the *lustral* tax, levied on the profits of commerce, the *copiatæ* or grave-diggers, whom the Church of Rome employed for the gratuitous burial of the dead; and Constantine, Anastasius, and Justinian, freed from all tribute the *ergasteria*, or offices at Constantinople for the same object.[4]

The poor being assisted from the ecclesiastical revenues, it was still an advantageous measure for them, which adjudged to the churches and the convents the property of the priests and monks who had

---

[1] St. Bazil and St. Gregory's epistles, among others, are full of petitions directed to the civil authority, in order to have exempted from taxes the charitable establishments they had founded. (Basil., ep. 142, 143, *ad percept.*, 284, 285, III. p. 235, 424, *seq.*) Basil writes to the assessor of Capadocia: "The property of the poor, far from being useful for those managing it, spreads itself into liberality, and the church is always more inclined to overreach her resources, than to reap benefit from her income." See, too, Greg. Naz., *Orat.*, 19, *ad Jul.*, c. 13, I. p. 371, et *Carm.*, II. p. 1014. . . "If Christ," says he, "chose to be born at the time of a census, it seems that his purpose was to teach collectors their duties of equity and mercy." (*Cf.* Ep. 67 et 68, *ad Jul.*, 98, *ad percept.*, 211, *ad Cyr.*, Opp., II. p. 60, 81, 176.)

[2] Cod. Theod., XI. 16, *De extraord.*, l. 21, 22, ann. 397.

[3] Cod. Just., I. 3, l. 2, 32, 33, 35, etc.; Nov. 131.

[4] Cod. Theod., XIII. 1, l. 1, ann. 357.

belonged to them, if they died intestate, without leaving either relatives or patrons. This was established by the new edicts.[1] In order that the part of the poor might be as large as possible, Justinian limited the number of ecclesiastics who ministered in the Cathedral of Constantinople, ordering the surplus of the revenues of this church to be consecrated to charitable and pious uses, specified by the donors.[2] Finally, he permitted, in case of scarcity, or for the purchase of captives, the vessels and other objects belonging to the sacred treasury, to be given in pledge, and even to be alienated.[3]

But, is this all that the Christian emperors did in behalf of indigence? Were they satisfied with seconding, by laws and regulations, the charitable action of the church and of its members? Did they not themselves allot any funds, any donation for this object, which they appear to have had so much at heart?

In the enumeration of their Christian largesses, we ought naturally to commence by setting aside the distributions already established under their pagan predecessors, the *congiaria* to the people, the *donativa* to the army. The extraordinary gifts on the days of installation, continued, as formerly, as long at least as it was permitted by the finances of the empire.[4]

---

[1] Cod. Theod., V. 3, *De bon. cler. et mon.*, ann. 534.

[2] Justin., Nov. 3, c. 1–3.

[3] Cod. Just., I. 2, *De sacros. ecc.*, l. 21, Nov. 120, c. 9, 10, ann. 541.

[4] As an example we may quote the rich *congiaria* which Constantine distributed to the people of his new capital, on the wedding-day of his two sons, corresponding with the 20th and the 30th anniversary of his reign. (Euseb., *De vit. Const.*, III. 22; IV. 49.)

It was the same with the regular distribution of bread and other provisions to the people of the great capitals; it was thought impossible, without danger, to withhold from the turbulent citizens of Rome this ancient tribute of prudence or of fear.[1] When Constantine had chosen a new capital, he thought that he could not refuse to it the privilege enjoyed by Rome; the inhabitants of Constantinople had their regular rations of provisions, which, reduced one half by Constantine, in consequence of a theological riot, were bestowed upon them again, in full, by that emperor, and afterwards were augmented by Theodosius.[2] Finally, as most of the supplies of grain, destined for these two cities, came from Egypt, it was necessary, for fear of seeing them frequently famished, to assure the same privilege to the inhabitants of Alexandria, who, from jealousy, would not have failed to intercept or retard the convoys. This new measure, already ordered by Diocletian, received an extension under Theodosius, the Younger.[3] Besides, in the intention of these princes, it was so little a measure of charity that Constantine, anxious to see the construction of

---

[1] After several attempts at reduction, just as useless as those made under Augustus, this tribute was confirmed by Valentinian the 1st. (Naudet, *Sec. publ.*, *ub. sup.*, p. 47.)

[2] Naudet, *Sec. publ.*, p. 48–50; Baldwin, *Const. Magn.*, p. 139, *seq.;* Gothof., *in Cod. Theod.*, V. p. 235; Sozom., *Hist. eccles.*, III. 7, etc.

[3] Gothofr., *ub. sup.*, p. 269; Cod. Theod., XIV. 26, *De frum. Alex.*, l. 2, ann. 436; Moreau de Jonnès, *Statist.*, II. p. 473. On Libanius's demand, Julian granted likewise a supply of wheat to the city of Antioch during a dearth. (Liban., *Leg. ad Jul.*, Opp. II. p. 152.

his new capital completed, caused the distributions of provisions, which he granted to them, to be given, not, as might be thought, to the poor without bread and shelter, but, on the contrary, to the possessors of houses,[1] so that it was necessary, as has been said, to be a proprietor in order to figure on this Golden Book of indigence.

Besides, in these distributions, there was absolutely nothing that recalled the Christian alms; neither priests nor deacons were charged with them, but the magistrates; they were made not in the hospitals nor at the doors of the churches, but from the height of the public places, to all citizens who were entered in the records of the *annona*.[2]

Perhaps we must see rather a measure of police than of charity in what the emperors did for the gratuitous burial of the dead at Rome and at Constantinople. Constantine allowed the church of the latter city the rent of nine hundred and fifty houses, (*ergasteria*) destined to support the same numbers of *lecticarii* or bearers for the interments. Under the reign of Julian, George, the Arian bishop, attempted to abolish this institution, which was re-established by the son of Theodosius. In the fifth century Anastasius added one hundred and fifty *ergasteria* more, with a supplementary revenue of seventy pounds of gold; Justinian confirmed this new donation, charging the patriarch of Constantinople to see that the interments were gratuitous for all those whose relatives should demand it, as well as for the institutions

---

[1] Cod. Th., XIV. 17, l. 1, 12, etc.

[2] *Ibid.*, XIV. tit. 17, *De annon. civil. et pane gradili.*

of benevolence.[1] Notwithstanding this, and though the sepulture of the dead had at all times been among the works of charity recommended by the church, we may believe that these measures, restricted, as we have seen, to the two capitals of the empire, were principally dictated by motives of public hygiene.

The marks of Christian charity are more perceptible in the new traits which we proceed to indicate.

Eusebius shows Constantine to us from the moment of his conversion, occupied with zeal in the relief of his subjects, himself distributing money, provisions, and clothes to the indigent of the provinces which he passed through, to the beggars whom he saw wandering about the public squares, generously repairing, by presents of lands, dignities and employments, the breaches which some families, formerly opulent, had suffered; assisting helpless widows, acting as a father to their children, establishing in marriage, and endowing poor orphans; in a word, doing good to all those who approached him, "shedding, like the sun, his vivifying influence on all who were within the sphere of his rays."[2]

The authors of those times speak with the same enthusiasm of the charities of St. Helena, the mother

---

[1] Cod. Just., l. 2, l. 18; Justin., Nov. 43 and 59, ann. 554; *Cf.* Leo 1, Nov. 12; Baldwin, *Const. Magn.*, p. 21, *seq.* This institution was still existing in Leo, the Philosopher's time.

[2] Euseb., *Hist. eccles.*, X. 6; *De vit. Const.*, I. 42–43; III. 1; IV. 28, 44. The same prince charged the bishop of Antioch with the distribution of thirty thousand bushels of wheat in a famine. After the war, he invited his soldiers to clemency, and gave them a certain sum for each enemy they saved. (Ryan, *Bienf. de la rel. chr.*, p. 196.)

of Constantine,[1] and of those of the Empress Placilla, wife of Theodosius.[2] Pulcheria, sister of Theodosius the Younger, after having established, during her life, many pious foundations, left her whole estate to the poor, and this disposition was ratified by her husband, Marcian.[3] Anastasius I. and Mauritius, each made considerable presents to the poor.[4] Tiberius II. paid to his own soldiers the ransom of the Persian captives, whom he sent back into their own country;[5] distributed to the unfortunate the treasure left by his predecessors, and replied to his mother, who reproached him with this excess of liberality: "The treasure will not be empty, if the poor are assisted and the captives redeemed; for the Lord says that such are real treasures."[6]

As soon as the Church had commenced founding almshouses and hospitals, and experience had shown the benefits of them, the Christian emperors displayed much zeal in enriching them and in augmenting their number. Constance re-established, at Constantinople, the hospital founded by St. Zoticus.[7] Valens, in the admiration which the charity of St. Basil inspired him with, gave to him, for his infirmary, some fine estates which he had in Cappadocia.[8] The Empress

---

[1] Euseb., *De vit. Const.*, III. 44, 47; Socr., *Hist. eccles.*, I. 17; Sozom., II. 2.

[2] Greg. Nyss., *Orat. funer. de Plac., ad fin.*

[3] On the charity of these two princes, see Sozom., IX. 3; Evagr., II. 1; Theophan., *Chronogr.*, ed. reg., p. 65, 91.

[4] Greg. Magn., *Epp.* VIII. 2, *ad Maurit.*

[5] Le Bas, *Hist. du moyen âge*, III. 1.

[6] Ryan, *ub. sup.*, p. 189.

[7] Du Cange, *Fam. Byz.*, *Const. chr.*, IV. 9.

[8] Theodoret., *Hist. eccles.*, IV. 19.

Eudoxia founded several hospitals in Palestine. Pulcheria had some built elsewhere, and joined *Xenodochia* to them for strangers, and *Xenotaphia*, or establishments, for their sepulture.[1] To all the magnificence of his reign, Justinian wished to add that of charity. The *Xenôn* of Sampson had been consumed during the sedition of Constantinople, with all its patients in it. He caused it to be reconstructed in greater splendor, and augmented its annual revenue. Near it, he founded two other similar hospitals, ordered a place of prostitution to be destroyed; conveyed its unhappy inmates to a monastery of penitents, which he had built on the site of the ancient palace, and joined to it a refuge[2] for women whom want might drive to shame. He afterwards re-established an old house for the poor, who were afflicted incurably, which time had destroyed; restored in the same manner and endowed many hospitals (*nosocomia*) in the provinces; had an asylum built on the road to Jerusalem, for pilgrims and the sick; finally he founded, in concert with Theodora, his wife, several *Xenodochia* for the inhabitants of the provinces, who came from all quarters to solicit, or to seek for fortune in Constantinople, and who, deceived in their hopes, and more miserable than before, wandered about in that capital without asylum and without resources.[3] Assuredly, it would have been better for Justinian not to have overwhelmed his subjects with imposts;

[1] Sozom., IX. 1, 3; Theoph., *Chronogr.*, p. 91.

[2] Παραψυχή.

[3] Evagr., *Hist. eccles.*, IV. 30; Procop., *De ædif. Justin.*, I. 2, 9, 11; Du Cange, *ub. sup.*

not to have exhausted them with interminable wars; not to have exposed them to the barbarity of the farmers of the public revenue;[1] in a word, not to have engendered misery to be afterwards relieved. But all the Princes did not repair, as he did, the faults of a bad administration; many ruined their subjects for quite other dotations than those of hospitals and of houses of penitents. After him, Justin, the Younger, Mauritius, Tiberius, and their successors, established also at Constantinople asylums for the sick and for the aged.[2]

At an epoch when the emperors disposed so arbitrarily of the fortunes of their subjects, and when their own individual property was confounded, for the most part, with that of the State, it is difficult to decide if the fundations of which we have just spoken, were of the domain of public or private beneficence. We incline, however, to the latter opinion. It seems to us, as to De Gérando, that in most of these cases the emperors acted rather as simple members of the church, though with the liberality befitting their rank,[3] consecrating to private deeds of charity funds which nothing would have hindered them, had they wished it, from lavishing upon ostentatious caprices.

But there are works of a nature more general, in which we see them acting as heads of the State, as administrators of the public fortune; such are the

---

[1] Evagr., *Hist. eccles.*, IV. 30.

[2] See the enumeration of them in Du Cange, *ub. sup.*

[3] De Gérando, *Bienf. publ.*, I. p. 500.

two foundations of Constantine, of which mention must be made.

Theodoret relates that this emperor ordered the provincial prefects to levy each year from the revenues of the cities, a certain number of measures of wheat, to distribute them to the widows, to women who took the vow of celibacy, and to those who fulfilled the duties of the sacred ministry. "He meted out this aid, adds Theodoret, much less according to the need of those to whom he accorded it, than to his own munificence."[1] Elsewhere, the historians, in relating this decree, only mention the churches and the clergy, among whom it is known[2] that the virgins and consecrated widows were included.[3] It seems then, that this was, on the part of Constantine, a deed of piety as much as of benevolence; one of those subsidies which the empire, having become christianized, accorded to the church for the necessities of its worship and of its ministers. However it may be, the allowance in question, soon became a subject of contention between the different Christian parties. The bishops were charged with its distribution: the orthodox church alone had enjoyed it at first. The Arians of Egypt and Libya, indignant at being excluded from it, accused St. Athanasius of having appropriated to him-

---

[1] Theodoret., *Hist. eccles.*, I. 11.

[2] 4th, Conc. Carth., can. 103, (Labbe, *Conc.*, II. p. 1207;) Chrys., hom. 30 *in Cor.*, c. 4, X. p. 274.

[3] Sozom., I. 8, ἐκκλησίαις και κληροῖς. Theodoret himself, when speaking of them in regard to Jovian, speaks but of churches, (*ub. sup.*, IV. 4.)

self the profits, and had decreed to themselves, by the Emperor Constance, the privilege of distributing it for the future.[1] Julian harmonized the two parties by suppressing the allowance. Jovian re-established it, reduced to a third, it is true, because of the famine which then raged;[2] but yet a considerable sum, according to Theodoret.[3] It existed still in the days of this historian, about the middle of the fifth century.[4] It is, probably,[5] that which Valentinian III. and Marcian, in their edict of the year 454 maintained. "As humanity makes it our duty, they say, to provide for the necessities of the poor, and to see that the means of subsistence do not fail them, we guarantee, in perpetuity, to the church, these subventions (*salaria,*) which heretofore have been allowed to them in different forms by the treasury."[6] Justinian in inserting this law into his code, seemed to pledge himself to a continuation of the same aid; however, it is observable, that in the enumeration of the public expenses, which he places to the charge of the municipalities, he makes no mention of any charitable establishment kept up at the expense of the cities or of the state.[7]

---

[1] Athanas., *Apol. cont. Arian.*, c. 18, Opp. I, p. 138.

[2] A new proof, perhaps, that it was an assistance granted to the church rather than to the indigent.

[3] Theodoret., *Hist. eccles.*, IV. 4.

[4] *Ibid.*, I. 11.

[5] Such is the opinion of Godofred, (*Not. in Cod. Just.*, I. 2. 12, p. 32).

[6] Cod. Just., I. 2, *De sacros. eccles.*, l. 12.

[7] Moreau, du *Probl. de la misère*, I. p. 295, note. Let us add that this portion of Valentinian's and Marcian's edict is not in the Basilios, which contain however its first paragraph. (Fabrot., *Basilic.*, V. 5, 1).

It is probable, then, that these subventions had already ceased, not only in the West, at the fall of the empire, but even in the East, since the reign of Justinian; and, in general, it is known that in the middle ages, the church counted for the support of the poor and of the clergy, much more upon the income from its own funds, than upon the annual allocations of the treasury or the contributions of the cities.

The other foundation of Constantine had much more the character of a work of charity, but it was of shorter duration.

It has been seen, above, that some of the pagan emperors, desirous of repeopling Italy, had established in that province, a certain fund for the maintenance of poor children, whose parents would engage to raise them. It has been also seen that this subsidy, wholly local and partial as it was, soon ceased from a failure of resources, which it was necessary to supply, occasionally, by private gifts. Constantine revived this enterprise upon a more extensive plan and with more Christian views. He saw in it, according to M. Naudet,[1] less an empire to repeople, or a population to renew, than human existences to preserve. He made of it the complement of his laws against exposition and parricide; perhaps, even as Gothofredus supposes, he yielded on this occasion to the solicitations of Lactantius, whose expressions[2] offer, in effect, some resemblance to those of the two edicts of Constantine. "Let there be published in all the province, said the emperor to the Governors of

[1] Naudet, *Des secours publ.*, *ub. sup.*, p. 79.
[2] Lactant., *Inst. div.*, VI. 20.

Italy, a law which shall turn our subjects from parricide. If any parents bring to thee their children, declaring, in view of their poverty, that they are not in a state to raise them, speedily furnish to them food and clothing, for assistance to new-born babes must be speedy. We place at your disposition, to this effect, the resources of the imperial treasury, together with our own."[1] In 322, he addressed the same recommendation to the Governor of Africa, adding these words, which clearly indicate the spirit of the law: "It is repugnant to our manners to leave unhappy children to perish of hunger, or parents to resort to an atrocious crime."[2]

This kind of assistance, analogous, on the one hand, to the poor-tax in England, on the other, to the communal and departmental reliefs used in France for abandoned children, like these, soon exhausted all the resources fixed upon to be consecrated to it.[3] The public and the imperial treasury put under contribution, were soon unable to respond to the demands of negligent or poor parents. In the interval, the wealth of the church had increased, she had opened her monasteries, founded her *brephotrophia* and her *orphanotrophia;* and to her the emperors

---

[1] "Fiscum nostrum et rem privatam." (Cod. Th., XI. 27, *De aliment.*, etc., l. 1, ann. 315.)

[2] *Ibid.*, l. 2.

[3] If we, however, compare this measure to the French law of 1811 upon the same subject, we cannot forbear acknowledging that it was superior to it in two respects. 1st. By admitting children to public assistance, but on the presentation of their parents, it did not make their abandonment on the part of the latter so easy. 2d. By assisting them in the paternal house, instead of having

henceforth referred the care of rescuing these poor creatures from the grave. Therefore the edicts of Constantine, cited above, were not admitted into the Justinian Code. Public charity exhausted, abdicated anew, and left definitively this charge to voluntary and private charity.

It appears, then, that as to charitable institutions, the part of the Christian emperors at this epoch, was much less to found themselves, than to recognize, to regulate, to guarantee, sometimes also to enrich with their private gifts, that which the church had founded. Every where the initiative had been taken by religious charity. Public charity only followed in the distance, and when it attempted to go ahead originally and alone, it soon found that it had strayed aside, and was constrained to withdraw.

---

them brought up with strangers or hirelings, it respected the bonds of the family, bonds that are never relaxed or broken but to the great prejudice of society itself.

RECAPITULATION AND CONCLUSION.

PAST AND FUTURE OF CHARITY.

WHATEVER portion of history we may study, it is only by numerous facts, drawn from authentic and contemporaneous sources, that we can flatter ourselves that we may recall the past, to serve as a light and guide to the present.

We proposed to do this in the preceding work. While attempting to seize the true spirit of Christian charity during the first six centuries, we have circumstantially related its efforts in the Roman world, what it did in behalf of the suffering classes, the works which it inspired, the measures which it dictated or obtained in their favor. We will now group the facts, which have just passed before our eyes in detail, to enable ourselves to form a general idea of the influence of charity during that period, and to draw from them, as we have announced, some summary inductions concerning the part it is called upon to fill in our days.

It is with misery as with all the other evils of this world which we must seek to relieve, but which above all, and as far as possible, we must strive to prevent.

At an early hour charity undertook this double task. By turns, it strove to relieve the privations which spring from indigence, and to diminish or dispel the causes of this scourge.

We are then called upon to distinguish here, as it is usually done, its subventive and its preventive action, and to recapitulate separately what it did in these two respects.

SECT. I. — SUBVENTIVE ACTION OF CHARITY.

THAT we may the better appreciate the subventive action of charity, let us compare it with that of the system of assistance in vigor among the Romans, at the same epoch; and, above all, let us recall the principles which serve as the basis of each of these two systems.

In the Roman subventive system, as in that which it is proposed to-day to substitute for charity, all property was thought to be held of the State,[1] which

---

[1] Troplong, *Infl. du chr. sur le droit civ.*, p. 121; Giraud, *Journal des écon.*, II. p. 91. "According to the principles of the ancients," says Mr. Boeckh, "the State comprehended all interests, and ruled over them all; . . . all citizens were agreed that the State had rights upon the whole of private property." (*Econ. pol. des Athén.*, transl., Paris, 1828, I. p. 86.) There is nothing more positive on this point than the following passage drawn from Plato: "I declare to you, in my capacity of a legislator, that I consider neither you, nor your property, as belonging to yourselves, but to your family; . . . and your family and their property as belonging still more to the state." (Plato., *des Lois*, lib. XI. transl. by Cousin, VIII. p. 303.) This principle established in an absolute manner in the East, brought into credit, as just seen, among the Greeks, received likewise, though in a somewhat mitigated form, a sanction in the Roman world. There it was derived from conquest. "War," says Troplong, "had given to the State the

could, at will, make use of it either directly or through a possessor, while relieving certain classes of persons. It was by virtue of this, that the State distributed to citizens the conquered lands; that it levied out of the public funds the *congiaria*, or gratifications given on certain days to the people or the army; that, out of the tributes paid by the provinces, it caused provisions to be daily distributed to the poor citizens of Rome. By virtue of this, again intervening in the relations of patron and client, it fixed the amount of the *sportula*, which they were to receive each day, and which the patron had to guarantee to them after his death.[1]

The Christian system traces the right of property still higher; it assigns to it a divine origin.

God, the Creator of all things, was also the supreme dispensator of all property.[2] He gave it to each, upon conditions which pleased Him; and one of these conditions was, that it should be used to aid those of His children who needed the necessities of life. But this was not an obligation of human and positive right; it was, as has been seen, an obligation purely religious and moral, based upon faith, prescribed to conscience, the observation of which was secured by no civil and even by no ecclesiastical sanction; whilst Roman as-

---

conquered territory; the victorious army occupied it only *collectively*. It was Numa who had made the first division of lands. But the original right of the State appeared in a multitude of institutions, particularly in the system of imposts." (Troplong, *de la propr. dans le code civ.*, p. 12–19.) It is found also entire in the system of Roman assistance.

[1] Naudet, *Secours publ. chez les Rom.*, *ub. sup.*, p. 82, *seq.*, 89.

[2] Troplong, *Infl. du Christ.*, p. 121.

sistance was ordered and guaranteed by law, Christian assistance was absolutely free and voluntary.

From this fundamental difference in the principles upon which they rested, flows that of their effects in the relief of want.

The Roman system, in creating for the poor a positive right to assistance, had the inevitable effect of excluding from their heart all sentiments of gratitude, and, at the same time, of infinitely raising their pretensions. Who believes himself obliged by those who only acquit a debt? Who is not rather disposed to believe that they do not acquit it fully enough, or soon enough? Never was legal assistance sufficient for the avidity of Roman citizens; their wants increased with the assiduity shown to satisfy them. In the first place, wheat was sold to them at a reduced price; after the year of Rome, 695, it was necessary to give it to them gratuitously. Under Augustus, it was distributed to them every fourth month; afterwards, it was every month, and after Aurelian, it was necessary to distribute it to them every day. In the beginning, only the eighth part of the citizens domiciled at Rome were assisted. After Cato, the Censor, it was the third; Julius Cæsar found that it was more than three-fourths of them. In vain, did he try, by sending out colonies, to reduce this frightful proportion. Under Augustus, the number of the assisted already amounted to more than two hundred thousand. At first, only corn or bread was given to them; subsequently oil and pork were added. Under Honorius, the distribution was for five months, four thousand pounds of bread a day. Under Valentinian III., it rose to more than ninety thousand.[1] Was the promised assistance momentarily exhausted, or was it delayed, the people of Rome, of Constantinople, and of Alexandria, manifested a dissatisfaction which soon arose to dangerous fury. In 359, the convoy of grain having been retarded a few days, Tertullius, the prefect of Rome, was near being torn into pieces by the populace. He escaped only by giving his children in hostage to them.[2] We have seen that, in similar cases, more than one emperor was in danger for his crown, and even for his life.

Christian assistance, purely voluntary, was not exposed to the same dangers. Without doubt, the funds of charity, known to be placed in the hands of the church, gave birth among the poor to an expectation which occasionally was exacting. Some of the assisted widows, on comparing themselves with their companions, were ready to charge their benefactors with injustice; and Chrysostom, in his Treatise on the Priesthood, enables us to see how their complaints and murmurs sometimes tried the patience of the bishop who assisted them.[3] Elsewhere, however, he renders a more honorable testimony of them; "In spite of their misery," says he, "you never hear them blaspheme. They often pass the night hungry and cold, and yet they do not cease to give thanks; they are grateful for the least farthing that is given to them, and are not offended with a refusal, contenting

[1] Naudet, *loc. cit.*, p. 19, 23, 64, *seq.*, Moreau, *du Probl. de la mis.*, I. p. 348–352.

[2] Amm. Marc., XIX. 10, p. 222, *seq.*

[3] Const. Apost., III. 14; Chrys., *De Sacerd.*, III. 16, I. p. 396.

themselves with the bread of each day."[1] Elsewhere, again, he describes the poor of the Church of Antioch, as silently waiting for alms before the sanctuary; and at evening, when they had not obtained from the passers-by the morsel of bread necessary to keep them alive, he shows them to us importunate, sometimes impudent, but never dangerous or malicious; and it was but in dreams alone that the avaricious, according to the same Father, were an object of the outrages and misdeeds of the beggars whom they had sent away.[2]

Roman assistance, in extravagantly exciting the pretensions of the poor, was at the same time degrading to them; for, it was only granted to them at the price of services and acts which were unworthy of free men. "The common people," says Cicero, "have but one means of obliging us, or of recognizing our good offices; that is, to follow us in a crowd when we are seeking honors. Let us suffer that those who hope all from us should also do something for us; it would be little if they did not give us their suffrage."[3] Thus, the patron, who, in the morning caused the *sportula* to be thrown to his client, counted through the day upon his escort in the forum, and in the evening upon his suffrage in the *comitia*. The Prætor, who, on the first day of the year, gorged the populace at his own expense, with meats and wine, counted, in return for this good cheer, to be promoted to new offices. Nero, in doubling and trebling these

---

[1] Chrys., hom. 30 *in Cor.*, c. 4, X. p. 274.
[2] Chrys., *ibid.*, et Serm. 5 *in Gen.*, c. 3, 4, IV. p. 668–670.
[3] Cicer., *Pro Muren.*, c. 34.

gratifications,[1] exacted in return that the usual acclamations should be doubled and trebled; he forced the people to offer incense, in his person, to the vilest wretch Rome had produced. Those Romans whom we have seen lately so insolent, then crouched before the son of Agrippina; they adored that parricidal but liberal hand. Besides, what better could be expected of a people brought up in mendicity? Nothing could be less discreet than alms at Rome. The list of the assisted, engraved upon brass, was exposed to all eyes. Each day they came, their *tessera* in hand, to receive the alms delivered to them from the highest public platform. Thus, at Rome, the police of assistance required it.

Christian charity had more regard for the poor. It respected, in him, the dignity of a child of God. In aiding him, it honored him; in relieving him, it elevated him. Not waiting that he should come to humiliate himself, it went about seeking the virtuous and timid poor; while relieving his poverty, it spared his modesty;[2] it protected in him that flower of delicacy which is the most precious guarantee of his virtues, and which is never withered with impunity.

Roman assistance, accorded in the name of the State, took no account but of the civil rights of the assisted; it remained a stranger to all moral considerations. Whether the indigent was laborious or idle, honest or vicious, economical or extravagant, whether his poverty was the result of his misfortunes or his

---

[1] Le Bas, *Hist. Rom.*, II. p. 212; Moreau, *du Probl. de la mis.*, I. p. 364.

[2] Leo Magn., Serm. 4, *De coll.*, Opp., p. 6.

faults, he was equally entitled to the legal subventions; and, if there were any preference, it was in favor of the intriguing, who knew how to gain protectors for himself;[1] of the beggar who knew how to render himself importunate; of the seditious, who could make himself feared. For a long time the sad effect of the civic *annona* had been foreseen. "When under the tribunate of Caius Gracchus, it was agitated to distribute, each month, a bushel of corn to the poor plebeians, Cicero says, that law was very agreeable to the people, to whom it ensured an abundance of food without the necessity of any work; but it displeased wise men, because it was calculated only to exhaust the treasury and to make the people live in idleness.[2]

The event proved that these fears were far from being exaggerated. Alms, indiscriminately accorded by the State, were not only an encouragement to improvidence and laziness,[3] but a premium to prodigality and to debauchery. The Roman populace was not only the most idle, and, as has been seen, the most turbulent, but it was also one of the most dissolute and the most given to debauch. Ammian paints to us these pensioned sluggards, busy from the dawn of day at playing dice, drinking in the taverns, brawling on the public squares, running to the circus

---

[1] Naudet, *ub. sup.*, p. 42.

[2] Cicer., *Pro Publ.*, *Sext.*, c. 48. Pericles was likewise reproached with having by the establishment of *theorical* funds, made his fellow-citizens lazy, greedy, talkative and profligate. Boeckh, *Econ. pol. des Ath.*, I. p. 356.)

[3] "Alimenta inertiæ," says Valerius Maxim.

and the theatre, to the shows of mountebanks, and every where where they had a chance to satisfy their greediness or gluttony.[1] Certainly, if, as Voltaire has said,[2] it was a *noble usage* to furnish grain to the people through three hundred and twenty-seven granaries, it was not at least by the nobleness of the sentiments which this usage inspired them with, nor the habits which it caused them to contract.

A reproach has sometimes been made to Christian alms, of an excessive indulgence for those whom it assisted; even in the times of which we have retraced the history, under the empire, of the imperious circumstances which forced it to enlarge its instrumentalities, we have seen that it did not always take a pride in the most severe discernment. What superiority, however, had it not, in this respect, over the assistance furnished by Rome! Its most abundant assistance was always for the unhappy, incapable of taking care of themselves; and if, in this category, it sometimes aided persons but little worthy of interest, never, at least, did it sacrifice the true poor to the shameless beggar; always it proportioned its benefits to merit, and its gifts to the good use made of them. The distributions made in the homes of the needy, furnished it one of the surest guarantees for that. The deacons, charged with these distributions, soon intimately knew each of the families assisted, and observed carefully the use made of the aid furnished. Later, when the multiplicity of wants had rendered this detailed administration difficult and almost impossible; when

[1] Amm. Marc., *Rer. Gest.*, XIV. 6; XXVIII. 4, p. 29, 534.
[2] *Dict. philos.*, Art. Charité.

vast establishments had become necessary, and the office of the deacons had been replaced, in part, by that of the hospitalers, the Church did not cease to exert an active oversight over the morals of those whom it assisted. According to an ancient usage, which Julian admired, and which he would have been willing to have introduced among the pagans,[1] it carefully distinguished the strangers and travellers furnished with a recommendation from their bishop, from those who were addressed to them as unknown and not yet tried.[2] It enjoined on the priests a serious inquest on the persons whom they entered upon the roll of widows and virgins to be assisted.[3] It struck from the roll those who, once admitted, lived in idleness or in disorder; it excluded from its hospitals and its monasteries, the vicious who would have carried the scandal of their bad examples there;[4] it checked and sent away the monks who only sought in the cloister a life less painful, or a subsistence more secure.[5] In a word, it remembered that before being the asylum of distress, it was, from God, a school of virtue and sanctification.

But let us pass by, if it seems well, the moral

---

[1] Greg. Naz., *in Jul.*, c. 111, I. p. 139.

[2] Letters given to persons of an established morality were called ἐπιστολια or εἰρηνικά. Those given to travellers, not fully recommended, (πρόσωπα ἐν ὑπολήψει) were called συστατικά. (Conc. Chalc., can, 11; Labbe, IV. p. 761.)

[3] Chrys., *De Sacerd.*, III. 17; I. p. 399.

[4] Basil., *Reg. fus. int.* 10, II. p. 352, *seq.*

[5] August., *De op. monach.*, XXVI. Pope Gregory the Great made numerous ordinances for the discipline of monasteries. (Lau, *Greg. Magn.*, p. 126–131.)

effects of the one and the other system of assistance, and let us limit ourselves to the comparison of their positive results, their material effects.

Roman assistance, emanating from power, embraced only those categories of persons which it suited power to attach to itself; first, the army which made and unmade emperors; then the people of some large capitals; then the slaves and the artisans enrolled in the public workshops. One whole category was excluded. If, upon a day of scarcity, some sufferers came to seek in Rome the bread they needed, a pitiless privilege closed its entry against them and drove away, without distinction, beggars, strangers, provincials, Italians even; every one who was not of the sovereign people, or necessary to its pleasures—citizen or player.[1]

Exercised in the name of the Common Father of all, Christian charity knew neither these exclusions, nor these preferences. To its eyes there were neither foreigners nor natives, nor citizens, nor subjects, nor people of the capital, nor people of the provinces. It extended over all the surface of the empire, like a vast tissue of benevolence. There was no city, no hamlet, which, with its church and its priest, had not its treasure for the poor; no desert which had not its hospitable convent for travellers. The compassion of the church was open to all. If, by a very natural preference, it first helped its own children, the pagans were never, at this epoch, formally excluded from its favors; and often, even, especially in the first three centuries, they shared in them abundantly.

[1] Amm. Marc., XIV. 6.

Roman assistance, exacted as an impost, only relieved certain categories of persons in oppressing the others. It was the money raised out of subjects, tributaries, and the proscribed, which paid for the magnificent liberalities of Augustus.[1] The crops of Sardinia, Sicily, Spain, Africa and Asia, were put under contribution to provision Rome. Egypt alone was taxed two hundred and seventy, then three hundred and twenty millions of pounds. This tribute was still increased under Tiberius; when it did not suffice, wheat was bought, but at a low price and prejudicial to the vendors.[2] Thus whole provinces were stripped, that some thousands of citizens in one city alone might live in idleness. What a leaven of discord and hostility in the State! Christian alms, on the contrary, asked as a favor, had, for him who gave them all the charm of a voluntary sacrifice; and, like all the sacrifices dictated by the heart, it fortified the sentiment that had inspired it. The Christian attached himself to his brothers whom he relieved with the same love one feels for a friend, on whom he has lavished his services. The richest offerings appeared to him light, he gave always with joy because he gave freely.

Exclusive and unjust as it was, did the Roman assistance, at least efficaciously, relieve those who received it; and did it wisely assert and proportion its aid to the necessity?

On the contrary, nothing was habitually more in-

---

[1] Naudet, *ub. sup.*, p. 67, *seq.*

[2] Dureau, *ub. sup.*, II. p. 431; Hegewisch., *ub. sup.*, p. 200.

sufficient, more precarious. As it had no other guarantee than the law, no other lever than constraint, it constantly failed before the resistance of men, or the force of events. Did a bad harvest, a war, a sedition, or a tempest, retard or diminish the supplies of provisions, no public resource, no individual sacrifice was there, to supply them; speculators, profiting by the public misfortunes, held back from consumption the little wheat that yet remained; the more rigorous the law appeared, the more the granaries closed, and the imperial treasury could only give that which it disposed of itself. The misfortunes of the empire came at last to dry up completely the sources of legal assistance. The gratuitous distributions, suspended at Rome during the revolt of Gildo, reduced afterwards to five months of the year, ceased after the definitive loss of Africa and of Sicily, and were, for a moment, re-established by Theodoric, only to cease definitively after his death.[1] At Constantinople, where they had also been from time to time interrupted, they were entirely suppressed by Heraclius, and replaced by an annual subsidy. of 600 pounds of gold, destined to keep bread at a moderate price.[2] These were all the traces which this institution, so vaunted, had left. It was the same with the gratuities so magnificent under the first emperors, so mean and soon null under the last. The founda-

---

[1] Gothofr., *in Cod. Th.*, V. p. 229; Naudet, *ub. sup.*, p. 57, 64; Moreau-Christ., *ub. sup.*, I. p. 351; Sismondi, *chute de l'empire Rom.*, c. 8; Le Bas, *Hist. du moy. âge*, p. 45, (ed. 1839.)

[2] Naudet, p. 50; Moreau de Jonnes, *Econ. dom. des Rom.* (*Journal des Econ.*, III. p. 64;) Moreau-Chr., *ub. sup.*, II. p. 294.

tions of Constantine himself, though suggested by a Christian thought, met the fortune of the other legal subsidies.[1] As to the distributions, to which law and usage subjected patrons, they ceased by the massacre or dispersion of the great families, and there soon remained almost nothing of all the resources of Roman assistance.

Those of Christian charity were, as has been seen, much more fruitful and much more durable. For it was the true source; instead of constraining the rich, it interested them, won them over, by persuasion, to the cause of the poor. A kind intermediarry between these two classes, which so many barriers separated before, it united them by a close sympathy; it caused to flow towards the unfortunate the treasures barrenly heaped up in the coffers of the rich. From the heights of society, till then frozen, petrified by egotism, it caused to flow vivifying fountains, which changed the face of the desert. At its word the monopolist opened his granaries; the miser poured out his gold; the vain woman stripped herself of her ornaments. In its ingenious activity, charity took upon itself all the forms required by the infinite variety of wants. By turns it satisfied the hunger; attended the old man in his infirmities; sat down, and prayed at the pillow of the sick; protected the widow; received the abandoned child; raised the orphan; assisted the dying; cared for man, and honored him, even in his inanimate remains. Did necessities increase; did misery threaten to intrude everywhere; charity was neither astonished nor discouraged by it. It organized collections, redoubled

---

[1] See above, Book II. c. 10, 11.

its solicitations, multiplied its resources by economy and learned to relieve, in mass, the evils which, before, it relieved in detail; it opened vast hospitals where each unfortunate person found suitable aid; or else, taking advantage of the spirit of renunciation, it sheltered poverty in the asylum of monasteries, and there assisted it at the same time with the products of toil and the gifts of piety. How many miseries of all kinds were succored by these diverse means! And how right was St. John, the Almoner, in saying that the *treasures of God* are inexhaustible![1] Without these precious resources, spread over the whole empire, without this charity, which, like a bountiful rain, watered all its surface, where would have ceased the sufferings of the wretched populations? What would have become of those peasants who, according to Gaudentius, bishop of Brescia, to escape death from hunger, had no other resource than the alms of the church?[2] Without the charity of a St. Patientius, a St. Gregory, how many thousands more would have been cut down by the famines of Gaul and of Italy! In fine, during the invasions of the Barbarians, amidst the sacking of cities and of provinces, what, without the devotedness of Paulinus, of Deogratias, and others like them, would have become of so many captives, whom no one would have redeemed; of wandering families, whom no one would have received; of fugitives, who would have

---

[1] Fleury, *Hist. eccles.*, XXXVII. 11, § 1.

[2] Gaudent., *Serm. de nat. dom.*, (*in Orthodoxogr.*, p. 1838.)

found hospitality nowhere![1] If it is true, as most historians confess, that the weight of imposts, misery and depopulation, were the most active causes of the ruin of the empire; and if the charity of Christians was almost the sole counterpoise offered to so many scourges, who can dispute with it the honor of having not only mitigated, but perhaps retarded, for many years, this catastrophe?

However it may be, its influence long survived the misfortunes of the empire. Whilst nothing remained of the institutions of Roman assistance, Christian charity, bequeathed to the Middle Ages, like a precious palliative, its innumerable foundations, its hospitals,[2] its monasteries, without speaking of its brotherhoods, associations of provision perhaps more than of charity, but also instituted under the auspices and patronage of the church.[3]

Unfortunately there is hardly a power in the world, however beneficent it may be, which, when it is not under the control of another power, or closely watched by opinion, does not, sooner or later, abuse the credit which it has acquired by its services. The laws by which Justinian had provided for the main-

---

[1] St. Ambrose asked the heathens of his time, where were the captives whom their temples redeemed, the poor they assisted, the exiles whose subsistence they secured. (Ambr. *contra Symm.*)

[2] In the Middle Ages, Constantinople had as many as 37 hospitals or hospices, the most of them dated from the epoch which we are now considering. (See their enumeration in Du Cange.) In the XIth century, the Emperor Alexis founded a hospital that contained, itself, 10,000 poor.

[3] De Gérando, *Bienf. publ.*, III. p. 61; Blanqui, *Hist. de l'écon. pol.*, II. c. 19.

tenance and faithful administration of the funds of charity, had had but little authority in the West. The church, the patrimony of which had always been considered as that of the poor, continued in the Middle Ages to receive, in their name, rich donations; but it often allotted to them only a small part; the rest served for appanages to the cadets of noble families, or sometimes to support idle prelates in luxury. The property of the hospitals, having passed successively into the ecclesiastical revenues, often profited the administrators more than the sick.[1] Rich monasteries were seen, limiting themselves, as to assistance, to distributing at their door some rations of soup and bread. As the spirit of charity disappeared, fanaticism took its place. The church, forgetting its ancient impartiality, excluded from its assistance, and even from its pity, those who thought otherwise than itself.[2] Finally, when industry began to revive in the West, the reproach could be made to some of the religious orders, of seeking less to favor than to paralyze the impulse; of fostering, by undiscerning alms, the spirit of improvidence and of inertness; of preferring daily to assist beggars in rags, rather than to encourage

[1] De Récalde, *Abr. hist. des hôp.*, p. 60, *seq.* See the grave charges raised in France, in the XVIth century, against the ecclesiastical management of the hospitals, (edicts of 1543, 1561, 1587;) Moreau, *Probl. de la mis.*, III. p. 358, note.; De Récalde, *ub. sup.*, p. 63.

[2] Hence, the remarkable development of industry and that of mutual charity, which we observe among some sects of the Middle Ages, among the Waldenses, the Albigenses, etc.; Ch. Schmidt, *Hist. des Cathares*, II. p. 156–161.

works which would have transformed them into free artisans.[1]

These abuses could not fail, at length, to provoke a lively and serious reaction.[2] It was a scandal to see property, that might have usefully stimulated industry, buried up or squandered away. The avidity of the clergy served for a pretext to that of the laymen. Kings, grandees, and people coveted, emulously appropriated to themselves, the spoils of the church. On the one hand, the possessions of the convents and hospitals were united to the public domain; elsewhere the administration of them was secularized;[3] almost everywhere religious authority lost the exclusive direction of the foundations of charity; from a purely ecclesiastical affair, which till then it had been, the assistance became an affair of administration and of civil police.

In thus returning, under different forms, to the Roman system, its evil consequences were soon seen to be renewed. The poor-tax, decreed in the name and by the authority of the State, has produced in England what the public distributions produced at Rome. By the side of blind largesses, the greater part of which impudence always receives, were measures of police, often cruel, always arbitrary and vexatious; enormous burthens always increasing and always insufficient, weighing upon agriculture and property; charity discouraged, as well as toil; the

---

[1] Du Châtel, *De la charité*, p. 42.

[2] Martin-Doisy, *Hist. de la charité*, p. 145; Mertz, *Armuth und Christ.*, p. 39, *seq.*

[3] De Récalde, *ub. sup.*, p. 62, *seq.*, 69, etc.

rich generous against their will, cursing in secret those whom they were forced to assist; the poor, ungrateful, discontented, improvident, dissipated, inclined to all kinds of vices, and capable of all kinds of excess; a swarming, miserable population, withheld only by force, and constrained to work only by the loss of liberty; finally, a frightful pauperism, daily growing worse, and extending like a leprosy over the whole country; such, in England, are the fruits of public assistance.[1] If it had not had the same effects in France, it is, as has been well explained,[2] because the aid has not been given like a debt; because the laws do not yet recognize the right of the poor to be nourished by the State;[3] because, up to the present

[1] See, on this matter, *Reports on adm. and oper. of the poor laws;* Lond., 1833; McFarland, *Recherches sur les pauvres*, c. 7, (Duquesnoy, *Rech. etc.*, V.;) Chalmers, *christ. and civ. econ.*, 1821, II. c. 10; Du Châtel, *De la charité*, p. 157, *seq.;* Naville, *de la char. lég.*, etc., etc. The fatal effects of the poor-tax have undoubtedly been tempered by the *poor-law amendment act* of 1834, which grants an assistance to valid indigents, only on the condition of an absolute seclusion in the workhouses. (See 2d *Ann. Report of the poor-law commissioners*, Lond., 1836.) But that condition, which was just for the idle only, has been found rigorous for such as were involuntarily so. The rule of *workhouses* has been softened; and it has been done with so little circumspection, that such houses ceased being an object of avoidance; hence, pauperism and the poor-tax have again risen in esteem. (Moreau, *ub. sup.*, III. p. 19, *seq.*, etc.)

[2] Du Châtel, *ub. sup.*, p. 287; *Journ. des Econ.*, X. p. 124. De Gérando, *ub. sup.*, I. p. 3, 454, *seq.;* Villeneuve, *ub. sup.*, II. p. 413–419.

[3] There are, however, several exceptions to be made on this general observation, especially as to foundlings. To cover France with public hospitals destined to receive them, as decreed in the

time, the public good sense has rated at their true value the disastrous principles of 1793, and 1848; because the funds consecrated to relief are raised only

---

ordinance of the 19th Jan. 1811, to place without distinction to the charge of the Departments and *Communes*, all those deposited in them, to spare those leaving them by means of revolving boxes (*tours*), from the shame of being known; was this not, as observed by De Gérando, to say to the public: "Whoever will get rid of taking care of his child, by giving the charge thereof to society, is invited to deposit it here, and will be dispensed from any justification." Was it not, in one word, to consecrate the right to assistance, and, what is worse, the right to libertinism?

It is undeservedly that, to support that state of things, they lean on the authority of two great names. The boxes have an Italian origin. St. Vincent de Paul was not their inventor; when he recommended to private charity poor children, starving almost with hunger, he meant assuredly not to encourage unnatural parents to remit theirs to the charge of the public. As for Napoleon, he could, with much convenience, multiply the hospitals and boxes; he always knew what to do with the children sent in; no one called him to account for the blood shed on the battle-field. But why should France, in time of peace, be loaded with such a burden? One hundred thousand foundlings on the hands of the State; just the treble of those in Necker's time; one million of foundlings of all ages, all deprived of their civil and family condition, though at least one-tenth are born legitimate; is it not for the country an immense load, and at the same time a serious danger?

It is feared the suppression of boxes would multiply infanticides. Remacle has proved, by the most plausible reasons and the best stated facts, that, in this respect, their influence is more dangerous than useful. But, suppose that the presence of the boxes should diminish the cases of infanticide, would it not increase, in a much stronger proportion, the cases of abandonment? Is the distance so great between two crimes? If the former inspires more horror, is it a reason to give so much encouragement to the latter? Now, experience furnishes here the most positive results. At

partially and indirectly from the tax-payers; in a word, because public charity, there, has put on, the least possible, the character of legal charity. Who does not perceive, however, all the defects of the best administered official charity? If it possesses the advantage, often illusory, of centralization, who does not perceive all that it lacks of delicacy, discernment,

---

Mentz, where formerly only 30 exposures took place within 13 years, there were 516 during the four years under the system of boxes, and scarcely one a year since their suppression. In the 52 departments, which, on the authority of the government, suppressed their boxes in 1834, the number of exposures fell suddenly from 35 to 26; from 1834 to 1845, the numbers of exposed children diminished in France by more than 30,000, though there was an increase of the whole population by 2,000,000. In such *departments* as never had open boxes, the proportion of foundlings is but 1 to 896 inhabitants, whilst it is but 1 to 291 in the *departments* which have one or more boxes. It is impossible not to take account of such results. It is agreed, generally, therefore, now to require the gradual suppression of boxes, their replacement by offices of admission, offering securities for secresy, for the cases in which secresy is necessary; finally, as much as possible, the conversion of support in hospices, into an assistance at home, granted to unmarried mothers, or to poor or sick parents, up to the entrance of the child into the asylum. A prefect has succeeded, by such assistance, judiciously given, in reducing in his *department* the number of exposed children from 124 to 5, from which four have been withdrawn by their mothers. See on this question, Terme et Montfalcon, *Histoire des enf. trouvés*, Lyon, 1832; Remacle, *des Hosp. d'enf. tr.*, p. 227, 234, *seq.*, 260, 341, etc.; De Gérando, *Bienf. publ.*, II. p. 301, *et passim;* De Watteville, *Statist. des établ. de bienf.*, 8–12; *Annuaire de l'écon. pol.*, of 1851, p. 166; la Mothe, *Nouv. étud. de législ. char.;* p. 28, *seq.;* 43, 106, *seq.;* B. Delessert, *Discour. à la ch. des Dép.*, 27th of May, 1836, and 30th of May, 1838; Rapet, *Journ. des Econ.*, XIII. p. 51, 54, 64, 195; *Revue des 2 M.*, 1846, etc.

and true efficaciousness? Who does not deplore the dangerous pretensions to which it gives place, and the inevitable abuses which it engenders?[1]

Shall we conclude that, *from this moment*, the State ought to free itself from the cases of benevolence, and refer them entirely to voluntary and private charity?

Such is not our opinion. The habits of a people cannot be changed in a day. The true way once abandoned, it is not easy to return. Charity, like religion, for a long time sustained by the State, could not, without detriment, be suddenly deprived of this patronage. The State, besides, here has obligations of more than one kind to fulfil. Having become, by the effect of political and religious revolutions, the possessor of the ancient funds of charity, it ought to consecrate them in part, at least, to their destination, until some other provision is made. In despoiling the church, it has inherited a part of its duties. Its position is, in this respect, the same as that of the ancient Roman government. When the poor citizens of Rome found themselves frustrated of their part of the *Ager publicus*, it was necessary to supply it by the

---

[1] See in the *Journ. des Econ.*, (X. p. 263; XXII. p. 153,) the sad particulars given by Vée and Villermé, sen., as to the manner in which assistance is given and received at Paris in the offices of benevolence. *Cf.* Dufau, *Lettres sur la charité*, p. 255, etc. Mertz and Schmidt gave analogous particulars on the effects of public assistance in Germany. L. Naville, on its effects in Switzerland and elsewhere. (Mertz., *Arm. and Christ.*, p. 39–50, Stuttg., 1849; Schmidt, *Ueb. Verarm. in Deutschl.*, 1837, p. 10; Naville, *de la charité légale*, etc.)

daily distributions.[1] Just so, when the lower classes in England found no longer their subsistence in the interior or at the door of the convents, it was necessary, to stop their vagabondage and their revolts, to establish the poor-tax;[2] and to-day, however heavy this charge may be, and to whatever abuses it may give occasion, there is not a sensible man who would dare to demand its immediate abolition.[3] In France, even where the misery is far from being so intense, and where the revolution of 1789, in passing the property in mortmain over into the domain of the State, has, by a happy compensation, opened to all classes an access to property, the sudden suppression of bureaux of charity and of the public houses of benevolence, would give occasion to regrets and perhaps to grave dangers.

But, if public assistance is one of those institutions which ought not to be touched, except with much circumspection and reserve, the preceding considerations authorize us to maintain that, far from extending, in this respect, the part of civil authority, it is necessary, on the contrary, to labor continually to restrain it, and to tend unceasingly towards a state of things in which private charity, of itself and from its

---

[1] Dureau, *Econ. pol. des Rom.*, II. p. 308.

[2] Blanqui, *Hist. de l'Econ. pol.*, I. p. 326–331.

[3] Chalmers himself was far from claiming it; he proposed transitory means, of which he had made an attempt in a parish in Scotland, and by which the poor-tax could be, according to him, suppressed without inconvenience, after one or two generations. (Chalmers, *Chr. and civ. econ.*, II. c. 11, p. 89, 94, *seq.*, 113, *seq.*; Du Châtel, *de la Charité*, p. 167, *seq.*)

own resources, can alone provide for the necessities of the indigent.[1]

---

[1] By confounding, as it was too often the case in this question, *human society* in general, with *civil society* or the State, *collective charity* has been likewise confounded with *public charity.* From the fact that benevolence, as all human works, must be practised in society, it has been wrongly concluded that it belonged necessarily to the province of civil society, and thus was one of the attributes of government. (De Gérando, *Bienf. publ.*, II. p. 498; H. Say, *Journ. des Econ.*, X. p. 124, *seq.;* Moreau-Christophe, *ub. sup.*, III. p. 524; Lamothe, *Legisl, char.*, pref., § 6, p. 91; Marbeau, *du Paupérisme*, etc.) We think, on the contrary, that in this respect, as well as in many others, the more the spirit of association will extend itself, the more the intervention of the State will become superfluous; that the State is, in our days, engaged in so many affairs, only because private associations do not occupy themselves with them, and that its action, necessarily coactive, always more or less alters the works it concerns itself with.

Is there any fear lest resources of private charity should be inadequate to the wants of it? It is easy to show, with Chalmers, that their inadequacy oftenest proceeds from reposing upon the State the care of filling up its deficiencies. These resources are, however, very extensive. McFarland states, that at Amsterdam, they collect often in a single charity-box from 1,000 to 2,000 liv. st. a day; that, in the boxes of Hamburgh and Leipzig, sometimes up to 200,000 liv. st. have been received in certain years. (*Recherches sur les pauvres.*, in the Recueil of Duquesnoy, V, p. 186, 213, etc.) In certain counties of Scotland the product of boxes sufficed fully for the wants of the poor. (Villen. *écon. pol. chr.*, II. p. 433.) In England, in spite of the tax, they valued in 1828, at more than one million sterling, the income of the establishments of private charity. (Buret, *de la Misère, etc.*, II. p. 305;) it has been since that time increased by more than one quarter, and today it is said, to amount to 37 millions of francs. (Moreau, III. p. 200, not.) In France, the private gifts to officers of benevolence and to hospices, after constantly increasing since 1800, arose for the 26 last years up to nearly 75 millions. (A. de. Melun. *Rapp.*

Thus, for the evils that are hopelessly unavoidable, and consequently to be relieved of necessity, in place of at once turning our eyes towards the State and regarding it as a second Providence, let us each examine what we can do individually; let us provide, each one of us, according to our means, for the unfortunate whom we know, and who are near us; let us each, like the first Christians, have our sacred treasure enlarged by a part of our savings, and from which we draw in favor of the necessitous.[1] Then, for the evils which call for a larger display of resources, let us address ourselves to a collective, but always private and voluntary charity. Let each

---

sur les hospices, Ann. de la charité, 1851, p. 9.) For Paris only, the donations and legacies officially known have gone up in 1843 to 158,000 francs, and 5000 francs of rent. (De Watteville, *Journ. des Econ.*, X. p. 136.) There are now in Paris nearly eighty private institutions of benevolence, the yearly resources of which are valued at two millions. (Moreau, III. p. 466, not.; Dufau, *Lettres sur la charité*, p. 49.) Finally, the subscriptions, in cases of extraordinary disasters, amount sometimes to a considerable sum; that for these made orphans by the cholera has produced 1,000,000 for Paris only. (Dufau, p. 103; Moreau, p. 530, not.) In Germany, private charity has founded in the space of one year only, (from 1848–1849,) more than forty institutions for orphans, or for abandoned and vicious children. (Mertz, *Arm. and Christ.*) In presence of these figures, how can we despair of private charity? How doubt but she will succeed in filling up the void which public benevolence will leave by withdrawing little by little?

[1] With private and free charity," says Duchâtel, "one may fear useless repetitions, the want of ensemble and proportion. . . . But let each one look round himself and relieve the misery within his reach; this is a complete organized system." (*De la charité*, p. 211, *Cf.* A. E. Cherbullier, *Des causes du paupérisme*, c. 8.)

church, each parish, each religious or benevolent association, assist from the product of the offerings of its members, the indigent within its sphere.[1] These churches, these different associations, will then know, let us hope, how to unite in case of need, either to relieve, by means of general collections, evils more extended, or to sustain, in common, general establishments of benevolence, dispensaries, hospitals,[2] houses for orphans' foundlings, for the deaf and dumb, the blind, the infirm or the sick who cannot be taken care of in their own families.[3]

---

[1] L. Naville, in his *Mémoire sur la charité*, crowned in 1834 by the *Académie française*, after signalizing the inherent misuses in public charity, traced the plan of a system of private associations, bound to each other by a narrow connexion, embracing by their various committees, the whole group of charitable works.

Among the modern associations devoted with the most success to the practice of charity, we shall mention that of the "Friends of the poor," at Hamburgh, under the direction of Miss Sieveking, and about thirty others, founded in various places, after the same pattern; then the numerous societies of benevolence which the work of the *interior mission* has brought out recently in all Germany, a work created for the welfare of the poor, under the impulsion of Wicheren, the director of the institution at Horn, near Hamburgh. See the *Fliegende Blätter* which he has published since 1843, and his work on the interior Mission, 1849. See too the reports (*Ueber die Leistung d. Weiblichen Vereins*, Hamb., 1832–1851), of which an interesting extract was published in Geneva, in 1844, and of which a more extensive analysis has been published.

[2] We except military hospitals, the support of which belongs to the State alone; it is but just that it should provide, at its own expense, for those who expose in its service their health and their life.

[3] To pretend to do without those establishments of charity collective, and to limit one's self in all cases to the cares of individual

As for the organization of these collective subventions, doubtless it can vary much. The institutions of the primitive church may be imitated; new ones may be established, or ancient ones appropriated to our times; the care of them can be entrusted to ecclesiastical, lay, or mixed administrations; they can be sustained by means of foundations or annual subscriptions. In all that, regard must be had to time and place, to the character and genius of the people, and it would be rash to pretend to fix any general rule.[1]

---

charity; or, as it has been said, to the *primitive deaconship*, is, in our opinion, a mere utopia, the mere attempt of which would involve grave losses of time, and a great superfluous expense. Public hospitals have been, undoubtedly, much misused, and are now misused. A great number of poor old men, for instance, admitted there without distinction, would be more conveniently, more economically, and for themselves, more happily assisted at home. But those misuses would be easily reformed, if hospitals again became institutions of private charity; but, it seems to us impossible, not to acknowledge for many cases, especially of sickness, the necessity of hospitals. (Droz, *Econ. pol.*, p. 318; A. de Melun, Rapport sur le projet de loi relatif aux hospices, *Ann. de la charité*, janv. 1851, p. 10; Dufau, *ub. sup.*, p. 159, etc.) As to the improvements to be made in the management of hospitals and *hospices*, see Lamothe, *Nouv. étud. sur la lég. char. etc.;* Watteville, *Essai statist.*, *Annuaire de l'Econ. pol.*, 1852, p. 150, etc., etc.

[1] Like Chrysostom, however, we do not hesitate to prefer the system of occasional donations, or else, that of periodical subscriptions, to that of fixed foundations, and especially of dotations of real estate. Among other advantages, this system had the advantage of less increasing mortmain, less of exciting the expectations of the poor; of keeping up the benevolence of the rich; of offering less attraction and advantage to cupidity; finally, of better yielding to the diversity of circumstances and the chances of want. How much more would the *hospices* and the funds assigned to

Besides, the mode of organization has only a secondary importance in things of this kind. What is essential is, that those who preside over them and cooperate in them, bring to them suitable dispositions of head and heart.

To be personally sure of the reality of the necessities; to watch over the use of the succors; to withhold them as soon as they will be no longer needed; never to render the assistance sufficient for it to tempt those who might dispense with it; never to raise it above the level of the resources which the poor can provide by his work; never to enter into obligations with him for the future, so to relieve him that he will never lose sight of his personal responsibility, and will always feel the consequences of his errors and faults; to abstain from those perfidious aids, which, by nourishing vices, perpetuate misery; these, among many others, are rules dictated by simple good sense, and from which the organs of benevolence ought never to depart.[1]

But what is still more essential to the efficacy of this virtue, is the purity and elevation of the motives from which it emanates.

The history of the first centuries is before us to testify to this: in order that charity may produce its

---

them be more equally divided in France, if the system of fixed dotations had not prevailed in their respect? How many foundations, very beneficent in their origin, which, in the course of time, have been found useless or displaced, and which, under this pretence, have become the prey of revolutions?

[1] De Gérando, *Le visiteur du pauvre;* Duchâtel, *de la charité;* Naville, *Mémoire sur la charité, etc.*

best fruits; it is not enough that it should be voluntary, it must flow from a religious principle, the love of God must have inspired it.

Alone, Christian charity is truly profitable, because it proceeds from motives perfectly disinterested and pure. The poor rarely deceive themselves concerning the motives which move their benefactors, and they are always tempted to make an abuse of the favors which are not dictated by the heart. When, in place of a true interest for their lot, they perceive motives of vanity, of prudence or of fear, in those who assist them, they only think of freeing themselves from the burden of gratitude, and of using, in behalf of evil passions, the sentiments, hardly honorable, under the influence of which they have been assisted.

Alone, guided by the true desire of doing good, religious charity does it, when, and as it is needed. It chooses with discernment the object of its gifts; it relieves, not the evils which are spoken of the most, but those most deserving of sympathy; it carries assistance where no one sees it; it penetrates into hovels where worldly charity never enters; it invests its favors with a delicacy of regard that raises the poor in his own eyes, but it adds also exhortations and good advice to them, loving rather to serve than to please, and doing good without ever flattering the passions.[1]

---

[1] "To act morally upon men," says Guizot, "one must love and reform them, inspire them with trust by love, and respect by severity. Severity and love are the two efficient powers upon the heart of men; for men have the instinct of their moral wants, as well of those which are heavy upon them, as those which please

Inspired by the love of God, it also inspires with the same love those whom it assists. Its presence in the abode of the poor, spreads there a perfume of piety which calms pain. By the good which it manifests, the poor feels that it is God who sends him; and if, at times, misery had veiled to his eyes the idea of a beneficent Providence; if, by stress of suffering, he had come to turn to heaven only looks of reproach and doubt, at the sight of the charitable friend who visits him, he recalls the compensations which God provides to misfortune, he lives again to faith, to hope, and applies himself to his task with courage, in expectation of Him, who will crown his efforts.

Alone, finally, by the sublimity of the model which it proposes to itself, by the extent of the sacrifices of which it is capable, Christian charity is always equal to the necessity. Whilst the State has never been able to dispense with its concurrence, it has for ages alone sufficed for the relief of indigence. For the State disposes of only a limited treasure, all the more readily exhausted; since, to fill it, it has recourse to means of constraint; whilst Christian charity holds the key of the heart, that is, of an inexhaustable

---

them. They are troubled, profoundly troubled with their imperfection, and they want to be relieved. Love felt and inspired, is both their most beautiful and their liveliest joy; they want to love and to be loved. To require much of them in virtue; to give them much in love; the great empire, I speak of the moral empire, is given on that condition." (Guizot, *de l'état des âmes*, Meditat, Paris, 1852, p. 4.)

treasure, and which, as one of the Fathers has said, finds there, where there is nothing, something still to give.[1]

SECT. II.—PREVENTIVE ACTION OF CHARITY.

POSITIVE privations, material sufferings, are not the only, nor the greatest evils which come in the train of poverty. The most deplorable, perhaps, are those which strike the attention the least; that state of dependence in which the poor is placed in the eyes of his equals; that precarious condition which deprives him of all security, all confidence for the future; that constant preoccupation of material wants, which hinders him from engaging in the noble occupations of the intellect; finally, when this situation is prolonged or aggravated, when poverty becomes indigence, when indigence degenerates into misery, then, the temptations, to which it exposes a being always in care for the morrow; it is the continual alternative in which it places him of needing bread or of obtaining it at the price of virtue and honor; it is, finally, the state of degradation in which we see so many thousand human creatures plunged, less by their fault than by the misfortune of their position.

In view of all these evils, engendered by poverty,

---

[1] "The poor," says St. Augustine, "is rich by his charity alone, and thus he has the means of giving to infinity. He gives what he has; has he nothing, he gives his affections, an advice, if he can, an assistance, if he can; and if he has no advice nor support to give, he gives a wish, a prayer." (Aug., Enarr. 2, *in Ps.* 36, VIII. p. 83, *seq.*

who can believe it enough to soften momentarily its privations, to give some provisions to those who were without any, to dissipate for a moment some cares, to appease some sufferings which will reappear the next day? Who does not, on the contrary, recognize that, if it is good to relieve misery, it is better still to prevent it or to cause it to disappear; to suppress, as far as possible, the causes of impoverishment; in fine, to place the indigent in the way of ameliorating his condition, of elevating himself by his work and economy, to that state of independence and security, which is one of the most precious privileges of a life in easy circumstances?

In this new point of view, it appears to us to be superfluous to pursue the parallel, which we have already established. It is well known that before the appearance of Christianity, the Roman government had done nothing for the extirpation of poverty; that, content with nourishing from day to day the population of Rome, it had not sought to raise the proletarians from their sad condition, and that its measures had rather swollen than dried up the sources of misery.

The same reproach has not failed to be made to charity. Because it merited it sometimes in the Middle Ages, it has been too readily concluded that it gave the same occasion for it in the first centuries. But this conclusion seems entirely contradicted by the facts which we have cited.

What, in effect, was this protecting tutelage, with which the church surrounded the feeble in the name of charity? When it rose up against the excesses of monopoly and usury; when, at the risk of incurring disfavor with the powerful, it censured their abuse of power; when it resisted Andronicus and Eutropius, Theodosius and Eudoxia; when, from the height of the Christian pulpit, it thundered against the modern Achabs; when it undertook the defence of the widow and the orphan, against unjust governors and faithless tutors; when it made itself the guardian of their deposits and extended over their threatened goods the mantle of ecclesiastical immunity; when it caused his house and his domain to be restored to the captive returned to his home, and to the poor debtor the instruments of his labor; when it protected the *Colonus* against the exactions of his master, the small proprietor against the barbarity of his tax-gatherer; when, raising its reclamations even to the throne, causing the maxims of charity to penetrate the hearts of sovereigns, it obtained from them protecting laws for these oppressed classes; was it not to struggle as efficaciously as possible against one of the principal causes of poverty; was it not, as far as its nature would permit, to hinder a crowd of Roman subjects from falling into the class of proletarians, or, lower still, into that of beggars by profession?

Several precepts and regulations of the Ancient Church, still prove the importance which it attached to preventive means. We have seen that the Apostolic Constitutions, in prescribing alms-giving and hospitality to the bishops, also prescribed to them to secure the prospects of orphans; to have them taught a trade to enable them to gain a living; to procure for them the instruments of their trade, in order that they should not need the assistance of others. We have seen St. Basil recommend to his monks to busy themselves ceaselessly in the education of youth, and to cause each child to be instructed in his profession. St. Ambrose reminded the faithful that good advice is often of greater worth than a favor,[1] and Chrysostom, that alms "are not given alone in money but in deeds, by patronage, and by the influence one lends to the unfortunate."[2] It would be impossible to speak or to act more favorably for the true interests of the poor.

But these efforts, well directed as they were, were to fail before the difficulties of the times. Charity, it must be acknowledged, and it is one of the lessons to be derived from this historical study, charity cannot suffice, alone, for the destruction of misery. By its influence it aids to a more equal division, to a better employment of riches; it encourages, seconds the virtues which create them, but it cannot create them itself; it is to intelligence and labor that God has reserved this power. Agriculture, which multiplies the products of the soil; manufactures, which fashion them for the use of men; commerce, which enriches each country with the productions of all the others; the arts, in a word, and the civilization which make them fruitful, these are the sources of the prosperity of a people; labor and saving, these are the means by which each man assures to himself a lasting part in this prosperity. Where these elements are wanting,

---

[1] Ambros., *De off min.*, II. 15, Opp., VII. p. 303.

[2] Chrys., hom. 25, *in Act.*, c. 3, IX. p. 205.

however active charity may be, then, necessarily, deprivation and embarrassment exist.

Now, from the fourth century, Roman civilization was in full decline; and, as to labor, in vain had the church sought to revive it; in vain had it lavished encouragements upon it;[1] hardly did it succeed, except in some religious communities, to give it any impulse; everywhere else, discredited by prejudice,[2] ruined by usury, paralyzed by despotism, crushed by the competition of servile labor, free labor disappeared in the wars and invasions which desolated the empire. No mode offered itself to the poor for escaping from his condition; slave or beggar, such was his only alternative. Instead of that ascendant movement which, in prosperous States, raises, one after another, the different classes above their primitive level, a general languor ruined the social body; commerce, industry, agriculture, all perished; poverty, like an hereditary cancer, transmitted itself fatally from father to son; it was a yawning gulf, a fathomless abyss, which charity was condemned to labor ceaselessly to fill, but ever without hope.

Are the circumstances to-day more favorable to the

---

[1] This beautiful passage of Chrysostom is known: "Let us not be ashamed of mechanical employment; let us not despise hand-labor; let us rather despise idleness and laziness. If it were shameful to work, Paul had not worked with his own hands, and would not have gloried in it, he would not have forbidden such as will not work to eat. Sin alone is shameful; now sin originates in idleness; idleness is a fertile source of iniquity." (Chrys., *Hom. in illud: salutate, etc.*, c. 5, III. p. 178–180.)

[2] Blanqui, *Hist. de l'Econ. pol.*, I. 40, *seq.* Moreau-Chr., *du Droit à l'oisiveté*, pref. p. 1–12, p. 201, etc.

extinction of misery? The extinction of slavery and the other conquests of modern civilization, do they tend to render the action of preventive charity more easy at the present time?

In one respect it might be doubted.

Every birth is laborious, that of liberty more than any other, and it is not in precipitating it that its dangers are diminished. It has been with the emancipation of labor as with so many other forms of liberty, which, from not having been sufficiently prepared and provided for, have caused dangerous perturbations in the fortune of nations.[1] Like the Roman freedman, who, thrown upon the streets without a *peculum*, was reduced to beg; like the negro of the colonies, whom a stroke of the pen declares free, but at the same time renders tributary to hunger; the workman, quitting the tutelage of his master, has found himself burdened with the care of his subsistence, and often in no condition to provide for it; the artisan and the manufacturer, pushed, without capital, into the lists of universal competition, has found himself dismounted in the first encounter; the law has freed him, need has put him into dependence; he is obliged to hire out his services, and to harness himself to the car of all-compelling industry. There, during some time, his condition seems prosperous, heavy salaries invite him to enjoy; delivered from all control, he enjoys without measure, and marries without foresight. But, suddenly a crisis comes on;

[1] "The most critical situation for man," says Sismondi, "is the passage from the state of servitude or serfage to independence." (*Etud. d'écon. polit.*, intr., p. 35.)

a distant war or a neighboring revolution breaks out; markets close; consumption diminishes; capital is called in; ruined by a disastrous competition, the manufacturer suspends production, or else a newly discovered machine replaces the hands of the workmen, whom the division of labor has transformed into machines, and who find no more employment for their forces. Thousands suffer with hunger by the side of the products accumulated by their labor. When, to the joyful shouts of the people, modern society abolished the last remains of serfdom, could it have been foreseen that it would have suffered so soon from the excesses of liberty? When the gigantic progress of industry has been applauded, could it have been foreseen that the class which would concur the most directly in it, would receive the least of its fruits, and that the profits of these pacific conquests would go, as formerly those of war had gone, to concentrate themselves in the hands of a small number?

But while regretting that the enfranchisement of the workmen has not been effected with more precaution and more gradually, let us not, on that account, fail to recognize the blessings of liberty. To it we owe the prodigious development of commerce, the wonderful success of all the arts. Favored by it, the products of agriculture, those of mechanical activity especially, have been multiplied beyond all expectation; the poor to-day procure at a low price the comforts, and even the enjoyments, formerly unknown to the rich. Everywhere the working classes to-day are better lodged, clad and fed, than they have ever been before; the average length of life has notably increased; now are rarely seen to rage those famines which, so frequently, periodically desolated the ancient world, and swept down especially the inferior ranks. As consumer, the workman has incontestably gained by the present state of things. He has hardly gained less as producer. The profit of him who farms on shares, which, under the Romans, was only the sixth or the eighth of the product of the soil, to-day is more than half; wages for work by the day have risen almost as much. The rate of interest, on the contrary, has fallen more than two-thirds.[1] Finally, if liberty has its dangers, has it not also its sweets? If it has its rude combats, has it not its crowns? Can the temporary subjection which springs from want be compared with the servitude, consecrated, riveted by the law? Is it nothing to the artisan, that he can choose his master, dispose in some manner of his lot? Is it nothing to see a career open before us, which formerly had been shut, to be able, by skill and labor, to attain a position heretofore inaccessible to the most persevering efforts?

[1] Thiers, *on Property*, p. 121, 137. But, it is not necessary to go back to the times of the Romans, to find a perceptible improvement in the state of the inferior classes. In comparing it with what it was in France half a century ago, we observe already a very advantageous and striking alteration. Thiers, *ibid.*, p. 136; de Gérando, *Bienf. publ.*, I. p. 175, *seq.*, 458; *des Progrès de l'Industrie*, 2d ed., p. 12; Léon Faucher, *Journal des Econom.*, XXI. p. 347; Th. Fix. *Observ. sur les cl. ouvr.*, *ibid.*, X. p. 18, *seq.*; XII. p. 107; Marbeau, *du Paupér.*, p. 190, etc. It is thought, in particular, that agricultural wages have almost quadrupled in France, since about six years, and have risen by one-fifth in the last thirty years. (*Journ. des Econ.*, 15th Oct., 1850; Moreau de Jonnès, *Ann. de l'écon. pol.*, ann. 1851, p. 378.)

As to the obstacles, assuredly still great, which the poor yet find upon their way, the recent progress of civilization tends each day to remove them. Intimations may be seen of an epoch, when, provided by instruction with new resources, they may offer to society more precious, and hence better remunerated labor; when they will no longer have to struggle painfully against the competition of machinery; when, from the elevation of intelligence they shall have been able to attain, they can defy that deluge of mechanical force, which everywhere to-day disputes the ground with them.[1] The spirit of associa-

[1] Plato, Aristotle and Cicero, thought mechanical labor to be humiliating for a citizen, and it was in order to spare him from it, that they wanted legions of slaves. "To the slaves, they said, come all that requires the use of corporeal power, to the citizen, what demands the practice of intelligence, except war to defend the city, and agriculture to support it." I confess, I feel for man, the same susceptibility which those philosophers felt for the citizen; I am jealous for the time spent by my fellow-creatures in labor that a beast of burden or an engine could perform better than they; I would like to see their strength, little by little, replaced by mechanical agents, and applying themselves, in a manner more worthy of them, to what claims the co-operation of reflection and thought; I would like to see man having the command over engines, rather than struggling with them; I would like to see him, while inanimate slaves would execute his most rudest toil, engaged in higher occupations and nobler leisure; and is it not for this very purpose that God has given him the empire over matter? Is it not one of the traits of the perfectibility that distinguishes our kind? and is it not in that sense that the material progress of modern times must serve the spiritual interests of mankind? Let us forbear to curse and to paralyze this movement, both salutary and providential, which momentarily wounds the interests of the working class, only because our institutions have not yet enabled them to bear it.

tion, in developing itself, will furnish them with new aid, will lighten their toils, facilitate their economy, will give a new value to their savings, perhaps will permit them to unite the benefits of capital to those of labor,[1] the advantages of cultivation on a large

[1] People have complained for a long time of the considerable profits capital levies upon labor, and of the discouragement which results therefrom. It is in order to free it from that state of dependence, that in the year 1830, associations of workmen were established, with the view of working for their own account, and afterwards partaking of a part of the profit, whilst the rest was to be capitalized. We do not speak here of those associations which were formed in 1849, with the aid of a subvention of the State, and which almost all have fallen, as soon as they were deprived of that resource. (Reybaud, Rapp. à l'Acad. des sc. mor. See *Journal des Econ.*, July, 1852.) Even those established spontaneously, though they have had more persistence and vitality, have not answered the hopes founded upon them. The difficulty they feel in the division of profits, in taking account of the relative skill of workmen who are upon a footing of equality, of maintaining among them the discipline and the unity of views necessary for the regulation of the work, of finding among simple mechanics the knowledge, the perception, the activity of mind, indispensable qualities for a good agent; finally, of striving with a small capital against enterprises powerfully sustained; such are the principal dangers, which they meet upon their way, and against which several have stranded. (Reybaud, *ibid.*) Experience shows, however, that such difficulties are not insurmountable; we have reason to believe, that for manufactures they do not require a great deal of money, a certain number of honest laborious workmen, sufficiently acquainted with each other, commencing their concern on a modest footing, but pursuing it with perseverance, would have, in the course of time, a chance of success. The principle of association, by itself eminently salutary and fertile, will become more and more so, in proportion as instruction and morality progress among the working classes.

scale with those of small estates.[1] Property itself, rendered more accessible to the laboring classes, will secure to them a less precarious position, will protect them against the effects of industrial crises, and promote among them a spirit of foresight and of *moral constraint*, which is vainly preached to the proletarian and simple day-laborer.[2] Agriculture, now too much

---

Several modern economists have traced plans for the organization of industrial associations. See, among others, the works of Ott (*Econ. soc.*, p. 308–326) and of Feugueray, (*l'Association ouvrière*, Paris, 1851.) We regret that those authors, the views of whom are praiseworthy in so many respects, admit the fatal principle of a momentary subvention from the State.

[1] In answer to the detractors of small estates, Passy has set forth the advantages of the small farming. He has showed that a country possessing sixty farmers could support a population of 140, whilst if it numbered only 30, it could nourish but a population of 100. Even he has maintained that small farming, deduction made of the expense of production, yields, extent of land and productions being equal, the largest net income. (*Mém. de l'Acad. des sc. mor.*, V. p. 708, *seq.*, 728.) It cannot, however, be denied that the want of workmen, farming tools, and beasts of burden, is on small farms the source of many disadvantages, loss of time, often also, loss of crops. But why should they not imitate in the farming of their estates, what they do in the driving of their cattle, and in the manipulation of their milk? Why should not the possessors of adjacent small lots associate to till them in common? (Buret, *de la Misère des classes lab.*, I. p. 241; II. p. 129; Rossi, *Cours d'écon. pol.*, II. p. 117, *seq.*) The principle of association, already applied with success to mutual assistance among workmen, to the economical purchase of goods, to the building of cheap houses, might be extended with the same advantage to the common use of farming tools, investments working out in common, and to a multitude of other objects. (*Revue Brit.*, March, 1852, Assoc. des cl. lab. en Angleterre.)

[2] Whoever has tasted the advantages of property and the comfort it gives, wishes to leave the same advantages to his children.

separated from mechanical and manufacturing pursuits, will one day be more closely associated with them.[1] A happy system of land-credit, will fer-

Parental love, self-love itself, if need be, tell him more in this respect than all sermons on foresight. But the workman, who lives from hand to mouth, has no scruple in bringing forth children, condemned to the same kind of life; he follows his instincts, eats, drinks, procreates without thinking of the next day. The most wretched populations are those which propagate most; it is a fact acknowledged by all economists. Malthus, himself, says that nothing multiplies so much as misery. (Montesquieu, *Esp. des lois.*, XXIII. 11; Sismondi, *Etud sur l'écon. pol.*, I. p. 129, 193; Rossi, *ub. sup.*, I. p. 400; III. p. 182, etc., etc.)

As to the advantages of the free division of estates, see, besides the Mémoire of Passy, above mentioned, De Gérando, *Bienf. publ.*, I. p. 235; Sismondi, *ub. sup.*, I. p. 203, *seq.;* De Villeneuve, *Econ. pol. chr.*, I. p. 304, 416; Droz, *ub. sup.*, p. 98, *seq.*, etc. It has been shown in a manner equally peremptory and eloquent, that the distress will not cease in Ireland, that even in England pauperism will diminish, but by a change in the distribution of landed property, a change which may be effected without a revolution, without violence, by the simple abolition of the substitutions, and of the legal privilege of primogeniture. (Beaumont, *de l'Irlande*, II. p. 189–234.) Then it will be necessary to facilitate the mutation and the fractioning of landed property, by simplifying the formalities, so long and so complicated, of deeds. This change is indeed in a way of being realized in England, by the associations for *acquisitions*, which unite a small capital to buy large estates, which the purchasers afterwards divide among themselves; and in Ireland, by the commission of the Parliament, charged with authorizing and making easy the sale of mortgaged properties of the nobility. Already, more than one million of acres have been sold, it is said, in this manner to industrious farmers, who come to fill up the voids made by the Irish emigration.

[1] The profits of the farmer are small but sure; those of manufacturing are precarious but higher. If the manufacturer would invest his savings in real estate securities, and the farmer in manu-

tilize the soil, and, at the same time, secure the

---

facturing concerns, the advantages of the two classes would be thus usefully combined. But agriculture and manufactures can be united in a manner much more direct and salutary. In proportion as communications become easier, it would be desirable that manufactures should transfer themselves from cities to the country, as it has happened in some parts of Alsatia, where the working man, brought up amidst an agricultural population, finally leases for a long term a property which he pays for with his savings, and which he cultivates in his leisure hours and transmits to his children. (De Gérando, *ub. sup.*, I. p. 219; Th. Fix, Observ., etc.. *Journ. des Econ.*, XIII. p. 43; De la Farelle, *du Progr. soc.* 2d ed., p. 210, 279; Grün, *de la Moralisat. des classes labor*, p. 35, *seq.*, etc.) A change, still more desirable, wherever it would be possible, would be that labor, now concentrated in manufactures, to the great material and moral prejudice of populations, should be disseminated into rural districts. In Tuscany, in some parts of the Vosges, in some places of Normandy, some valleys of Switzerland, etc., every peasant family had its loom, its weavers, its embroiderers, its watchmakers, its engineers, who, in the winter leisures, or in the intervals of field-work, get the means of compensating for bad crops, of buying, or making fertile, new lands. "In the Canton of Apenzell, where embroidered muslins are manufactured, each family," says Zuber, "is at once agricultural and manufacturing, and especially well-educated, sober and religious. . . The workman in Apenzell, notwithstanding his strength, spends but twenty-five cents a day, and earns ten-fold." (*Journal des Econ.*, XIII. p. 43, note.) The contractors and manufacturers, for whom those industrial agriculturists are working, find, on the low price of hand labor, more than the equivalent of the savings which would result for them, from the coming together of their workmen on the same spot; and, moreover, what an advantage for the latter, who are thus left to their simple and peaceful habits, to the intimacy of family life, who are kept sheltered from bad influences, temptations and wants, in a word, far from those centres of poverty and corruption, found among the most of manufactures! (Audiganne, des classes ouvrières en France, *Revue des 2 Mond.*, 1851, 15th Nov., p. 737, 747; 15 fév., 1852, p.

gains of the working class.[1] Free trade, rendered more complete, will make each nation profit by the abundance of all the others, at the same time that it will permit each one to give itself up entirely to the kind of production in which it is the least exposed to see itself supplanted.[2] Finally, by the facility, already so marvellous, of the means of transport, the moment will come, we doubt not, for colonizing so many fertile and still uncultivated countries, of pouring into them the surplus population of our old world, of securing employment there for so many inactive hands, and of opening to Europe new places for the supply of provisions, and new markets for its industry.[3]

670; De Gérando, *des Progrès de l'ind.*, p. 35, 36, note, 84, *seq.*; note; Grün, *Moralis. des cl. labor.*, p. 39, *seq.*; de la Farelle, *du Prog. soc.*, p. 279.)

Moreover, under whatever form the union of agriculture and manufacturing be operated, we do not hesitate to see in it, as well as in that of labor and of property, one of the elements the most essential, henceforth, for the destruction of indigence.

[1] The *Land-Credit* (*crédit foncier*) established in Prussia and Poland, in about the middle of the last century, and long since demanded for France, as a means of disencumbering the soil, has been decreed by Louis Napoleon. (*Journ. des Econ.*, March and April, 1852.)

[2] On the advantages of free trade, and the fatal results of protection, see the works of Dunoyer, Blanqui, M. Chevalier, etc., etc.

[3] They complain of the excess of population, and they do not ponder, says Thiers, that in Europe, the three-fourths, in other places, nine-tenth, on the whole globe, $\frac{999}{1000}$ of the land, are still uncultivated. (*De la Propr.*, p. 129), and among them, some of the most fertile countries of ancient times. As to the difficulties, which have hitherto prevented their colonization, and have hindered the efforts of so many emigrants, those difficulties, already partly removed, will be so more and more.

These are some of the resources to be expected from the actual and future progress of civilization; they will permit each day's struggle with misery to be more successful.[1]

It is for the science of economy to hasten the development of these resources and to turn them to profit, especially for the good of the laboring classes.

But would science believe itself able to dispense with the co-operation of charity?

Where, then, would it find the motive for its researches? In an investigation which has for its object the greatest possible good for the greatest number, what more powerful motive than the love of man could animate and encourage its labors?

Besides, to what more enlightened guide could it apply? What more trustworthy light could direct the researches of economists?

Dr. Chalmers, somewhere,[2] deplores the division which he observed in his times between charity and science. This complaint can be conceived of only in regard to a false science or a false charity. Whereever there is good to be done, what better guide could be invoked than love? With equal intelligence, is not the most devoted friend the safest adviser? and the most tender mother, is she not also the most vigilant? One can be deceived, without doubt, in loving; but, it is much easier to be deceived in not loving. He whom a true sympathy for his equals animates, who sighs from the bottom of his heart over their sufferings, will seek with anxiety for the

[1] Thiers, *ub. sup.*, p. 422.

[2] Chalmers, *Chr. and civ. econ.*, I. p. 3.

means of relieving them, will receive from all sides the light of experience, and call all true science to his aid; and, if he possesses a clear and accurate mind, it will be he who will discover the true remedy. Let us believe that, if till now this has been sought in vain, if so few steps, or rather, if so many false steps have been taken in the solution of this important problem, it is because, heretofore, politics have had more to do with it than charity. In the sufferings of the poor, some have seen only a danger for the rich, and for their only remedy, have said to the poor, "resign yourselves, abstain;" others have seen only an occasion for overturning, for their own advantage, all social order, and have raised and armed the poor against the rich. Some, wholly occupied with the multiplication of production, have excited wants in order to stimulate activity, and encouraged all to enjoy, for the purpose of stimulating labor. Others, seeing in cheapness of production the sublimity of economical science, have, above all, exalted vast establishments, large farms, without thinking of the thousands of cultivators discharged and perishing of hunger in honor of the *net product*.[1] Here, the subsistence of the poor has been rendered excessively dear in behalf of the interest of proprietors or manufacturers; elsewhere, it has been proposed to rob the capitalist for the advantage of the workman. Always, in a word, as with the pagans, one portion of the

---

[1] Sismondi speaks of a noble Scotch lady, who, in the space of nine years, out of speculation, turned out 15,000 inhabitants from her estates, and converted her fields into pastures for sheep. (*Etudes*, I. p. 213.)

human race sacrificed to the other portion, always the good of some sought in the ill or the ruin of others!

Is it believed that these iniquitous or disastrous remedies can, for a moment, sustain the regard of charity? By this one word: "Love thy neighbor as thyself, whatsoever ye would that men should do to you, do ye even so to them;" it causes all false systems to fall, unmasks all sophisms, and tracks out, under all their disguises, the egotism of castes and the injustice of despoilers. Charity would not coldly condemn one part of the human race to hopeless privations;[1] nor would it teach the poor to seek their

[1] The reproach we apply to Malthus, in the practical part of his work is, not having recommended celibacy to the workman till he be able to bring up a family; the advice in itself is good, and many wise men, even Fathers of the church, had given it before Malthus. We reproach him with having stopped there, and with not having sought other preservatives against poverty. What would we think of a physician who, called to see a sick person, would prescribe only diet for him, without endeavoring to cure the disease which made diet necessary for him? Why? The most of your fellow-creatures are in a situation which condemns them to the saddest isolation, and in your extensive book you have nothing to say, but, that they must submit? You do not examine if a better economical system, a wider development of the spirit of association, a more extensive liberty of trade, a better constitution of work, an easier access to property; finally, to say the word, the destruction of manifest abuses, monopolies and unjust privileges, would not make the situation of the workman better? Pessimist, to the excess in regard to population, you show the most complete optimism in respect to the rest! You are surprised at your system having been found inhuman! You are astonished at having been considered as the advocate of the rich, rather than of the poor! That there may be an exaggeration in the reproaches addressed to you, that your intentions have been calumniated, this is beyond

happiness at the expense of the rich; it knows that lasting, real good is never obtained by injustice. Rome, enriched with the spoils of nations, was, in its turn, ignominiously stripped of them; the same fortune to-day awaits the classes of society who would think to elevate themselves upon the ruin of others. With whatever colors spoliation may be decked, let it be disguised under the names of community, progressive impost, right to credit, right to work; let violence, that no one would dare to propose

doubt; but a system capable of bruising so many generous souls, of wounding the most delicate and the purest feelings, must be altogether false in some part.

But, truly, Malthus had an excuse that the most of his disciples have not; he was an Englishman, and he wrote for England, for a country wherein all situations are occupied upon the soil, and where the most part of the inhabitants live upon the wages of some manufactory, constantly glutted with their own products. But how does it happen that a system suggested by quite local circumstances, has found such blind admirers on the continent? Let us, however, except the city of the pontiff, odd contrast! In our days, Rome, endows and marries poor girls, whilst Protestant England preaches celibacy! Is it not that each of these countries suffers with the exaggeration of its proper principle, and tries to remedy it by an exaggeration, in a contrary direction? France will do better, we think, if she follows, in this respect, the maxims so sound and so just, of some of her economists. . . Man, says Joseph Droz, should aspire to marriage, as to the situation the most suitable to his nature; but he must first make himself worthy of it; and this thought may become a powerful vehicle for the young workman in his labor. When opinion excites to marriage, it increases a wretched population; it would also have results, but happy ones, if it would teach the working class that marriage must be the reward of labor and economy. (Droz, *Econ pol.*, p. 311, *seq.; Cf.* De Gérando, *du Progrès de l'industrie*, p. 81 *seq.*, note.)

in his own name, be proposed in the name of the State; all that would be gained would be by the destruction of labor, one common level of misery. "The savage," says Montesquieu, "cuts down the tree to gather the fruit;" this is the image of the prosperity which socialism promises: to-day pillage, to-morrow famine. Such is not the counsel of charity. Animated by a universal benevolence for men, it holds an even balance between them all; from their union, not from their mutual hostility, it makes them expect their common advantage; it teaches that it is by the good of all that the good of each must be sought.

It knows, also, that the temporal good of the poor is never attained at the expense of his morality. Far from it, those doctrines, which, under the pretext of animating industry, discourage economy and temperance, excite in the poor man an extravagant thirst for enjoyments, which, long before satisfaction, may turn him aside from all his duties! Without exhorting him to asceticism, a virtue of another age, a necessity of an epoch of suffering and destitution, without prescribing abstinence for the sake of abstinence, privation for the sake of privation; on the contrary, in showing ease and well-being in the future to him as the legitimate reward of his labors, it recommends to him, meanwhile, the moderation of his desires, sobriety and economy, which establish on a firm basis the prosperity of individuals and of families.

If it desires to see the riches of a country multiply, it desires still more to see the general comfort promoted. It protests against those narrow systems which look only to the abundance of production, without regard for their distribution.[1] Splendid castles surrounded by desert fields, immense manufacturies peopled by miserable and wasted laborers, please it less than the shop of the workman at his ease, or the farm of the happy cultivator. It aspires less to augment the opulence, to swell the superfluity of a few, than to render a state of well-being accessible to the greatest number; and, as has been said, "to enlarge the circle of those who are invited to the legitimate enjoyments of life."[2]

It is for it, the true and impartial friend of man, to direct the science of economy for his true good, to point out to it its dangers, and to preserve it from deviating from its true end; in short, if there is any where an efficacious remedy against indigence, it is for charity to discover it, or, at least, to recognize it among the dangerous specifics, the trial of which has caused so many evils.

That remedy, whatever it may be, will require, always and above all, the co-operation of the poor. It is, then, upon the poor, that it is necessary to act, in the first place, to engage him in the way in which he will find the amelioration of his lot.

Nothing, to appearance, more easy; nothing, in reality, more difficult. There is nothing which men, ordinarily, are less able to comprehend than their

---

[1] "Upon reading certain economists," said Joseph Droz, "one would believe that productions are not made for men, but men for productions." (*Econ. pol.*, p. 73–76.)

[2] Blanqui, *Hist. de l'écon. pol.*, I. p. 25; II. p. 146; Sismondi, *Etudes*, pref.

true interests. Ignorance, obstinacy and prejudices, scatter on the way of goodness a crowd of obstacles, which only charity can always surmount. She alone finds in the consciousness of her intentions and in the fervor of her zeal, the persuasive accents which triumph over prejudices and disarm distrust; the patience which waits for, seeks and finds at last, the favorable moment, the perseverance stayed by no check, that sacred tenacity, to which alone that of routine yields. "The greatest of all powers," said Turgot, in his Memoir to Louis XVI., "is the proved desire to do good." And that great minister would have proved this himself, had it not been for the retirement and premature death which deprived France of him. But, to limit ourselves to more modest examples, it is by the power of his charity that Oberlin drew his parishioners from the apathy into which misery had plunged them, and obtained from them works which, in less than fifty years, transformed a wild valley, lost in the depths of the Vosges, into a fertile and prosperous country, capable of nourishing in ease, a population five times more numerous than formerly.[1]

But, if the amelioration of the fortune of the poor man depends, above all, upon his own energy; if, in the intentions of Providence, he must be the master-builder of his own prosperity, it is by no means true that he can always succeed by his own efforts. Who has not seen families laborious, honest, economical, poor, yet full of virtue and of courage, who, nevertheless, have not been able to rise out of their con-

[1] *Notice on J. Oberlin*, Paris, 1826.

dition? How many artisans who, with true talents, have vegetated all their lives! How many whose toil has been smitten with sterility, or who, upon the eve of success, have seen their savings, painfully amassed, all engulfed! They needed only an advance, a protection, an advice, and this resource failed them at the decisive moment.

It is here that the devotedness of charity becomes particularly necessary. It is she that, in this struggle against poverty, in this painful ascent to the promised land, faithfully attends the indigent, who, without ever substituting her efforts for his, encourages and sustains him, removes obstacles from before him, aids him in difficult passes, lends a hand where he fails, raises him when he falls, and never forsakes him till he arrives at the end. When each man, in the sphere of his relations, will exercise about him a beneficent patronage;[1] when the master will show an affectionate care for the interests of his domestics; when the manufacturer, regarding himself as the father of his workmen, will never separate his advantage from theirs, will of himself offer them the most equitable conditions, and will have constantly before his eyes their moral interest and their advancement;[2] when the rich proprietor, instead of wasting his income in

---

[1] On the benefits of patronage, see Cherbulliez, (*Des causes du Paupér.*, Paris, 1853.)

[2] Several great manufacturers in France, are renowned for the exact discipline they cause to reign on their manufactories, as well as for the paternal care they have for their workmen. (De Gérando, *du Progr. de l'ind.*, p. 83, 97 · *Revue des Deux-Mondes*, 15 fév., 1852, etc.)

some capital, where his presence attracts a crowd of adventurers and rogues, shall prefer to remain upon his estates, and, by his example, keep his cultivators there; when, instead of making a vain display, he will employ his leisure and his fortune in advancing some useful science, in developing some branch of industry, in propagating the best methods of culture, in caring for the interests of his poor neighbors, in founding and directing institutions profitable to all; these would be inestimable services rendered to the indigent.

We live no longer at a time where the rich man can believe that he has acquitted himself towards society, solely because he manages his own fortunes, spends his revenues and agreeably employs his leisure. No; I trust, in this, the wisdom of the ancients more than that of our age; all luxury is not a gain for the order of society.[1] Have not a first, and a second experience, sufficiently convinced us? For some workmen, whom your pomp supports for a time, for some frivolous occupations, which your fashions sustain for a day and destroy the next, your example spreads around you the contagion of vain and sensual tastes. That artisan, to whom you seriously think you are doing good, asks himself why he is not, himself, the idol who is to be adored under those festive garments, why his palate is not to relish those delicate meats and exquisite wines. All his gains are consumed in aping your expensive pleasures; he works no more

[1] On the principle which should direct the rich in the use of his fortune, see the wise reflections of Joseph Droz. (*Econ. pol.*, IV. 1, p. 323, *seq.*)

from a sense of duty, he works to shine, to enjoy. But if he could enjoy and shine without work! Thus covetousness is inflamed, temptations rise, one victim more drawn into the gulf of misery, one torch more for the fires of revolution. O, what gifts of Providence, which might be in the hands of the rich a fruitful source of prosperity, and which have been but a source of ruin!

As for charitable offices, just as for alms, nothing can replace individual action; the good one does, about himself and in full intelligence of it, is by far that which profits most. But the poor do not all find enlightened guides and generous protectors at their doors; and, among the services which their condition needs, many require time and care which few of the rich can bestow. It is here, then, indispensable, as in regard to subventive charity, to unite the action of individuals and of associations.

Hence, the numerous establishments created by collective benevolence; infant and other asylums, gratuitous schools for infants and adults, institutions for orphans, societies of apprenticeship, agricultural colonies,[1] intelligence societies, societies of patronage for prisoners and the discharged,[2] for young workmen, workshops, refuges, houses of Providence, peoples' banks, savings' banks,[3] and family banks,

[1] De Morogues, *du Paupérisme et de la mendicité*. On the colonies of foundlings established in Algeria, see *Ann. de la charité.*, Avril, 1851.

[2] Consult the works of Tocqueville, Beaumont, Charles Lucas, Moreau, etc.

[3] On the origin and the progress of that admirable institution, see the Report of M. Navier, in the session of the fourth classes

provisional and retiring funds, &c., there are so many institutions by which efforts have been made to aid the labor and the economy of the poor, and thus to prepare for him an access to a happier state.[1]

Among these institutions, which only need to be more extended to produce all the happy fruits that are expected of them, those which appear to us, above all, to claim a new development and a direction more conformable to their end, are the establishments of instruction.

We have seen that the question is, to give, at last, to the laboring classes that education which, in the natural order of things, should precede their emancipation. The question is, since no one is charged with conducting them, to put them in a condition to conduct themselves, to use well, for themselves and for society, the liberty which they have acquired. It has been said, "among the causes of misery, the most active is the insufficiency of the intellectual and moral forces of the people."[2] The lot of the laboring man

of the Institute, 24th of April, 1850; the notice of A. de Candolle, Genève, 1834. The Annual Reports of Benjamin Delessert; the notice nécrologique on this philanthropist by A. de Candolle. (*Bibl. univ.*, 1847, p. 546, 558;) the Annuaires of polit. econ., etc.

[1] A more complete enumeration will be found in the following works: Dufau, *Lettres sur la charité*; De Watteville, *Ess. Stat. sur les établ. de bienf.*, Paris, 1847; Moreau, *du Probl. de la mis.*, III. p. 201, *seq.;* 491, *seq.*, etc.; Villeneuve, *ub. sup.*, II. p. 364; De Gérando, *Bienf. publ.*, pass., and for more recent institutions, *Ann. de la char.*, 1851, p. 95, *seq.*, 281, 344, etc. For the institutions of preventive charity founded in Germany and in other protestant countries, see the *Wicheren's*, *Fliegende Blätter*.

[2] Passy (*Journal des Econ.*, XII. p. 50); Garnier (*Ibid.*, XV. p. 105;) M. Chevalier, Th. Fix (*Ibid.*, xiii, p. 121; x, p. 41); de la

will not be efficaciously guaranteed, he will not obtain advantageous conditions from his master except in proportion to the intelligence and fitness which he can manifest in his service, and the perfection of the work which he can offer to him;[1] he will not be protected from the dangers of being unemployed, except in as far as he can appreciate the causes which stimulate or retard the movements of labor, and, by the development of his inventive faculties, shall be able to pass easily from one occupation to another; when one branch of industry fails him, to create new ones and secure new sources of profit.[2] The elementary instruction, then, which he receives in our schools, is not enough. It is necessary, without scientific apparatus, but with a wholly practical clearness

---

Farelle, du *Progr. social* p. 41; E. Buret, *ub. sup.*, etc. Buret calls education "the moral baptism of man." The Académie Française has long since proclaimed the same truth. (*Rec. des Discours*, ann. 1834, p. 714, etc.)

[1] In our days, the working-man, the most honest clerk, the most intelligent, is frequently associated in the profits of his employer. In Prussia, the overseers of estates often receive as an encouragement, besides their fixed salaries, a certain part on the neat product. In other places, manufacturers secure for their most recommendable workmen premiums taken from the annual profits. It is from the extension of those various usages that man can, until a solid establishment of industrial associations be founded, hope for the progressive emancipation of the working class, the reconciliation of capital with work. "In proportion," says Rossi, "as intelligence is more required in works, salaries tend to be converted into profits." (*Cours. d'écon. pol.*, III. Séances de l'Acad. des sc. mor., 1851, p. 326. *Journal des Econ.*, XII. p. 242. See the example of the company at Orleans, quoted by M. Chevalier, *Organ. du Trav.*, p. 276.)

[2] Rossi, *ub. sup.*, I. p. 319.

30

and precision, to teach him the general principles of domestic and social economy,[1] and the technical knowledge proper to render him skilful in the exercise of his business.[2] It is necessary, above all, by a good method of instruction, to develop in him the habits and the faculty of reflection, to form in him, by this means, a sure judgment which will guide him in all the circumstances of his life, make him healthily appreciate his position, foresee and avoid the chances which threaten him, calculate the consequences of his determinations, and discern good from evil counsels.[3] But what is more necessary than all that, is, to prevent in him, by education, the vices engendered by misery,[4] to inculcate in him the virtues of his estate, marked with the seal of religion: labor, the foundation of all the others; probity, which claims confidence; justice, the indispensable bond of associations; temperance, which preserves to the

---

[1] *Journ. des Econ.*, pass., Rossi, *ub. sup.*, p. 397; Willm., *Educ. du peuple*, c. 5, § 14, 15; de la Farelle, II. 4, etc, *ub. sup.*

[2] Locke had already insisted upon this point and proposed the foundation of working-schools. Following his maxims, the industrial schools in England, known by the name of *Mechanic's Institutions*, the imitation of which is strongly recommended in France, were instituted. (*Revue des Deux-Mondes*, March, 1850; de la Farelle, *ub. sup.*, p. 310, *seq.;* Th. Fix, *Journal des Econom.*, XII. p. 296; XXIII. p. 30, etc.)

[3] It is especially for that purpose that Pestalozzi has established his system of teaching, the appreciation of which, under this point of view, was put up for competition by the Acad. of *mor. politic and sciences.* See the Report in the Compte Prendu of the Sessions of that Academy, ann. 1850.

[4] "Misery," says M. Chevalier, "will lose ground only on condition that morality will gain it."

workman his faculties and his forces; economy, which makes him free by the creation of a capital; prudence, which leads him to proportion his expenses to his resources; the just desire of ameliorating his position, with the fixed design of tending to it only by legitimate ways; submission to inevitable privations, with the elasticity which ever urges him on to perfection. Such is the direction which private charity ought to strive to impress upon the instruction in the schools which it creates for the people.[1]

As for the State, we do not pretend to deny the part which it may claim in popular instruction. It can, in still other respects, second the action of charity. It can, in times of extraordinary crises, employ on the public works the workmen thrown out of employment. It can, as a means of regeneration, and at the same time of repression, found agricultural colonies for discharged prisoners, and workhouses for beggars. It can exercise a useful oversight over apprenticeships as well as over the work to which children are held in manufactories.[2] It can, again, in default of sufficient private associations, constitute itself, provisionally, the depository and guaranty of the savings of the working man, the treasurer of assurance for families.[3]

---

[1] See on this subject the reflections of Grün, *de la Moralisation des cl. labor.*, Paris, 1851.

[2] See the law of 1841.

[3] It is in that spirit that the most of the measures proposed by the *Commission de Secours*, and adopted by the National Assembly, have been conceived. (See the Reports of Thiers, *Moniteur* of 27th Jan., 1850, and of Melun, *Ann. de la charité*, March, 1851;) particularly the funds of retreat and insurance for working-men, created by the law of the 18th of June, 1850.

But, in general, for all the methods within the province of benevolence, an indirect action is that which appears to us best suited to the State. Let us recall again, here, the experience of the first centuries. As much as the Christian emperors failed, when they attempted, by positive and direct measures, to relieve or banish misery, so much was their action salutary, when they limited themselves, in the sphere of their functions, to the repression of injustice, the protection of the feeble, the support of right, the retrenchment or restraint of abuses which endangered the prosperity of their people.[1]

Let the Christian governments work to-day in the same spirit. With all necessary prudence, but with an indefatigable perseverance, let them apply themselves to the destruction of the abuses which perpetuate misery, to the suppression of injurious restraints, unjust monopolies and ruinous protections; let them cease from lavishing in puerile festivities, from consuming in the struggles of ambition or of false points of honor, the resources of their subjects. Let the imposts, reduced to what the indispensable services of the State require, weigh less heavily upon the indigent. Let the machinery of society be simplified, the fiscal laws modified, so as to render property more accessible to those most capable of turning it to profit, and, thus, less tributary to the

---

[1] "Fraternity," says Troplong, "tempers the character of legislation, and brings mankind into precepts; it inspires the power with benevolence and equity; it wants it to have justice as a principle, and the general welfare as an end." (*De la propr. d'après le Cod. Civ.*, p. 66.)

government and lawyers.[1] Let the savings of the workman be a sacred treasure, against which, under pain of public execration, no one dare lift a hand.

To see to security, internal and external, to protect the rights of all, to guarantee the property, the liberty, and life of each citizen, such is the object of civil society, the end for which governments are established. Let them fulfil this mission with a scrupulous constancy; let them hold in check evil passions, and it is not to the rich only that their firmness will be of profit; under favor of the public confidence which they will promote, capital will circulate, industry will flourish; labor will have all its energies; the poor, himself, assured of gathering and transmitting the fruits of it, and, at the same time, protected from the temptation and the hope of political subversions, will expect his prosperity only from his own good and loyal efforts; he will give himself entirely to his task, and will close his ears to those who flatter him with views other than his happiness.

It is thus that I understand the action of governments for the gradual extinction of misery. Let us not charge them with more extended cares. They will do enough for charity if they solidly establish the reign of justice; they will make enough rich, if they make no poor, do enough good if they hinder evil. But does any one think that this course, to be embraced with courage and achieved with perseverance, exacts, especially in our days, less of devotedness, of

[1] Sismondi, *Etud. sur l'écon pol.*, I. p. 106; M. Chevalier, (*Rev. des Deux-Mondes*, July, 1850;) Villeneuve, *Econ. pol. chr.*, I. p. 314.

self-denial, of charity, in a word, than the most of the deeds to which this title is habitually reserved?

Charity under all its forms, in all its manifestations, has, then, a great mission to fulfil in the present. Alone, it is insufficient; we have acknowledged it; but, seconded by civilization and labor, it can do much more to-day than in the first centuries. Its influence was reduced then to a more equal distribution of resources, which diminished from day to day. Now by exciting and directing the researches of science, by placing the poor on a way which ought to conduct him to a state of well-being; in lending to him the co-operation of its proper individual and collective activity, in removing, little by little, the obstacles which come from the social system, charity can succeed in always circumscribing, and in insensibly destroying the scourge of misery. It is with joy that we see this truth better and better recognized in our times. To-day charity is worthily avenged of the disdain of its detractors. It is no longer the preachers, the moralists who proclaim its necessity, and extol its benefits; it obtains the suffrages even of the economists; it sees, inscribed in the list of its admirers, the names of the most distinguished men of science.[1]

"Yes," some discouraged spirits will say, "Christian

---

[1] Duchâtel, *De la char.*, p. 335, *seq.;* Sismondi, *Etudes*, intr., p. 10, *seq.;* Villeneuve, *Econ. pol. chr.*, intr., p. 88, III. p. 583; Droz, *Pensées sur le Christ.*, p. 134; Cousin, *Justice et Charité*, p. 66; Thiers, *de la propr.*, p. 318, etc. "The part which fraternity has played in the world is immense," says Chevalier; "that left to her is magnificent. There is more virtue for the amelioration of the existence of the feeble in these words: 'Love each other, like brothers,' than in any capital created or to be created." (*Revue des Deux-Mondes*, July 15th, 1850.)

charity, doubtless, has great secrets, and is capable of great things; but, where is it, to-day? It has disappeared with faith. Never was it more necessary, and never more rare. Attempt, to-day, with the eloquence of a St. Cyprian and of a St. Basil, to obtain the least of the devotedness which they formerly obtained."

Let us not confound the motives of charity with charity itself. Each age has its means of persuasion, its principles of action which are peculiar to it. True, we can hardly expect, in these days, to see rich men, persuaded that the world is about to be destroyed, seeking to redeem their past faults by the entire abandonment of their property. That even is hardly to be desired. But, if some of the motives, which formerly animated charity, have lost their influence, others, even by their sublimity, are destined to obtain still more than they ever had. God, the father and protector of all the human race; all men united in Him by the bonds of a close fraternity; the love of our equals, inseparable from the love of God; our present and future happiness, proportioned to the energy of this double love; beneficence, the necessary consequence, the natural expression of all lively and sincere charity; these are truths which, for being ancient, have lost nothing of their certainty, and which furnish an unshakable basis to this duty. Proclaimed by the greatest Author of Revelation, sealed with his blood, shown upon the cross, confessed by all eminent minds and elevated souls for eighteen centuries, dear to the Christian, recognized by all true philosophers, in accordance with the clearest notions of our intelligence, and with the noblest instincts of our hearts, confirmed by all that experience and sane reason reveal to us of the designs of Providence, far from having anything to fear from the progress of the age, they are destined to shine with an ever-increasing brightness, as men become enlightened. The only thing, then, is to cause these truths to enter deeply into the mind of the people. Let public and private education inculcate them to youth; let the ministers of religion give them emphasis in their instructions; let the learned, whose influence has contributed but too much to enfeeble them, apply themselves to make them evident. Finally, let all those who have the happiness of recognizing them, confess them openly and manifest them in their deeds; and, if charity no more effects the same prodigies as formerly, it will work out still more marvellous, and, above all, more fruitful and more durable ones; to it will be due not only the relief, but the elevation of the suffering classes, their attainment to an increasing state of ease, of well-being, of independence and of morality.

To the work, then! The times urge, not because of the dangers which misery could beget; if our sole aim was to conjure them, perhaps already it would be too late; the times urge, because our brothers suffer, and it will never be soon enough to relieve them. Were the shocks which still threaten social order to reach us to-morrow, to-day even, it is necessary to labor for the good of the disinherited classes: we must do for them, and for God in them, what it would be no longer time to do for ourselves.

THE END.

www.ingramcontent.com/pod-product-compliance
Lightning Source LLC
LaVergne TN
LVHW010150110826
845151LV00002B/472

* 9 7 8 1 4 2 5 5 3 7 8 7 6 *